No Better Place

Than in the Center of His Presence

A Daily Devotional

By Bob Pangburn

Sixth Printing: 2007

Library of Congress Control Number: 2002092506
ISBN: 978-0-9638693-0-2

Printed in the United States of America
Morris Publishing
3212 East Highway 30
Kearney, NE 68847
1-800-650-7888

Cover picture is a photograph of the marble statue of Christ overlooking the
City of Silverton, Colorado, taken by the author's wife, Mary Beth.

DEDICATION

This book is dedicated to the SonBeams singles ministry of Sweetwater Church of the Valley. It was through the loving encouragement received from this group of individuals that I experienced the freedom to move in the gifts of the Spirit.

To those individuals that entered the doors of the SonBeams classroom I express a deep appreciation and love to each and every one.

ACKNOWLEDGMENTS

A very special acknowledgment to my wife, Mary Beth, who encouraged me to commit this material to book form;

And to my daughter, Nancy, who, while bedfast and recuperating from a severe illness, edited and proofed the original manuscript draft;

And to Pastor Jack Enright who wrote the biography and also proofed the original manuscript.

CONTENTS

"...write thee all the words that I have spoken unto thee in a book," Jeremiah 30:2 (KJV)

FOREWORD

The Holy Spirit, like a mighty wind, is blowing again, and with fresh breath from heaven is leaving a deposit to encourage many on their earthly journeys. Bob Pangburn has yielded himself as a sensitive vessel to hear the whisper of the Spirit, and with God's direction has presented these "whispered words of comfort and encouragement" in this daily devotional book.

Daily devotions are as necessary to the Christian life as daily food is to the body. I believe that as you read these devotions, their precious words of truth will stir your spirit, help you to live with new power, and manifest many works of God's grace. Like trees planted by water, those who meditate in the Word of God night and day shall bear much fruit. Be blessed and then become a blessing.

Dr. Glenn Foster

INTRODUCTION

While attending family camp during the summer of 1987, our Pastor, Glenn Foster, challenged us to step out further in the Spirit than we had ever been before. That night my wife and I began to minister to others in a capacity not previously experienced by either of us. A few days later I began to hear the Spirit speak to me more plainly in my personal daily devotions, so I began to write as He spoke.

On the pages of this book are some of the words whispered by the Spirit in those early morning hours. As I wrote them I began to share them with my wife. Later the Spirit said to share them with others so I began to read and distribute them to the SonBeams, a singles ministry of Sweetwater Church of which my wife and I were the directors.

The title of this book, **NO BETTER PLACE - THAN IN THE CENTER OF HIS PRESENCE**, was chosen because the Spirit's message is that: God loves His children regardless of who they are; He is always near no matter the circumstance being experienced; our relationship with God is based solely on the truthfulness of His Word, not on emotion or how we feel; and that there is indeed no better place to be than in the center of His presence.

As you read these words may you experience the joy of God's unconditional love and faithfulness in that Better Place.

January

Crossing Over

CROSSING OVER
Joshua 1:1-7; 3:14-17

January 1

Child, do not be afraid. Do not be discouraged. You are about to cross over into the Promised Land; a land flowing with milk and honey; a great land; a land of abundance. But let not the crossing frighten you. It is the door, the avenue to great things. It is where the wilderness experience is left behind, and the place of prosperity is entered into.

Beloved, the wilderness is past. Your inheritance is before you, but you must cross over the waters to receive it. Simply place your foot into the unknown, and the obstruction and barrier will recede.

And though the waters of lack and adversity seem to mount up around you, you shall soon enter in. Yes, you shall enter new territory, and there shall be a new beginning, where lack does not exist. You are at the crossing. Look up and keep your eyes fixed on Me. You shall not be drowned. You shall not be overwhelmed, for I go before you, and cause you to walk on dry ground with your feet firmly planted on solid rock. You shall reach the other side without harm.

Yes child, come and cross over. Come in faith to the promises I have given. Come and possess the land before you. It is your inheritance, and it is good.

January 2

A DEPOSIT OF HIS SPIRIT
2 Corinthians 5:5

My child, I have robed you in My righteousness, and you are a new creation. Old things are passed away, and all things are now new. I have given you My Spirit as a deposit of that which is to come. And beloved, My Spirit teaches you all things. My Spirit leads you, guides you, and instructs you. He leads you

9

in paths of righteousness. He guides you into all truth. He instructs you in the way that I want you to go.

O child, listen to His voice. Listen carefully. Listen prayerfully. Listen quietly. Listen at all times, for He is ever present to do the work I have sent Him to do. He will instruct you in ways that please Me. So listen and hear His voice, and obey His counsel.

Yes, listen My beloved, for the just, the righteous, shall walk by faith. Their faith is in the leading of My Spirit. Their faith is in the Word that I have spoken. Their faith and confidence is in what I say I will do.

O let there be no doubt. Let there only be faith and trust, for this pleases Me and it produces beautiful fruit, which is the fruit of My Spirit within you. Yes loved one, all things are new. Believe it. Walk in it. For I have proclaimed it and My Spirit makes it so.

January 3
HE IS OUR ROLE MODEL
1 Thessalonians 1:6

Child, I have set the example for you. I have given you the model to follow. So follow Me with a heart of love, seeking always My presence in everything, for I am your role model.

Beloved, I am loving, kind, compassionate, and forgiving. I am your Heavenly Father, full of wisdom and truth. I am mighty and powerful, performing great signs and wonders.

So child, come and follow My lead. Imitate Me like a child loved dearly by his Father, one that wants to grow up to be just like him. O how proud and pleased that Father is.

I too, dear one, am pleased and proud of My children. I show them off to the universe. So imitate Me in word, thought, and deed, and your joy shall be full. And you shall please Me in every way.

January 4
FINDING CONTENTMENT IN EVERY CIRCUMSTANCE
Job 36:11

Child, in Me, you can find contentment in every circumstance, in every situation, in every pressure, in every test and trial, in every lack, and in every abundance. I am your contentment. I am your everything. Nothing else matters, for I am in control. I am your sufficiency.

So beloved, when the difficulties come, remember that your contentment is not in wanting your way, but in what pleases Me. Also know that I do not leave you to suffer alone. No, I rush to your rescue. I come to your aid with good things.

But child, contentment is not in things. It is in Me. And I remain the same always. Even when everything around you changes, and it looks like things are falling apart, rest in the truth that I never change. I am the same. My love and compassion remains the same. My grace and mercy is the same. My care and provision remains the same. Indeed, I am the same yesterday, today, and forever.

So dear one, focus thoughts on Me, not on your circumstances, and you will have victory, peace, and contentment in your life. Your heart will be in tune with Me, and nothing will shake you.

O beloved, I am the good God. Let your confidence and trust find rest and contentment in Me.

January 5
HE RESCUES AND DELIVERS HIS OWN
Genesis 14:14-20

Child, I rescue and deliver My own. I bless My own, and you are My own. And I strengthen you for battle, even when the odds are overwhelmingly against you.

Beloved, I cause you to triumph over your enemies.

I help you take back what the enemy has taken from you. I have given you My strength to do impossible things, to face impossible situations, and to do impossible tasks.

So follow Me with singleness of purpose, knowing that I am for you. Yes, follow Me knowing that I am the God of miracles and that I rescue you out of all your troubles.

January 6
AN ANOINTING THAT IS REAL
1 John 2:20, 27

My child, I have anointed you with My Spirit. Yes, My Spirit is within you, and He is real. He is the anointing. And that anointing, My Spirit, teaches and instructs you in all things. He teaches you godliness, righteousness, and holiness. He teaches you love.

O beloved, you have an anointing. Know it. Believe it. As the priest and kings of old were anointed with oil that ran down upon them from the top of their heads to the bottom of their feet, so are you anointed with My Spirit.

So child, come walk with Me in your anointing, and we will have sweet communion together. Minister to others in this anointing, and you will see miracles happen. Go about your daily work in this anointing, and watch the Spirit do great and marvelous things. Yes beloved, you have an anointing.

January 7
THE BENEFACTOR OF HIS GRACE,
THE RECIPIENT OF HIS LOVE
Malachi 3:16.18; 4:2.3

Loved one, you are one of My children. You are more than a treasured possession. You are one of My precious jewels, and I grace you with all heavenly favor, because I care for My own. I jealously watch over you. I guard you, protect you, and make My face to shine upon you. I arise within you in all My glory and splendor. I bring you healing and great joy. O child, I favor you. You are the benefactor of My grace, the recipient of My love. So be encouraged for you are Mine, no one can snatch you away. You are loved and blessed beyond measure. Your enemies cannot touch you, for in order to do so they must go through Me, and I am greater than any enemy. I am greater than anything in the world.

Beloved, I bring you great joy. Is not this good news? So rejoice, I am in control, and you are safe and secure in Me.

HE FINDS NO FAULT IN ME
Jude 24

Beloved, I am the one who keeps you from falling. I am the able one. I am the one who presents you to the Father with great joy. All the work has been done, and I present you faultless. Yes, you are presented in My righteousness, and this brings great joy to My heart.

Child, in Me you have been made perfect. I find no fault in you. There is no condemnation. I have washed you in My blood, and have cleansed you as clean as new fallen snow. I remember your sin no more, for you are perfect in My sight. I have declared it so.

Beloved, your life is now hid in Me. And there are no shadows, no dark areas for I have redeemed you. I have placed you in right standing with your Heavenly Father. I present you faultless, and I keep you there. I will not let you fall, for those who place their trust in Me shall not be put to shame. O child, rejoice with Me, for I have done a marvelous thing. I keep and I protect you. I present you faultless with great joy.

January 9

DECLARED RIGHTEOUS
2 Corinthians 5:21

My child, I indeed have justified you. I have declared you righteous. I have done this, because I love you. Dear one, it is received only by faith. It is faith in Me. It is faith in the finished work that I have done.

Beloved, did not I take your sin upon Me, and pay the penalty in full? Did not I rise again in fullness of life? Yes, and I did it for you. I did it so you would have hope. I did it so you would have life eternal, even life in abundance. I did it so you would be declared righteous, even declared to be the righteousness of God. O child, believe it. Believe that you are righteous, for in so doing it unlocks all of My promises. It unlocks the doors of heaven. O loved one, have not I declared in My Word that I watch over and care for the righteous?

My dear one, blessings are the natural result of righteousness. So are the sufferings. They take place to conform you more and more into My image. They take place to permit My righteousness to grow more and more in you unto that perfect day.

Child, I have placed within you, by the power and presence of My Spirit, a great hope. It is the hope and assurance that you can daily walk in My presence, in My grace, and in My glory without any hesitation, reservation, or condemnation.

Loved one, it is yours. So learn the walk of righteousness. Learn the walk of hope. Learn the walk of My presence. Learn the walk of death to self. Learn the walk of being alive unto Me. Learn the walk of Christ in you the hope of glory. O beloved, I have declared you righteous. Come and enjoy its benefits.

ANOINTED WITH THE OIL OF GLADNESS
Isaiah 61:1-3

Beloved, I have chosen you and anointed you. I have anointed you with My Spirit. I have anointed you with the oil of gladness.

Yes, gladness is yours. Even though it is My joy and gladness, I give it to you. I have anointed you with it. I have poured out upon you gladness of heart, not doom, sadness, sorrow, or mourning. It is the oil of gladness, the oil of joy.

Beloved, I have brought you into My presence, into the very center of My being. I have taken up residence in you. I have given you My Spirit. I have promised to guide you until I call you home.

O child, does this not make you glad? Does not joy overtake you when you consider that you are in My presence, when you consider that I care for you? Yes dear one, there is a river whose streams make glad the City of God. And though sorrow may be for a season, joy comes in the morning. It comes with dawning of hope.

So beloved, rejoice and be glad, for I have anointed you with the oil of gladness, the oil of joy.

THE PRAYER OF THE RIGHTEOUS
Isaiah 56:1-2, 7

Beloved, I have heard your prayer. It is the prayer asking Me to mold, bend, melt, break, and to conform you to My image. It is the prayer desiring to learn how to become fervent and effective in your prayer life. It is the prayer that says, "Do, Lord, whatever it takes to bring praise, honor, and glory to your name."

O My child, I am answering your cry. I have given you an everlasting name, and I am conforming you to

My image. I am bringing you joy in the house of prayer. Your prayers are being answered, dear one, not necessarily as you think they should, but they are being answered.

So do not become depressed or discouraged, but rejoice in your Lord, for I am accomplishing My purpose in your life. Just look around. Are there not opportunities to trust Me? Are there not opportunities to praise Me? Are there not impossible things that provide opportunities to see miracles happen in your life?

O My child, be content in My righteousness, for it is perfect. Nothing can be added or taken from it. And you, loved one, are being made perfect as you receive more and more of My righteousness, which is daily being revealed to you.

January 12
DRINK OF HIS SPIRIT
1 Corinthians 12:12-13; John 7:37-38

My child, I have a message of love, awe, wonder and blessing for you. For indeed, you are part of My body, and I dwell in you, and you dwell in Me. You are an important part of My body, as are all the parts.

Dear one, I give you My Spirit to drink. That sweet refreshing drink that is yours moment by moment. It is that fresh filling of My Spirit, of My presence, of My power, of My mercy, and of My grace.

Yes child, drink of My Spirit. Let your fellowship with My Spirit spring up from within you continually, as a river of living water overflowing to those around you.

O loved one, that refreshing drink of My Spirit causes you to thirst no more for the things that do not satisfy, or things that do not last. For, child, My Spirit quenches all that. My Spirit refreshes and brings life to your spirit, soul, and body.

Beloved, My Spirit is beautiful, and He provides everything you need. So do not let your heart be troubled, but rather come to My fountain and drink of My Spirit for as long as you wish. Yes, come daily from now throughout all eternity.

See My child, do not I love you and give you all things, all spiritual blessings? For you can fellowship with Me continually, drink of My Spirit as often as you want, and go boldly into the Father's presence at anytime with your praises and your petitions.

Yes dear one, drink of My Spirit, and know that you are a very precious and important part of Me.

January 13

HE IS FOREVER IN CONTROL
Psalm 147:1-20

Child, I am the God of wonder, power and might. There is nothing I cannot do. Nothing is too difficult for Me, for I was before all things, and through Me all things came into being, and by Me all things hold together.

Beloved, I am the Alpha and Omega, the Beginning and the End. Everything is totally wrapped up in Me. I am in charge of it all. Nothing takes place without My knowledge, permission and intervention. Nothing can take place without it being first woven into My plan and purpose. For I am, and forever shall be in control.

Yes child, the enemy is out to steal, kill and destroy. But I came to give life, and to give it more abundantly. Know beloved, that the enemy is defeated. Know that all the work has been completed, for I accomplished it in My resurrection.

So dear one, rest in the fact that everything has been paid for and that My work finished all the requirements. Yes My child, rest in Me for I have made every provision for you. And whatever comes your way, whether it be severe tests and trials, or intense attacks of the enemy, rest assured that I have made a way. Rest in the fact that there is nothing that I cannot handle.

O child, let go of everything. Turn it over to Me. Cease from trying to fix things, and come into rest. Simply rest in Me, for I have already overcome every challenge that can come your way. So go about your day, doing the tasks before you, but rest them in Me.

O beloved, I live in you My purposes to fulfill. I turn mountains into molehills, raging storms into streams in the deserts, and floods into fountains of blessings.

So rejoice, dear one, the best is on its way. Today is better than yesterday. And child, look for Me in everything. Praise Me in everything, for you shall always find Me in praise. O beloved, there is nothing I cannot do, for indeed I am in control.

January 14
GROUNDED, STRENGTHENED, AND SETTLED
1 Peter 5:10-11

Beloved, I fix you firmly in Me. I establish you. I settle you. I cause your roots to go down deep in My love. I ground you firmly. Nothing can tear you away from Me.

O child, be alert. Be self-controlled. Be aware of that which takes place around you; for the enemy would try to devour you, to cause you harm, to cause you to lose your joy, and to cause you to lose your fellowship with Me. Be alert to his intentions. Watch the situations carefully, so he does not get a foothold. Simply resist him, being steadfast in the faith that you have in Me, and he will flee from you.

So beloved, be sober and vigilant. And though you go through the fellowship of My sufferings, know that I am always at work within you. This work, dear one, is to establish, firmly ground, strengthen, settle, and to place a hedge around you.

My child, I bring you into the power of My presence so nothing can move or shake you. This causes no interruptions in our fellowship; no condemnation in your heart; peace to exist no matter the circumstance; and a constant glow of My Spirit within you.

SPEAK TO THE MOUNTAIN
Mark 11:22-24; Hebrews 11:6

My child, there are mountains in your life today, but be of good cheer for they can be removed. Have not I said that you can speak to the mountain, and it will be cast into the sea? Have not I said to ask in prayer, and you shall receive?

Dear one, this is accomplished when you cast aside all doubts and believe what I say is true. Yes beloved, believe that speaking to the mountain will remove the mountain. Believe that what you ask in prayer you will receive, for it will be brought into existence.

My child, this means to settle all doubts. It means to trust Me completely. It means to believe that My Word is My Word. It means that I am capable of doing what I say I can do. And I will do it, for child, I keep My Word. I do not lie.

So loved one, speak to the mountains in My name, and they shall be removed. Ask in prayer believing, and you will receive. For My Word is true and I will do what I say I will do. Yes, speak to the mountain, and it shall be removed, because I have said it would be so.

HE WATCHES OVER ME BOTH DAY AND NIGHT
Psalm 121:1-8

Child, I am the one who watches over you, both day and night. I am the one who keeps you from harm. I am the one who protects you. Yes, I do all this because you are Mine, and I love you so. Beloved, My thoughts are never far from you. You are always near and precious to Me. And I place a hedge of protection around you that none can penetrate without permission. For I am mighty and powerful, eager to deliver.

So My child, you have nothing to fear, for your life is hid in Me. I hold you close and whisper that I love you. I tell you to fear not, for I will go before you. I tell you that I will strengthen, help, settle, and uphold you. I will rescue you from your enemies. I will set you upon a rock, upon solid ground. I will honor you, and those around you shall yet praise Me for what I do.

O rejoice, dear one, for My Word is true. I indeed watch over you, both now and forever more.

January 17
BLESSING AND PROSPERITY
Psalm 128:1-6

Child, there is blessing and prosperity to those who fear Me, to those who trust Me without doubt, and to those who seek Me first. Have not I said that those who place their trust in Me shall lack no good thing? Have not I said to ask, and you shall receive? Have not I said to have faith in Me, and nothing shall be impossible to you?

O beloved, I indeed lavish you with My love, My protection, My provision, and My care.

January 18
TOTAL COMMITMENT
Matthew 16:24-27

Beloved, I call to you to take up your cross daily, and come follow Me. I call to you to make and keep your commitment to Me. The commitment to sell out completely to Me. The commitment to make Me first in your life. The commitment to follow Me even to the death if need be. O child, there is no better place to be than in the center of My presence in total commitment to Me.

Loved one, I do not promise an easy path. I do not promise that there will be no tests or trials. I do not promise that there will be no pressures or discomfort. But I do promise strength in the trial. I promise deliverance, a way out of the pressure. I promise to make the crooked places straight.

And I promise to go through the sufferings with you, and to bring you out on the other side. I promise you life in abundance. Yes, I promise to bring great blessing out of the midst of difficulty. I promise that following Me, in total commitment, brings great peace.

Beloved, I did not call you to serve yourself, but I called you to serve Me with your whole heart, no matter the cost. In so doing, loved one, there is great reward. O My child, great peace have they who love My law, who follow Me without reservation, who say, "Whatever you want or need from me to bring praise, honor and glory to your name, so be it Lord, for I am completely yours."

January 19

SEE OTHERS AS GOD SEES THEM
1 John 4:11

Child, I am teaching you to love one another. For this is My command, that you love one another. O loved one, look not at the outward manifestation of My people, but see them as I see them. See others as My children. See them as a son or daughter of their loving Heavenly Father. Look past their faults and failures. Look past the flesh. Look past the old nature, and see Me in their life.

Yes beloved, look for Me in others, for I am there. Look only for Me. Do not try to find areas to justify your dislike, but rather look beyond that which you do not like and see Me, for that is what I do with you. O loved one, I do not see your sin, faults and failures. No, child, I look beyond that, for I have proclaimed you righteous. I remember your sin no more. So, look at others as I see them. Look at them through the eyes of your Savior.

And dear one, receive them in love for love covers a multitude of sin. See them as righteous. See Me at work in their lives. Yes, look beyond what you see, and look for Me, and you will find Me there.

Beloved, it pleases Me for you to love others, for it is My love within you manifesting itself. Yes, those I bring across your path, I bring for a purpose. So, love one another.

January 20
BE STRONG IN THE LORD
Ephesians 6:10

My child, be strong in My strength, for My strength is made perfect in weakness. Know that I am your strength. Have not I said that the joy of the Lord is your strength? Yes, I strengthen you, I uphold you, and I keep you from falling. And I equip you with everything necessary to withstand the attacks of the enemy.

O beloved, I have conquered the enemy, and the victory is yours. I have conquered the world, the flesh, and the devil. I have conquered sin and death

So pray and give thanks, for I am your strength. Pray in the Spirit at all times, for this is strength. Pray all kinds of prayers and requests, for there is strength in knowing that your Father hears and answers prayer. O child, be strong in the Lord, and in the power of His might.

THE REMOVAL OF ALL FEAR
Isaiah 43:1-2

Beloved, I am removing all fear from you, for I am your helper. I am your peace. I am your deliverer. I am your fortress. I am your God. Nothing is impossible for Me. So fear not, for I am totally in control. Know that in the center of My presence there is no fear, only peace. Even in the most difficult circumstances, there is peace like a river. O beloved, this is where I want you to live. Not in the presence of fear and anxiety, but in the very presence of your Lord. And those who seek Me and My presence, shall lack no good thing.

FILLED WITH ALL THE FULLNESS OF HIS PRESENCE
Ephesians 3:19

Child, I am at work within you. Do you not see it? I am filling you with all the fullness of My presence. I am strengthening you. I am encouraging you. I am building up your confidence in Me. I am giving you understanding and insight.

Yes dear one, I am at work in you by the power and presence of My Spirit. I am at work within you by the very presence of My unlimited love, which is new and fresh every morning. It does not fail. There is no measure to it. It is limitless and super abundant.

Child, I am filling you with the very fullness of My presence, and nothing shall be impossible for you. For out of My love, power, and presence I do awesome and mighty things both in, and around you. All of this is to My honor and glory. Yes beloved, I am filling you with all the fullness of your God.

January 23
GRAPES IN THE DESERT
Hosea 9:10

Beloved, I am the one who found you. I am the one who chose you. I am the one who made you righteous. I love you, and I am pleased that you are Mine. Loved one, you are refreshing and beautiful to Me.

My child, I am making you pure and holy. Yes, it is already done in the Spirit, but I am also accomplishing it in your daily walk. Beloved, I multiply your seeds of righteousness. Seeds for you to sow. So sow seed, for they will not return void, but will produce a bountiful harvest of righteousness, and a beautiful harvest of goodness, kindness, and love.

My child, you are pleasing to Me. So come and enjoy My presence. Come and let us labor together in love. Come let us plant seeds of righteousness. Come let us water them with our tears. Come, My loved one, and watch them grow.

O look around you. Look at what you have sown. Do you not see it bearing fruit? Beloved, come and see the beautiful fruit ripe unto harvest. Yes My child, you are like finding grapes in the desert, beautiful, refreshing and pleasing to behold.

January 24
A PRAYER OF SUBMISSION
1 Corinthians 7:17

Beloved, I have placed you where you are, and I open doors of opportunity and blessing for you every day. So, learn contentment where I have placed you, for I am the one who has planned and ordained your life for you.

My child, learn, no matter the situation or the location, that I have called you to serve wherever I lead. For I call you to go, and I call you to stay. What I

24

desire from you is the willingness to do what I ask you to do. And what I desire from you is your prayer of submission saying, "Here I am Lord, use me wherever you want."

Beloved, know that where you are right now is where I want you. But also know that I can change that in a moment. So, work where I have you as if you will be there the rest of your life and expect miracles, blessings and prosperity.

But, My child, keep your heart and ears open for My leading, which may take you to other places, people, and lands. For I, the Lord, am on the throne, and I have work to do, and I am sending laborers into the harvest field.

So loved one, be content where I have you today. With expectation look for Me in everything, for I am there. O child, know that My promises, blessings, and prosperity are yours wherever you are, for they come from Me, and not from your circumstances or location.

Dear child, when I am ready to move you to new places, you will know it. I will show you ahead of time. I will open the right door. I will settle you elsewhere for My purpose. But today you are where I want you. So, give yourself totally to where you are, and serve Me with your whole heart in this place.

January 25
YOUR CALLING AND ELECTION IS SURE
Romans 11:29

Beloved, your calling and election is sure. It is secure. I have chosen and called you. It was not because of your works that I chose you, but, rather it was because of My mercy and grace, received by faith.

Yes child, I have chosen and called you for My purpose, to accomplish that which I please. For you are one of Mine, and I love you so.

So let not the cares and the anxieties overwhelm

you. Let them not distract you, for I have called you for a purpose, a divine purpose. O recognize each day that this is true.

Dear child, come, walk with Me daily. Yes, let it be moment by moment, in the attitude that I am fulfilling My purpose in and through you. And loved one, know that I am always near, ready, able, and willing to help you through anything.

Beloved, My purpose is to bring praise, honor, and glory to My name. My purpose is that none should perish but that all come to repentance. My purpose is to conform you to My image. My purpose is to make you holy, pure, and blameless. My purpose is to bless you. My purpose is to be a Father unto you.

Child, I did not choose you at random. I did not just call to hear Myself call. O no, there is purpose for I have a plan, and each day, today, is a new beginning in the fulfillment of that plan.

So beloved, come! Hear My call. Yes, come walk and rejoice in the calling of your God. Child, your calling and election is sure.

January 26
DELIVERANCE IS AN ATTITUDE
Psalm 126:1-6

Child, I am the God of deliverance. Indeed, I rescue you out of all your troubles, and I bring joy and gladness to your heart. O loved one, deliverance and joy are experienced in the attitude of your mind. Yes, in the midst of trial, in the midst of difficulty, you can have peace and joy that transcends all understanding. For deliverance is in the mind. It is an attitude.

Beloved, it is in how you perceive the situation. Yes, I deliver you from situations, for I am a God of the impossible. But dear one, I deliver you from your self, from your attitude. Do you not see that in the pressure there is opportunity to be renewed in the attitude of your mind? So, let not the pressure over-whelm you, but overwhelm it with a mind fixed on Me. For in the midst of difficulty I am there. In the center of the fiery furnace I am with you. In the isolation of the desert I am ever near.

O child, look up and rejoice. I still am in control. I will lead and guide you, and I will show you what to do. I will whisper quietly to you which way to go. I will not let you down. So, no matter the situation, know that I am in control, and that all I require of you is to believe that I am. Simply believe Me and trust Me without a shadow of a doubt, and let Me show you what I have in store for you.

Beloved, I am the God of My Word. So, rejoice and be glad, for indeed, I do great things. I am your deliverer. I provide for your every need even to the thoughts that renew your mind. Have not I said that you have the mind of Christ? O child, I turn attitudes into instruments of joy.

January 27

IT IS A GOOD THING TO GIVE THANKS
UNTO THE LORD
Psalm 136:1-3

My child, it is a good thing to give thanks unto the Lord, for I alone am worthy of praise. I am the one who goes with you, and delivers you from all your troubles. I am the one who sees you through the storms and comforts you in the time of need. I am the one who gives you everything you need for life and godliness.

Beloved, I am the one who forgives all your sin and makes you righteous. I am the one who lives in you, in power and might, My purposes to fulfill. I am the one who brings things into being from that which does not exist. I am the one who tells you to fear not for I am with you. I am the one who heals you of all your diseases. I am the one who watches over you, and protects you. I am the one who gives you peace in the midst of trial.

Child, I am your God. I am your Heavenly Father who is filled with love, compassion and care. See, I do not leave you without hope. No, I come to your rescue. So, give thanks for great is your God and greatly is He to be praised.

January 28
THE FEAR OF THE LORD IS THE BEGINNING OF...
Psalm 111:10

My child, you are blessed and I continue to bless you. Have not I said that blessed is the man whose delight is in the law of the Lord?

Beloved, the fear of the Lord is the beginning of wisdom. It is the beginning of blessing. It is the beginning of favor with the Father. It is the beginning of righteousness. It is the beginning of Godliness. It is the beginning of compassion.

Child, it is the beginning of being rooted and grounded. It is the beginning of death to self. It is the beginning of praise, honor, and glory to Me. It is the beginning of being unmovable and unshakable. It is the beginning of generosity. It is the beginning of revelation.

O beloved, blessed is the man who fears the Lord. And this is only the beginning. There is no end.

January 29
FULL RIGHTS OF A SON
Galatians 4:5-7

Beloved, you are a son of God. You are part of the family, and you have the full right of a son of God. Child, you have the right of My love. You have the right of fellowship with Me. You have the right of My security. You have the right of My protection.

And beloved, you have the right of My caring. You have the right of feasting at My banqueting table. You have the right of My comfort. You have the right to My provision. You have the right to My name. You have the right to My life.

O child, I have placed My Spirit within you giving you the right to call Me Father. And as My child, you have the right to an inheritance reserved just for you.

So loved one, come and enjoy My presence. For you are family with all the rights and privileges thereof.

January 30

THE GOD OF POWER AND WONDER
Psalm 111:1-9

Child, I am a mighty God. I am the God of power and wonder. I do awesome and majestic things. I demonstrate to a sick and dying world My faithfulness and My power to change the impossible into reality.

Beloved, I show you great and mighty things. I lay before you land to possess, new things to do. And I am capable of giving you that which will bless you, and bring honor to My name.

Yes child, My ways are perfect. My precepts are pure and just. So, come without reservation and trust Me for the miracle you need. Have you not seen My hand at work? Have you not experienced the impossible? Have you not received when you thought there was no way to receive anything? O beloved, I am the God of wonder and miracles, and you are the beneficiary of all that power and majesty.

January 31

HE IS THE ONE
Psalm 76:1-12

Child, in praise I am known, and in worship I am found. O dear one, I am in control. I am the One who is to be feared, and to be trusted wholeheartedly with awe and reverence.

I am the One who crushes the enemy. I am the One who brings great deliverance. I am the One who sets the captives free. I am the One who performs great signs and wonders, who makes the lame to walk and the blind to see.

I am the One who assures you that no weapon formed against you shall prosper. I am the One who is for you, not against you. I am the One who makes you a conqueror. I am the One who fights your battles, and gives you the victory.

I am the One who makes crooked places straight, and who levels mountains and raises valleys. I am the One who leads you through the wilderness, and brings you safely to the other side. I am the One who makes even your enemies to be at peace with you.

I am the One who tells you to fear not, for I am with you, and to be not dismayed, for I am your God. I am the One who will help, uphold, and strengthen you. I am the One who made you My child and an heir of everything that I am.

And I am the One who lives in you by the power and presence of My Spirit, providing strength, wisdom, understanding, joy, and peace that no one can take from you.

Yes beloved, I am for you, and if I am for you who can be against you? So, rejoice and praise Me, for I am found in your praise

February

Safely Through the Storm

February 1
SAFELY THROUGH THE STORM
Psalm 107:28-32

Child, I bring you safely through the storm and through the troubled waters. And though the waves swell to great heights, they shall not overtake you, for I bring you into a safe haven.

O beloved, know that each storm lasts only for a season, and that each storm is unique in its activity and intensity. But know that I use each one to conform you a little bit more to My image. O loved one, know that I rescue you out of them all.

So child, when the winds blow and the waves roll, look not at them. Keep your eyes on Me and together we shall rise above the storm. We shall walk on the water together. And it shall not overwhelm you, for I am with you. It shall not overtake you, for I am your God. It shall not bring you under, for I am the Lord of all.

O beloved, rejoice and give thanks, for I do great things. Yes, listen for Me. Reach out and hold My hand. Trust Me dear one, for I guide you safely home. Child, this storm shall pass.

February 2
WHAT HAPPENS IS TO ADVANCE HIS PURPOSES
Philippians 1:12

O child, know and rest assured that all that happens to you, yes, everything, is not to make you miserable. It is not to make you unhappy. It is not to destroy you. It is not to bring you discouragement or despair. It is not to make you ashamed. But rather, beloved, it is to advance My name in your life and in the world. It is to further My plan and purpose. It is to help you grow and mature. It is for you to come to know Me better. It is to advance and lift up My name.

Dear child, it is for instruction in godliness and holiness. It is to conform you to My image. It is to reveal self and death to it. It is to bring you into rest. It is to reveal Me and My life in abundance.

Beloved, My purpose is to continue to do the good work through you. And I will carry it on to completion. So rejoice, even in the difficult and pressure times, even in times of opposition. Yes dear one, rejoice for I am advancing Myself in and through you.

O child, think not of yourself as a failure, but rather think of Me as your victory in every situation. So, no matter the detail, I am greater than any situation. Yes loved one, there is great peace to those who love Me and My Word, who see Me in all things.

February 3

AN ACTIVE GOD
Psalm 145:20

Beloved, I am an active God. I am alive and powerful. I do not sit passively by and let the world run itself. I do not turn you loose to flounder about without help and guidance, but rather, I actively and jealously watch over you.

Dear one, I have given you a manual for wisdom, guidance, correction, and comfort. I have placed My Spirit within you to live through you in all My power and might. I have given you great and precious promises; promises that are for you to claim and use daily. And I speak to you moment by moment, giving life, healing, and instruction.

O child, I have given you Myself. I have given you Me, and with that gift comes everything that I am. I have made you a partaker of My divine nature. I have given you authority to use My name. So rejoice, My beloved, for your God watches over you even while you sleep. Yes, I am an active God.

February 4
MANY PRESSURES, BUT HE HAS
OVERCOME THEM ALL
John 16:33

My child, indeed, there are many pressures. There is great tribulation. There is much trouble, but be of good cheer, I have overcome it all. I have overcome the world, and it is subject to Me. So, faint not at the pressures, for I ever live so that you might have peace.

Beloved, like a shield, let Me go before you in the midst of the trouble. Like a big brother, let Me stand up to the bully before you.

O child, rest in the fact that I go before you and fight your battles. They are already won. All you need do is claim the victory.

Beloved, it makes no difference what the pressure is, I have already overcome it. I have already declared peace to you in the midst of the difficulty.

So, see Me surrounding you in all of My power and might, and in all of My strength. Hear these words, dear one, "Peace be still." Yes, My peace I give unto you, for My child, I am your peace.

February 5
HIS WAYS AND HIS THOUGHTS
Isaiah 55:8-11

My child, My ways are above your ways, and My thoughts are above your thoughts, for I am the Lord God, the Omniscient One. And My ways and My thoughts are pure and holy. There is no deviation in Me; no evil thing in Me.

Beloved, I am kind and I loving. I keep My Word. I do not say one thing and do another. No! My Word is true and faithful. There are no shadows in It.

Child, when I say that I lead you forth with joy and peace, it is the truth. When I say the mountains and the hills shall break forth with singing, they will do just that, for there is no mountain too difficult for Me.

O beloved, as I overcame all the obstacles, so in Me you also are an overcomer. And the mountains shall only be opportunities for My Word to be made manifest and real in your life. Indeed, they shall break forth into singing, and the trees of the field shall clap their hands. And you shall rejoice at what I am doing in and through you.

My child, I have great things in store for you. I have places for you to go, and people for you to see. And I send you to a dry and thirsty land with food and drink to quench the most famished and thirsty soul.

O beloved, there shall be rejoicing, and My name shall be honored and glorified. You will be awed at what I do. For My ways are above your ways, and My thoughts are above your thoughts. I lead you in them so that they may become yours to possess. So My child, go out with joy, and be led forth with peace.

February 6

THE PROMISES OF HIS WORD ARE TRUE
Ezekiel 12:21-28

Beloved, what I say is so. What I promise is true. What I have written is accurate, and not one Word shall remain unfulfilled.

Yes child, the promises of My Word are true. They shall be fulfilled without delay. For indeed, if I spoke them, they are as pure as refined gold, and more precious than fine jewelry.

So dear one, think not that I delay performing My Word, or that I have forgotten, or that I don't care, or that My words have no substance. Everything I have spoken, and everything I have written is true and shall be made manifest. You shall see it.

Beloved, those words whispered to you by My Spirit are also true and accurate, for they too are based on

My Word. O dear one, I am God of My Word. I honor My Word. My Word is good, and you may count on it. So, rejoice in the fact that I do not lie, but that I do what I say and bring to pass what I promise.

February 7
GREAT COMPASSION
Psalm 119:156; Isaiah 63:7

Beloved, I am the God of great compassion. I am not hard, stern, or cruel, but rather I am slow to anger, always ready and willing to forgive. I abound in love and mercy. My love and compassion fail not, and to them there is no end.

Yes child, I am moved with compassion. Did not I, out of compassion, feed the multitudes? Did not I, out of compassion, weep over the city of Jerusalem? Did not I, out of compassion, cause the blind to see, and the lame to walk? Did not I, out of compassion, cleanse the lepers, and cast out demons?

Beloved, did not I, out of compassion, die for a lost world? Did not I, out of compassion, take your place on the cross of Calvary? Have not I filled you with that same love and compassion for the needs of others?

O child, there is no limit to My compassion, for it is beyond measure. So, rejoice today, in that I am ever mindful of you. Rejoice in that I have compassion for you. Rejoice in that I watch over you and protect you, and that I jealously guard those who are Mine.

Beloved, I know that the pressures are great, but remember, that out of My great compassion, I deliver you according to the integrity of My Word.

February 8
HIS SPIRIT MAKES UP WHAT I LACK
Romans 8:26,27; Joel 2:29

My child, I have poured out My Spirit upon you. I

have anointed you. And My Spirit helps you in your weakness. He makes up what you lack. He fills you with Himself, and He lives within you. He intercedes for and through you. He takes your prayers offered in the Spirit, and directs them to Me, and I hear them and I answer them.

O beloved, My Spirit within you is mighty. He is powerful. He keeps everything under control. Yes, through My Spirit, I have provided you with all of everything you will ever need.

Child, My Spirit brings unity. He is the bond of peace. He is the one who loves others through you. He is the one who expresses love through faith. It is My Spirit that reaches out in love to those around you. It is My Spirit that sees others as I see them.

So beloved, let your life be free to follow the leading and nudging of My Spirit. Listen to His voice. Hear His gentle persuasion, for He is there. And keep the door of your heart and the gates of your ears open to hear Him. For He speaks to you often, and tells you this is the way, walk in it.

O child, My Spirit is the one who has given you the gifts that you possess. Yes, I pour out My Spirit upon you, and He helps you in your weakness. You lack nothing.

February 9
CONTENTMENT IN ALL THINGS
Philippians 4:11-12

Child, I bring great peace and contentment, even in the midst of trial and pressure. For contentment comes from relying upon My strength and sufficiency for everything and in all circumstances. O loved one, you have much to learn, and I have so much to teach you. One of the lessons to learn is contentment in all things, whether you have plenty, or whether you have nothing.

37

Beloved, contentment is not based on having all you want. It is not based on an easy life. It is not based on wealth, fame, or fortune. But it is based upon relying on My strength in every situation.

So child, learn contentment. Learn to experience peace in the midst of lack, and in the midst of plenty. Learn that the extremes are brought together in My sufficiency. Dear one, you can do anything, go through anything, withstand anything when you are focused on Me and not on the situation.

O beloved, fear not. I do not leave or forsake you. Come, rest in My provision and strength, and you shall experience contentment in all things. Remember child, contentment is knowing that, regardless the condition, I am greater than any circumstance. It is a mind satisfied with My sufficiency in the midst of each and every situation.

February 10
HE GIVES ME THE DESIRES OF MY HEART
Psalm 20:4

My child, you are indeed a delight unto Me. I delight and joy over you with singing. For you have sought Me with a sincere heart. Yes, loved one, the desires of your heart are pure, and to the pure I reveal Myself pure. The desires of your heart are blameless, and to the blameless I reveal Myself blameless.

O beloved, I know you desire My Word. I know that you desire My fellowship. I know that you desire to serve Me. I know that you desire to be obedient. I know that you desire to follow Me wherever I lead you. I know that you desire My name to be high and lifted up. I know that you desire death to self and to be conformed to My image.

So My child, I give you the opportunities to receive your heart's desire. They are always before you. Yes, I cause you to triumph. I cause you to succeed. I cause your enemies to be at peace with you. So, see Me in each and every circumstance, even if it looks totally disastrous. Consider it is an opportunity to die to self, and to be found alive in Me.

Beloved, I am the one who rescues you. I am the one who keeps you safe. I am the one who keeps you from falling. I am the one who trains you for battle. I am the one who goes before you. I am the one who is your shield. I am the one who broadens your path. I am the one who gives you the victory.

So rejoice, child, if I am for you, who or what can be against you? I am your rock and your refuge. I am your strong tower to which you can run and be safe. Yes beloved, I delight in My children.

February 11

I AM BLESSED
Deuteronomy 30:9-16

My child, I am the one who cares for you, blesses you, and prospers you. Indeed, I bless those who diligently seek Me, those who delight in My precepts.

Beloved, those who diligently seek Me with their whole heart, I will not refuse. Those who love Me and walk in My precepts, I will not despise. For I have promised, I have given My Word that I would bless and prosper those who follow Me with their whole heart.

So child, let it be well with you, for I am near you. Yes, My Word is near you, even in your mouth. And My Word and My Spirit shall lead you, and you shall walk in paths of righteousness. O beloved, come and enjoy the abundance of your Lord. Enjoy the provisions I offer you. Enjoy the land and its fruit, for it is yours to enjoy. Yes, I bless My people.

February 12
SAVED TO DO GOOD WORKS
Ephesians 2:8-10

Child, it is not your works that saves you, rather it is by My grace. But I saved you to do good works; works that I have planned for you to do; works planned before the foundation of the earth; righteous works; works of obedience; works that brings life; and works that produce spiritual acts and deeds.

Beloved, My purpose for your life was planned long ago. And you indeed have a purpose. I have a plan for your life, and you shall fulfill it. I have a plan, and you shall walk in it, for that is the desire of your heart. Yes, I know that your desire is to love and serve Me with your whole heart.

So rejoice, child, you shall know what I want you to do. For I reveal to you in advance My will. You shall not miss out on anything. So, think not little of where I have you today, for there is purpose there.

O beloved, when you are where I want you, there is power, strength, and purpose. So, even when I say wait, and even when I say to be still and know that I am God, know that for that moment, you are exactly where I want you to be.

Yes child, I shall not let you miss out on anything. You have a calling, a ministry to do, and you shall do it. But be sensitive to My Spirit and to My Word, and you shall go forth to do what I have in store for you to do. For you are My handiwork, designed to do what I have planned for you to do long ago.

February 13
LET YOUR CONFIDENCE RISE
Isaiah 54:14-15

Child, there is nothing to fear. There is no reason to be in doubt. There is no reason to be discouraged, for I am with you. I am the one who sets up, and the one who puts down. Nothing is impossible to Me. So, let your confidence in Me rise and consume you, for is not this truly your strength?

Yes beloved, when I say be strong, it is to be strong in My provision. It is to believe without doubt. It is to trust and be confident in Me, even when things look totally impossible, and all around you everything seems to be against you. It is to trust when there appears to be no answer and no way out of the impossible situation.

Child, your strength comes from your confidence in Me, in who I am and in what I do. It is in the truthfulness of My Word and My faithfulness to it.

Beloved, I am sending you across this river, through all the opposition, and I will bring you safely through to the other side to a land of promise. And even though there be enemies, I shall deliver them into your hand. So rejoice and take heart, for I am with you. There is no need to fear.

February 14
PURE AND HOLY THOUGHTS
Proverbs 14:15; 21:29

My child, I search the thoughts and intent of the heart. I know My people better than they know themselves. I know that the thoughts of the flesh are carnal, but the thoughts that My Spirit brings are pure and holy.

Beloved, My Spirit is at work in you daily to bring you into holiness of thought, heart, and mind. And He has beautiful thoughts, holy thoughts, and fertile thoughts for you to dwell on. Thoughts for you to take down deep into your heart where they can sprout, take root, and grow. Thoughts that can spring up and permeate your entire being.

O child, listen to Me and you will hear what I say.

You will receive the revelation of My Word, not like My disciples who misunderstood what I spoke about so often. But, dear one, you will grow in the nurture and admonition of your Lord.

Beloved, read, listen, and meditate on My Word, for it is My thoughts and My ways. My Word is perfect, converting the soul. So, hear what I have to say. Listen to My thoughts and you shall never go astray.

Child, when you take off on the thoughts of the flesh, the world, and the devil there is only destruction, remorse, and sorrow. But when you exercise My thoughts, there is life, joy, peace, and hope in abundance.

So rejoice, My loved one, because My Word, My thoughts are alive, and they quicken you. They make you alive. O come, listen to Me often. Yes, moment by moment, and you shall never be disappointed.

February 15
IN HIS PRESENCE
THERE IS FULLNESS OF JOY
Psalm 16:11; 27:1-6

Child, in My presence there is fullness of joy. O loved one, there is no better place to be than in the center of My presence. And My presence is with you at all times. I never remove it from you.

Beloved, to enjoy My presence means to be aware constantly that I am ever present. Being aware of My presence lets Me be involved in everything you do and say. It allows Me to be in control of your thoughts. It lets Me be Lord of your life.

O child, know that My presence is with you. Know that you can boldly enter into My presence. Know that My presence is peaceful and yet it is powerful. Know that in My presence you can come confidently, while yet in awe of My majesty and splendor.

Yes beloved, be aware and be at home in My

presence. For indeed, there is fullness of joy in the presence of your Lord.

REST
IN THE MIDST OF GREAT DIFFICULTY
1 Peter 4:12-13

Child, know that this light affliction is only for a little while. I use it to bring you to maturity, and to channel great blessing. O loved one, know that the sufferings you go through are to bring praise, honor, and glory to My name. For through the pressures I bring you into a new and fresh relationship with Me.

Yes beloved, I turn impossibilities into miracles and obstacles into stepping stones. So, look to Me always. Let Me move within your life, for I am refining you and removing self. Let all murmuring and complaining cease. Let criticism and animosity vanish like a vapor. O dear one, let nothing else move you other than following Me.

My child, continually commit and submit yourself to Me. Entrust yourself to Me for safekeeping, and I will establish and strengthen you. I will settle and quiet you. I will give you rest, even in the midst of great difficulty.

February 17
TESTS AND TRIALS, OPPORTUNITIES FOR GROWTH
James 1:2-4

O child, be glad and rejoice when the tests and trials come, for they are opportunities for you to grow. Know, loved one, that I turn trials, tests, pressures, and even disasters into stepping stones to maturity. I use them to teach perseverance and patience. I use them to bring you into the fullness of your salvation. I use them to make you complete, so that you lack nothing.

O beloved, none of My promises fail, but they remain true and fixed forever. I indeed am with you. Nothing can stand against you. And I am bringing you to maturity. I am causing you to grow. And it is in My Word that you find strength and hope.

My Word speaks of all that is yours. It tells you that every provision has been made. It tells you to rejoice, and to count it pure joy, when you encounter trials of many kinds. For by these, loved one, I bring you into a far greater experience of My presence, power, and peace regardless the situation, condition, or circumstance.

So child, do not lose heart, but know that your God is at work in your life. And be not bitter, or despair, or lose faith over the difficulties, but rejoice for you are being made whole. You are being made complete. You are coming to maturity. O loved one, I am ever near to walk through the trial with you; to take the burden from you; to carry it for you; and to be your deliverer.

February 18
TRUST HIM TO HONOR HIS WORD
Joshua 1:9

My child, place your hope and your confidence in Me, for there is nothing that can deter what I have planned for you. Therefore, be encouraged. Do not be afraid, anxious or dismayed, but hope in Me. Trust Me to honor My Word.

Beloved, I tell you that I am with you wherever you go. I tell you that I am your friend. I tell you that you are My workmanship, created to do what I have planned for you to do. I tell you that I will complete in you that which I have begun. I tell you that the testing of your faith brings maturity, so that you lack nothing.

So child, do not let yourself despair. Do not ride on

the tide of your emotions. But rather trust Me, and believe what I say. And I say that I am with you always to accomplish My purpose in your life unto the praise, honor, and glory of My name.

LIVE WITH CONFIDENCE AND BOLDNESS
Hebrews 10:19-23

My child, live and move with confidence and boldness, with a heart full of assurance that I am, that I care, and that My Word is true. O never lose your confidence in Me, for that is what keeps things happening in your life. Yes, that confidence and faith is the spark that ignites the power of the living God in you. So, be bold and confident in your faith and trust in Me. Let nothing stand in the way.

Beloved, I have completed all the work, and I am now seated at the right hand of the Father. There is no need to struggle, for I have already made provision. There is no need to fight, for I have already won the battle.

So child, rejoice in what you have in Me. Am not I greater than any problem? Am not I greater than any enemy? Am not I greater than any possession? Am not I greater than any lack? Am not I greater than any man? Am not I greater than any principality or power?

O yes beloved, I am and I always shall be. And I am available to you at all times. So, rejoice and be bold. Be confident in the greatness of your Lord.

February 20

THE EXPECTANCY OF BETTER THINGS
Romans 15:13

Beloved, I fill you with joy and peace. I fill you to overflowing. I fill you with a super abundance. It is yours. You have it. I have already given it to you, so simply walk in it. Let it surface. Let it be manifest, for you already possess it.

Child, I have done a complete work in you, and I fill you with hope. I fill you with the expectancy of better things, and the best is yet to come. Loved one, it is for you I am returning, and this is the best yet to come. I am conforming you to My image, and that is the best. I watch over you and protect you, and that is the best. I prosper you in health, joy, and peace and this is the best. I give you great and precious promises, and they are the best.

So child, look not at today and say yesterday was better. No, look at today and say it is better than yesterday, and it will continue to get better for the best is on its way. O loved one, today is better than yesterday. Today's blessings are for today. Today's hope is for today.

So rejoice, for I fill you with peace, joy, and overflowing hope by the power and presence of My Spirit.

February 21
THE POWER WITHIN ME
Colossians 1:11-12

Child, I am able to do far more than you can ever ask or think, and I can do it through you. For I am at work in your life in great power.

Beloved, the power that is within you is the greatest power there is. It is the power of My Spirit, which is the same power that created the entire universe. It is the same power that raised Me from the dead and seated Me in the heavenlies. And this same power is at work in you. It is encased in love. It is life changing and alive.

Child, nothing compares to the power of your God at work within you. So, use this power. Release it. And as you do, you shall see miracles take place all around you. O release it, dear one. Release the power of My

46

Spirit, and you shall be awed and amazed at what I do through you.

LET NOT YOUR HEART BE DIVIDED
2 Corinthians 6:17-18

O child, let not your heart be divided, for you cannot serve Me and the world at the same time. Have not I said to come out from among them, to be separate, to not touch the unclean thing; and I will receive you, and be a Father unto you, and you shall be My child? So, My dear one, let nothing come between us. Let nothing come before Me, for the best place to be is in the center of My presence, doing what pleases Me.

Beloved, you cannot serve two masters, for you serve either one or the other. It is as simple as that. So, let nothing such as money, position, relationships, wants or desires, hold an attraction to you. Let them not be your master, for if they are your master, then I am not. And if I am not your master, you are short-changing yourself.

Child, if you seek Me first and My righteousness, and serve Me only, then these things shall be added unto you. But they are not to become your master. You are not to become enslaved to them, but rather, they are for you to enjoy and use to further My kingdom. O beloved, serve only Me and do it with your whole heart, undivided, pure, and holy.

HIS CARING MEANS...
Matthew 10:26-31

My child, walk in truth. Walk in the light of My revelation. Walk in illumination knowledge. O walk, where I lead you to walk. Beloved, when I say that I care for My children, it means that I care for you. It means that you are precious to Me. It means that I do not leave or forsake you. It means that I am always with you. It means that I rush to your protection, I hurry to your side.

Child, it means that nothing happens to you without My knowledge and permission. It means that I allow your growth to take place. It means that I take your every situation and circumstance and turn it into good. It means that I make every provision to meet every need.

It means, beloved, that I am providing only the best. It means that you can boldly enter into My presence. It means that nothing can harm or destroy you. It means that I am your refuge and your strength. It means that I hear your cry, and am attentive unto your prayers.

It means, My child, that I have everything under control. It means that everything is all right. It means that I love you, and give you My joy and peace. It means that I visit and fellowship with you daily. It mean that I walk and talk with you. It means, dear one, that your God is mighty, and yet He enjoys your companionship, and will never let you go.

It means, beloved, that I am filled with compassion. It means that I am faithful and true. It means that I am forgiving and hold nothing against you. It means that the God of the entire universe is your Heavenly Father, and you are His child.

February 24
THE BATTLE FOR YOUR MIND
John 3:6; Ephesians 6:12

My child, know that you wrestle not against flesh and blood, but against principalities, powers and rulers of darkness. Know that they are ever trying to get you to gratify the cravings of the world, the flesh, and the devil. Know that your worst enemy is self, for the flesh gives birth to the flesh, while the Spirit gives birth to the Spirit.

Yes beloved, your warfare is spiritual. It takes place in the mind, whether to satisfy the lust of the flesh, or the leading of the Spirit. That is why I have said to be renewed in the attitude of your mind. Let not the flesh dominate your thinking, but let the Spirit be in control.

Child, as you think, so you are. It is the thoughts of a man that rules his life. If the Spirit is in control of your thoughts, of your mind, you shall be led forth in peace, and you shall overcome the world, the flesh, and the devil.

Yes, the war is for your mind, so let My mind, the mind of Christ, be in you. Let My mind be your mind. Let My thoughts be your thoughts.

So, listen for the Spirit in every situation, and in everything you do or say. In every thought you think, let it be of the Spirit, and you will not fulfill the lusts of the flesh. Instead, you will have sweet communion with your Lord, beautiful fellowship with the Spirit, and a pleasing response from your Heavenly Father.

February 25
GROW NOT WEARY IN WELL DOING
Galatians 6:9

My son, do not grow weary in well doing. Let not the work of the Lord be a burden to you. Let not that which you are daily engaged in become toilsome and bothersome. But rather let Me fill you full of joy. For the joy of the Lord is your strength.

Beloved, I strengthen, encourage, settle, and give you peace. Know that the Lord your God is the one who gives the increase. He is the one doing the building. He is the one putting everything together.

So child, fret not. Do not become discouraged, even

49

when you suffer for well doing. But seek to please Me in each and every situation, and I will give the increase.

O beloved, each day look with anticipation for manifestations of My presence, and let not your heart be troubled. For I am the one doing the building. I am the one that makes you peaceful. I am the one that gives the increase. So, rejoice and be glad, for in this you shall find your strength.

February 26
THE GOD OF THE IMPOSSIBLE
Genesis 18:14

Child, there is nothing too difficult for Me, for I am the God of the impossible. I make crooked places straight. I level mountains and raise up the valleys. I quicken the dead, and bring into being things from that which does not exist. I bring order out of chaos, and abundance out of loss.

So rejoice, beloved, for what you see happening around you, the tests and the trials that assail you, I will turn into positive things. I will work them together for good. And continue being faithful where you are, and pray for those who are hurting around you. For I am God, and nothing is impossible for Me.

February 27
GARMENTS OF SPLENDOR
Isaiah 52:1; Zechariah 3:1-5

My child, where there is no vision, where there is no revelation of Me, the people perish. O loved one, I have clothed you in garments of splendor, in rich garments, costly and at great price. I have given you the precious garments of righteousness, and you are clothed in them.

Beloved, you are so beautiful in them, for they

shine as bright as the noonday sun. You are robed in splendor, and you are beautiful to Me. There is perfection in your garments. There is not one spot or wrinkle, for they are ornate and magnificent, and awesome to behold. O child, I am raising up a people arrayed like the world has never seen. And My people shall shine brighter and brighter unto that perfect day.

Yes dear one, you are clothed in My righteousness. Let this encourage you. Let it bring boldness to your life. Let it bring rest to your soul. Let it call forth praise from your lips, and let it bring forth My Word from your mouth.

O beloved, none are as beautiful as My people, for I do not see them in the flesh but rather I see them perfect. I see them complete and whole. I see them in right standing with the Father. I see them as innocent children.

So My child, put on your garments. Enjoy them. Walk around in them. Let them be seen. For indeed, they are beautiful, yes, beyond description. O loved one, I delight in My children. I reveal Myself to them, and I clothe them in rich and fine garments, garments of splendor and beauty. Is not this a revelation? O yes, My child, and much, much more.

February 28

POWERFULLY AT WORK WITHIN ME
Colossians 1:28-29

Child, know beyond a shadow of a doubt, that I am powerfully at work within you. Know that My Spirit and My Word are powerfully at work in your life.

So rejoice, dear one, and let Me do My work through you. Let not your heart be troubled, but rather rest your life in Me. Know that I am in you, your hope of glory. Know that, "Greater is He that is in you than he that is in the world." Know that the world, the flesh, and the devil have no control over you, when I am permitted to work powerfully in you.

So beloved, free Me to do what I came to do. Let your life be an instrument in My hands, and you will see awesome things take place. Yes, rejoice, for I am powerfully at work within you.

February 29
SEE THE COMPLETED WORK
1 Thessalonians 5:16-18; Philippians 4:4

My child, approach each circumstance as though it was completed. See it as totally accomplished. Yes, see it as if it were already past, and that the outcome was a blessing. See it as completed according to My will, and in so doing you will find Me in each situation.

So, see the completed work now, for beloved, this is how I look at everything. This is how I see you.

March

A Special People

A SPECIAL PEOPLE
1 Peter 2:9

Beloved, you indeed are a special people, for you are of the family of God, My family. And I have given you My name, the name that is above every name. I have made you a son. I have chosen you as one of My very own. You are part of My holy nation. I have made you a royal priest. And it does not yet appear what you shall be, but I have great things in store for you.

O child, I brought you, My chosen one, out of darkness into marvelous light. I did this so that you could show forth the praises· and greatness of your Lord and Savior. Loved one, the position you have in Me is great and without compromise. It cannot and will not change. Nothing can remove you from My family, and from being My child with all its rights and privileges.

Yes, you and all My children are special. I have made it so, and I have made every provision for My own, My holy ones. Nothing is lacking. So, rejoice, for you are Mine, not as a slave, but as a child, an heir.

O child, do not I indeed pour out blessings upon blessings in these last days? So, look up and rejoice. Come walk above the things of the earth, and you shall live where nothing can move or shake you. For I have promised never to leave or forsake you, both now and forevermore.

Yes dear one, you are a special people, a holy nation, a royal priest in the household of your God.

HE HAS MET ALL MY NEEDS
1 Peter 4:1-2

Child, it is My will that you have the same attitude as I, that you be conformed to My image, and that you

54

become like Me in every way. I set the example. O beloved, I took care of all your need in My death, burial, and resurrection. All your spiritual need, all your physical need, all your material need I have met.

So, look to Me and let your life be free to receive all that I have for you. And think it not strange concerning the tests and trials, for they come to strengthen you. They come for Me to bring great blessing to your life. They come so that I may be exalted and lifted up. They come not to tear you down or to defeat you, but to give you an opportunity to walk in victory and abundance in Me.

O rejoice, child, for the best is yet to come. See Me in each circumstance, each trial, and each suffering, for out of these situations I bring beauty in the place of ashes, and order out of chaos.

O dear one, commit to My will, and continue to do good. So shall your days be blessed both now and forevermore.

March 3

HE DOES WHAT PLEASES HIM
Psalm 135:6

Child, I alone am the God of the universe, there is no other. I am in control of it all. I have established principles and precepts that are consistent with My character. I do great and awesome things. I can do anything. I do what pleases Me. And it pleases Me to call things into existence from that which exists not. It pleases Me to be your Father, and to watch over you at all times.

Beloved, it pleases Me to be loving, kind, and compassionate. It pleases Me to bless My people. It pleases Me to clothe, feed, and shelter them, to meet all their needs. It pleases Me to see My people seeking Me with their whole heart.

It pleases Me to receive their praise and adoration.

It pleases Me to receive their worship and devotion. It pleases Me to receive their obedience and fellowship. Yes beloved, I do what pleases Me and I do it out of the goodness of My heart.

March 4
HE IS THE AWESOME GOD
Nehemiah 4:14, 20

Beloved, I am the awesome God; the god full of love and compassion; the God to whom nothing is impossible. I am the God whose Word is true and trustworthy; one who does no wrong.

And I am the God who is pure and holy, righteous in all His ways. I am the almighty and the all-powerful God. I am the God of all wisdom and understanding. I am the God of faithfulness and perfection. I am the God who is mindful of you.

Indeed child, I am the awesome God. I created the heavens and the earth, and I hold all things together by My right hand. I bring into being things from that which exists not. Yet, I am ever present and attentive to the cry of My own.

So rejoice, beloved, I am with you always to fight for you, to rescue you, to lead you, and to guide you in the way you are to go. I am ever present to comfort you, and lift you up. For I delight in My children, I rejoice over them with singing.

Yes child, your God is awesome, and He watches over you. He cares and delivers all those who place their trust in Him.

March 5
NOTHING CAN SEPARATE US FROM HIS LOVE
Romans 8:35-39

O My child, nothing can ever separate you from My love. Yes, no fear, no pressure, no trouble, no person, nothing can separate you from Me, absolutely nothing. For you are Mine. You are My child, and you shall always be My child. No one or nothing can separate My love from you.

Beloved, I loved you so much that I laid My life down for you. I hung on the tree to save you. I did this so you could receive all My love and be adopted into My family. I did this so there would be a way for you to be the recipient of My unlimited and unconditional love.

Child, I made the way possible. And if I made the way possible for you to be in right standing with Me, is not your daily life of importance to Me? Do not I supply all your needs? Do not I meet your every need? Do not I tell you that all things work together for good?

Beloved, do not I say that you are an heir, that you are Mine, and that I will never leave or forsake you? O dear one, recognize that what you go through, the trials, the tests, and the pressures are only training and proving grounds. They are preparation. They bring maturity.

But, My child, nothing, absolutely nothing will cause Me to love you less. Nothing will cause Me to cease from loving you, for My love has been given without condition. So, rejoice in the fact that, no matter what, nothing shall separate My love from you.

March 6

LIVE BY THE SPIRIT
Galatians 5:16

Beloved, a simple command I give you today: Live by the Spirit. In everything you say and do, in every thought, word or deed, let it be by My Spirit. O child, this will keep you from the tradition of man. This will keep you from that which is unclean. This will open doors for you to great and mighty things. Yes, live by the Spirit.

Dear one, living by My Spirit puts to death the desires and lusts of the flesh. Living by the Spirit gives power and life to a weary soul. Living by the Spirit means victory over the world, the flesh, and the devil. Living by the Spirit means that the carnal desires no longer keep you in bondage.

Beloved, living by the Spirit brings joy and peace. Living by the Spirit means that I am radiant in and through your very being. Living by the Spirit means the sharing of My love with those around you. Living by the Spirit means seeing signs and wonders take place before your very own eyes. Living by the Spirit means everlasting joy, even when the circumstances appear just the opposite.

O child, living by the Spirit means that you are pleasing Me. So, live by the Spirit, and let the fruit of the Spirit be super abundantly manifested in your life. Yes beloved, live, walk, and be led by My Spirit, and you will be blessed.

March 7
NOTHING JUST HAPPENS
Romans 8:28

Child, I work all things together for good, for I am in control of all things. Nothing just happens without My intervention, for I have a plan and purpose. So, beloved, when it appears that everything is falling apart; when it seems that hell itself is being unleashed; when you think that you are all alone and that everyone is against you; when you are being attacked by the world, the flesh and the devil; know that I am at work bringing forth the very best in you, and for you.

Yes child, even in sickness, I can be manifest and glorified, for I can use illness to promote growth and to bless others. So, do not be discouraged, for I have not forgotten you. You shall not be overtaken by what you are going through, for I will strengthen you, I will help you, I will uphold you, I will deliver you. Many shall see and be awed at your God, and they too shall desire My presence in their lives.

O rejoice, dear one, I am in control. Nothing in your relationship with Me is by chance. I allow things to take place in your life for a purpose.

March 8
LEARNING TO TRUST HIM COMPLETELY
2 Samuel 22:30-37

Beloved, I am the one in control. I am in charge. For I have created all things, and I keep all things in existence. I hold it all together. Without Me nothing would exist, and nothing would take place. There is nothing too difficult for Me?

My child, I know the circumstances, but have not I said to look not at what you see, but look to Me for I am the God of the impossible? I am the God of miracles, but you will not find the miracles in yourself or in the works of man, rather you will find them in Me. For I am the one that arms you with strength and makes your way perfect. I am the one that enables you to run through a troop and to leap over a wall. I am the one that is your refuge and your shield.

O beloved, look not at what you see and say what shall I do, but look through the circumstance, and see Me in the midst of it. See Me in everything, and release yourself from the circumstance, and let Me walk you through it. Let Me hold your hand. Let Me tell you this is the way, walk in it.

Child, there is absolutely nothing to fear, for I am in charge. And if the whole world around you should come tumbling down, say like Job: "Though He slay me yet will I trust Him." Do not place your hope in things, or in your work, or in your relationships, or in your possessions, or in your reputation, but place your hope in Me, in My reputation. Beloved, this is what counts. This is what brings release. This is what brings victory. This is what turns darkness into light. Yes, hope and trust in Me is what counts.

So, release all the anxiety. Release all the fear. Release all concern, and let Me fill you with the peace of My presence. Let Me take the cares and dispose of them in the manner I choose.

O child, this is learning to walk with Me through everything, through the night, through the shadows, through the valleys, through the storm, yes, through all things. This is learning not to be shaken by what goes on in and around you, but to be strong and steadfast in the Lord. This is learning to trust Me totally, no matter what. So go today rejoicing in the knowledge that your Heavenly Father cares and is with you to help you. O trust Me child, for I indeed am in control, I am indeed in charge.

March 9
HIS STRENGTH IS MADE PERFECT IN WEAKNESS
2 Corinthians 12:9-10

Beloved, My strength is made perfect in weakness. Yes, in the weakness of the flesh, in the weakness of your soul, and in the weakness of your abilities, My strength is made perfect. Even in the weakness of the wilderness experience, even in the weakness of great difficulty, and even in the weakness of extreme pressure, My strength is made perfect.

So rejoice, for when you are weak, when you feel helpless, when you think that your God doesn't care, when you think that the task is too big, and when you think surely that the Lord could better use someone else, remember that My strength is made perfect in weakness.

Loved one, all that I ask of you is a submitted heart, and a willingness for Me to work through you; a willingness for your God to share His strength through your weaknesses. This is a willingness to rejoice in your weaknesses, knowing that in those weaknesses, I reveal My strength.

Yes child, My grace is sufficient in any and all circumstances. It is sufficient even in your weaknesses. For it is in your weaknesses that My power is demonstrated.

O dear one, this means a total dependency upon Me. It means that your weaknesses produce nothing in and of themselves. But rather it means that I can take those same weaknesses and turn them into strengths.

So beloved, rejoice in your weaknesses, for I shall reveal Myself in and through them. Think not that you cannot do this or that, but know that in Me all things are possible. Know, dear child, that your weaknesses are opportunities for Me to reveal My strength. They are opportunities for Me to reveal My grace. And beloved, they are opportunities for Me to do miracles, signs, and wonders.

O child, is not this good news? Yes, My strength is made perfect in weakness.

March 10

HIS HAND IS UPON ME
Ezra 8:22

Beloved, My hand is upon you to watch over you, protect you, and keep you. Yes dear one, I care for My own. You can trust Me, for those who trust Me shall lack no good thing. They shall be guarded and protected. They shall be fed. Their enemies shall be at peace with them. No harm shall befall them.

So child, look to Me always. Look not at the trials or difficulties, but look past them and see Me. Look for My leading. Look for My guidance. Look and see the answer to your prayers.

For indeed, beloved, My hand is upon you to bless you, to bring you joy, to give you peace, to comfort you, and to lift you up. So, rejoice and know that in Me all things are possible. Know that My hand is upon you.

March 11
SHARE YOUR FAITH
Philemon 6

O child, be active in sharing your faith. Let it not lie dormant. Put it into action, for faith activated can move mountains. It can level the valleys and make the crooked places straight.

Beloved, an active faith shares with others what I do. It praises My name and lifts Me up. It says My God can do anything. It says that God is in control. It says God has a plan and a purpose for each and every one. It says that though He slay me, yet will I trust Him. O loved one, it stands the tests.

Child, by an active faith you come to know Me better, and you come into a fuller understanding of the good things I have in store for you. Yes dear one, activate your faith. Use it. Share it with others. Put it into action moment by moment, and let nothing move you, for faith in Me keeps you on a steady course.

Child, sharing your faith brings hope and comfort to those around you, and it also brings a reward of blessing to you.

March 12
GOD IS LOOKING FOR FAITHFULNESS
Matthew 25:19-21

Child, I am looking for faithfulness. I am seeking those who will humble themselves and be faithful in little, for if you are faithful in little I will make you ruler over much.

O beloved, think not that what I ask of you is beyond achievement or possibility. Indeed, I am the one who gives you the strength and ability to carry out My plan and purpose. Your role is the choice, the willingness for it to be done.

So child, be steadfast and unmovable. Let nothing deter or sway you. Be not embarrassed of your Lord, or of your faith in Him. Be not ashamed to take a stand for Him, for have not I said that those who put their trust in Me shall never be put to shame?

O beloved, follow Me wherever I lead you. Do what I ask of you. Be not afraid of the mockers and of the scoffers, but simply say: "Here am I Lord, send me." And you shall find rest and peace, for there is no better place to be than in the center of My presence, doing what I ask you to do. And child, there are no better words to hear than, "Well done, faithful one, enter into the joy of your Lord."

March 13
REST ASSURED THAT YOUR GOD IS NEAR
1 Peter 3:12

O child, is there any doubt that I watch over and care for you? Is there any reason to think otherwise? Does not My Word tell you clearly that I see and hear you? Does it not tell you that I live within you? Does it not tell you that I deliver you? Does it not tell you that I answer your prayers? Does it not tell you that I am attentive to your need?

And beloved, does not My Word assure you of My unfailing love? Does it not tell you that I am your protector, your shield, your fortress and your strong tower? Does not My Word tell you that I am your hiding place? Does it not tell you that I instruct you and teach you in the way you are to go?

O child, rest assured that your God is ever near. Rest assured that your Heavenly Father is with you and in you, full of love and compassion for you. Yes, rest assured that I care for you and will never turn My back on you. O rest assured of your confidence in Me.

March 14
IT IS HIS WILL
Romans 12:2

Beloved, it is My will that you live a holy and blameless life, both at peace with Me and with your fellowman. It is My will that you be holy, even as I am holy. It is My will that you put into practice the things that I have spoken, the things I am teaching you.

And My child, it is My will that you be patient in My timing. It is My will that you be filled with My Spirit. It is My will that you listen to the Spirit of the Living God who dwells within you. It is My will that you be conformed to My image. It is My will that you love and comfort others. It is My will that you grow in grace and knowledge of Me. It is My will that you take authority over the world, the flesh, and the devil. It is My will that you seek Me first. It is My will that you love Me with your whole heart.

And loved one, it is My will to provide for you. It is My will to bless you. It is My will to call you child. It is My will to make you a son and an heir. It is My will to give you My name and the authority that goes with that name. It is My will to live in you. It is My will to watch over you. It is My will to lead you and guide you, and to instruct you in the way you are to go. It is My will to endue you with power.

O child, it is My will to love you with an everlasting, unlimited, total, and complete love.

March 15
A WILLING AND OBEDIENT HEART
Hebrews 13:20-21
Beloved, it is I that work in you both the willing

and the doing of My good pleasure. It is I that creates a pure and clean heart within you. It is I that gives you everything you need. It is I who fully equips you to do what pleases Me.

Child, I have placed at your hand all the equipment, tools, and resources necessary to do My will. I do not ask you to do that which you are not equipped to do. I do not ask you to do what I want you to do in yourself. No, I do the doing through you. All I need from you is a willing and obedient heart.

O beloved, I desire a heart that responds to My leading and to My call. I desire a heart that says: "Yes, Lord, whatever you want, I am willing and available." I desire a heart that says: "Not my will but thine be done." I desire a heart that lets Me set in motion the work I want to do.

Yes child, I do My work through you. You are a vessel, an instrument, a tool that I choose to use. So, offer the sacrifice of praise, and continue to do good. And share with others, for in this I am well pleased. In this, I am doing My work.

O beloved, do you see this? Do you hear My voice? Do you understand what I am saying? It is so simple. All I am saying is that I do the doing, and that I equip you with everything needed, or required to do what I want to do through you.

March 16

EVERYDAY MIRACLES
Jeremiah 32:17

Child, nothing is too difficult for Me, for I am the one who created the heavens and the earth, and everything in them. Nothing was made without Me, and I hold all things together.

O beloved, look around you. Is not what you see beautiful and miraculous? Do you not see creation and miracles everyday? Examine the flowers. Are they not beautiful and exquisitely designed? I made them, you know.

And look at the majesty of the mountains and the strength of the raging rivers. I made them also. Look at the wonder of a raindrop and the intricacies of a snowflake. Are not they the products of My hand? Look at the conception and birth of a tiny baby. Is not this a miracle? O yes, loved one, I put all these natural laws into existence.

So, look around and appreciate what I have done, and what I am doing. Know that I am doing a great work in your life. Know that there is nothing impossible, or too difficult for Me. There is no situation that can withstand My presence.

So rejoice, beloved, and be glad. Rest in My Word, and in My strength. For all things are possible with Me. Rest in the fact that I am with you and in you in all My power, might, and strength. O dear one, I am ready and willing to do great and marvelous things.

March 17
BELIEVE WHAT HE SAYS
John 14:1, 12-14

Child, do you believe what I say is true? O loved one, what I tell you is not a lie. What I say is My Word, and it is not false. It is not illusion or convincing words, just to make you feel good, and then to be snatched away like the wind. No, My Word is true, for I speak only the truth. I do not lie.

Beloved, when I say you shall do the same works as I did, you shall do them. When I say that greater works you shall do, then you shall do far more works and miracles than I did. But they are not done in yourself. You do them through Me. For you are in Me and I am in you, and the life you now live is My life living in and through you.

My child, when I say that whatever you ask in

doing My works, I will do it. When you ask for a healing, I will do it. When you ask for an anointing, I will do it. When you ask for a miracle, I will do it. I will do whatever you ask in My name to glorify the Father.

Beloved, My Word is true. And I equip you with everything you need to do the work I have sent you to do. So, ask for people to come to know Me. Ask for healing of the body. Ask for the blind to see and the lame to walk. Ask for the disease and affliction to flee. Ask that the immune system function. Ask and I will do it, for I said I would honor My Word.

RECONCILED TO THE FATHER
Colossians 1:22

O child, remember always that I love you. Know that it was out of My immense and immeasurable love that I brought you into right standing with the Father. Know that I reconciled our differences.

Beloved, I love you and I care for you. I know what you face each day. I know the joys and the sorrows. I know the gladness and the pain. I know the happiness and the disappointments. For I also was a man like you, acquainted with grief and sorrow.

Yet child, I overcame. I was obedient unto death, and because I was, it resulted in your reconciliation to the Father. Yes, I atoned for your sins. I became the sacrifice. I, who knew no sin, became sin for you. I, who was tested and tried, did not let sin have dominion over Me. But rather, I took authority over it and became the victor.

Beloved, I did this for you. I did this so you could have hope. I did this so you could have the victory. I did this so that sin should not have dominion over you. O child, I did this out of My love and grace, so you could find mercy and help in the time of need. I did this so that you could have fellowship with Me. I did this so you could know the love of God. I did this so you could share that same love to all.

March 19
HE RUSHES TO MY RESCUE
Job 5:19

Child, I know and I understand all that you are experiencing. I am aware of the hurts, the problems, the difficulties, and the struggles. But, loved one, know that all you need do is to cry out to Me, and place your total trust and confidence in Me, and I will rush to your rescue.

Beloved, I have rescued you many times. There were times when you were not aware that it was I doing so. There were times when I kept you from harm. There were times when I met your needs. And there were times when you were ill. Yes, many times I place a hedge of protection around you.

O loved one, I have placed My Spirit within you, and My Word has been spoken over you. So rejoice, child, for all that you are facing, all that appears to be swallowing you up, shall be brought under your feet. You are more than a conqueror through Me. Only trust Me with your whole heart. Yes, I rush to your rescue, and I fill you to overflowing with joy and peace.

March 20
WHO ELSE IS LIKE HIM
Isaiah 57:15

O child, who else is God like Me? Is there any other? Who else can give you peace and calmness of soul even while the storm rages? Who else can speak comfort to you when you are hurting, and when you feel all alone, and that no one cares?

Who else heals your body and makes you whole? Who else restores and refreshes you daily? Who else leads and guides you, and helps you make the right decisions? Who else gives strength to the weary and joy in the midst of sorrow? Who else has written your name down in the Lamb's Book of Life?

Who else has given you eternal life? Who else has made you His child and has become your Heavenly Father? Who else has given you His name and made you His heir? Who else makes provision for your every need, all that you need for both life and godliness? Who else has given you written words that become alive within you?

Who else has made you His dwelling place? Who else has given you His Spirit and made you spiritually alive? Who else has said that He would never leave you or forsake you? Who else has said that those who trust in Him would lack no good thing? Who else says that He is your friend, one that is closer than a brother? And who else loves you with an unlimited and unconditional love?

O beloved, I am the one, and if I be for you nothing can be against you.

March 21
LOAVES AND FISHES
Luke 9:10-17

Beloved, you have asked for My sufficiency, and I have heard your call. And I have answered, and will continue to answer? Have not I taken care of you in the past? Have not I brought you through tests, trials, dangers, and difficulties?

O child, consider where you are today, and where you were yesterday. Have not I piloted you through treacherous waters? Consider, dear one, how I fed the five thousand. Did not I welcome the people? Did not I speak life and healing to them? Was not I moved with compassion? Did not I care for their physical needs, as well as, their spiritual needs?

Beloved, did not I take what was available, bless it, multiply it, and feed the people? Was not there far more left over than when I began? O yes, loved one, there was a super abundance. There was no lack. For everyone ate and was satisfied.

So child, consider the wonders of your Lord and Savior, for I still take little and make it much. I still am your sufficiency. I still multiply the loaves and the fishes. I am still moved with compassion. I know the needs. So, say not, or even think that your Lord would abandon you. Think not that there is lack. Think not that I am insufficient.

But, My beloved, give to Me what is available, and I will multiply it. I will make it grow. I will make it sufficient, so that there will be more than enough. So, go now and rejoice. Leave the multiplication to me, and you will be awed at what I do.

O child, look through the difficulty and see Me satisfying you, even with twelve full baskets left over.

March 22

ASK THE FATHER
John 16:23-33

O child, have not I said that you could ask the Father for anything in My name, and He would give it to you? So ask, loved one, and you shall receive that your joy may be full.

Yes beloved, this is My Word. I spoke it. It is true. I do not lie. My Word is not a double standard, which is good for one and not for another. It is for everyone. I did not speak it to bless only a handful. I spoke it so that all would be blessed. It was spoken so you could receive all that you asked.

Yes child, whatever you ask in My name the Father will give it to you. So, believe what I say. Do not doubt, but put your faith into action. Speak it. Speak a good confession. For if I said it, and I did, it is true.

70

O loved one, let not the pressures convince you otherwise. For I have overcome the pressures. I am the one that overcame the world, the flesh, and the devil. The enemy has no place in your life.

So believe, My child, let there be no doubt. Ask in My name, and you shall receive so that your joy may be full.

DEATH TO SELF
1 Corinthians 15:31; Romans 6:6

My son, to be in Me is life eternal. But there is the need to die to self, and to count it as dead. Yes, self must die if I am to be high and lifted up. My child, is it not your prayer that My name always be glorified in and through you? Is it not your prayer that I be Lord of your life?

So rejoice, My dear one. I am at work in your life. I am answering your prayer. I am bringing you into a deeper and fuller relationship with Me. And the more death there is to self, the more I can be manifest in your life.

O child, you have tasted and you know that I am good. You know that in Me you lack nothing. You know that I do not withhold any good thing from you. You know that this is the day that the Lord has made, and that you are to rejoice and be glad. It is a day of celebration, not mourning or grief.

O beloved, remember that I watch over you and care for you. Know that I am bringing you into the fullness of My resurrection power, as you die daily to self and become alive unto Me.

HOPE IN HIM
1 Timothy 4:10

Child, I am the God of hope, there is no other. And I bring hope for today and hope for tomorrow. For hope in Me brings life in abundance. Hope in Me turns darkness into light, and sorrow into joy.

Beloved, hope in Me says: "Though He slay me yet will I trust Him." Hope in Me believes that all things work together for good. Hope in Me knows that I am in control of each and every situation. Hope in Me makes Me Lord of your life.

Dear child, hope in Me sees only the good. Hope in Me brings love and compassion to the needs of others. Hope in Me brings commitment to Me. Hope in Me settles all doubts. Hope in Me says: "Everything is all right."

Child, hope in Me believes that I rescue you out of all your troubles. Hope in Me believes that I hear and answer your prayers. Hope in Me makes for sweet communion between us. Hope in Me expects and receives miracles. Hope in Me says that my God can do anything.

Beloved, hope in Me says that nothing shall be impossible. Hope in Me believes that in weakness I am your strength. Hope in Me believes and claims all My promises. O loved one, hope in Me believes all this and so much more. So, hope in Me with great expectation, and you shall not be disappointed.

March 25

FAITHFUL AND OBEDIENT
2 Chronicles 31:21

Beloved, I am looking for faithful and obedient men and women. Those who place nothing else above Me. Those who will not rob Me or cheat Me. Those who will give Me their all. Those who will not hesitate to follow where I lead.

And I am looking for those who will hold back nothing from Me. Those who say: "Lord, here am I, and here is everything I own. Here is my heart, my mind, my thoughts, my words, my deeds, my actions, and my possessions. I am yours, Lord, do with me as you want."

It is such, My child, that I am molding and shaping to My image. It is such that I can use for My glory. It is such who do not count the cost. It is such that lead many to righteousness. It is such who I can place in the front lines. It is such who will follow Me wherever I lead them.

O child, faithfulness and obedience gain My favor. So, be faithful and follow Me. Be obedient and walk in My precepts, and you shall see the hand of the Lord become more and more evident in your life. O rejoice, beloved, I am still working on you.

March 26

LET PRAISE ALWAYS BE FIRST
Hebrews 13:15

In everything, child, praise Me. Let praise always be in your heart and on your lips. Let it be the first thing in the morning and the last thing at night. Even in the night seasons let praise flow from deep within.

Yes beloved, send your praises first. And as you face each new day, let your praises rise. Over each issue, each problem, each difficulty, and each pressure let praise be the first thing that comes from your lips. My child, send praise first over every situation. Let praise prepare the way for victory. O dear one, I inhabit the praises of My people.

HE CREATES MASTERPIECES
Ephesians 2:10

Beloved, know that He who has begun a good work in you will complete it. Yes, I will finish it, and you will know that I am the one doing it.

O child, what I begin, I do not let lie dormant. I do not start something and then not finish it. No, I take what I start and I bring it to perfection. I make it perfect. I make what I do holy. I sanctify it. I make it pure. I do a good work.

Beloved, what I create is masterpieces. It is not practice. It is not something to be discarded. For I create and bring into being things that are beautiful and lovely, things of splendor and majesty. I create masterpieces, and that is what you are.

Child, you are not worthless. You are not something to be cast away. O no, you are a masterpiece of My work, and I do this by the power of My Spirit. And dear one, I hear your cry. I know your heart, and I tell you that you are beautiful. You are My child, and I walk with you, and talk with you, and tell you that I am your friend.

O beloved, come and walk with Me in the beauty of My presence. Come, fellowship with Me in the quietness of the day. Come, let Me fill you with Myself. Yes, put the self-life to death, and let My resurrection power surge through your entire being. For I am building a temple, and I will finish it. I will complete it, and it will be perfect. For you are that temple, and I dwell within.

THE SECRET OF BLESSING
Psalm 119:89-94

My child, the secret of blessing is to walk in My precepts, to heed My commands, and to follow My Word. O loved one, let My Word so fill your life, that living it becomes as natural to you as breathing. For My precepts are divine, and they are life giving.

O hear Me, beloved. Love Me with singleness of purpose, and with a pure heart. Yes, love Me and serve only Me. Love Me with all your heart, with all your mind, with all your soul, and with all your strength. And let that love lead you into keeping My commands, into obeying My Word.

Child, in keeping My Word, you are brought into pleasant places. In walking in My precepts, you will do nothing but prosper. In living My principles there shall only be life to everything you touch.

O beloved, know that there is no other. Know that I am the one who brings you into the land you are to possess. Know that I am prospering you. Know that I have promised that all shall go well with you, that you shall enjoy long life, and that you shall increase.

But child, know that I have promised this on the condition that you love Me with your whole heart, mind, and strength. Yet, you can walk in that love by simply choosing to do so, by choosing to follow My precepts.

Loved one, My principles and My precepts are pure. They are unmovable. They are My ways. They are the ways that lead to an abundant life. So, remember Me always. Do not forget to speak of Me and My precepts at all times, for in so doing you will never be disappointed, and your life will be the better.

Child, you will see the fields grow and bloom, the vineyards will yield their fruit, your house will be filled with good things, and you will eat and be satisfied. It is true, beloved, for I keep My Word. There is no other like Me. Does this not cause you to rejoice? Is this not blessings far more than can be counted? O child, this is My way.

March 29
A STRONG CITY
Isaiah 26:1-2

Child, My dwelling place is a strong city, and I fortify it with impenetrable walls of My salvation. O dear one, My people make up that city. And you are a part of it, for I have opened up the gates to you. I have clothed you in My righteousness, and have given you My name. I have given you My Word filled with great and precious promises.

Beloved, in My city, behind the walls of salvation, you can find strength and comfort. You can find peace and prosperity, joy and gladness. You can find protection and security. For I have brought you to a safe refuge, a strong tower, a city that cannot be shaken. The enemy cannot come and take you away, for I have defeated him.

Child, have faith in what I say. Believe it, for it is true. You are forever protected and cared for by your Heavenly Father in the city not made with hands. It is the city that will remain forever. It is the city that will never pass away. It is the city that is full of righteousness, truth, and holiness. It is the city of the living God.

March 30
WALKING IN THE LIGHT
Ephesians 5:8-10

My son, come and walk as a child of My light, for in so doing you will be found pleasing to Me. Beloved, these are the things that please Me: allowing me to live

My life through you; manifesting the fruit of the Spirit in your life; being filled with My Spirit; having a thankful heart; singing and making melody in your heart; and receiving your praise and worship.

So child, come walk in the light. Let My Spirit expose within you what must dissipate in the light of My presence. Let nothing hinder or block your walk with Me. O loved one, hang not on to things that are temporal, things that do not last, things that erode and fade away. But hold fast to that which is good, that which is righteous and true.

O beloved, place yourself before the light of your Lord, and examine yourself to see what needs to be exposed. See what needs to be turned over to Me, and let it go. For I love you, and I have given you My Word, and My Word brings life. It brings conviction, instruction, and discernment. It brings the light of revelation. So, walk as a child of that light.

Yes child, come to the mirror of My Word, and you shall see the things that need to go and the things that need to stay. And as you come daily to that mirror you will see, more and more, a renewing taking place in your life. O dear one, walk in the light of My Word.

March 31

ALIVE IN CHRIST
Ephesians 2:4-5

Dear child, I have lavished you in My love. I have immersed you in My grace. I have rescued you and redeemed you. I have set you free from sin and death. O loved one, My grace, My loving kindness, is more than sufficient, for it abounds unto you.

Beloved, I have identified you with Me. I have made you one with Me. You share in My death, burial, and resurrection. And I have made you a partaker of My divine nature. I have seated you in the heavenlies. I have given you authority. O loved one, I have made you alive to demonstrate to the world My greatness, power, love, mercy, and grace.

Child, I manifest Myself in you. In you I live My life. In you the glory of your God is revealed. In you I bless others. In you I turn weakness into strength. In you I demonstrate My mighty power. In and through you, I minister to the needs of My people. For you are My handiwork, created to do good works that I have prepared for you to do. O rejoice, child, I have made you alive.

April

All the Days of My Life

ALL THE DAYS OF MY LIFE
Isaiah 46:3-4

Child, know that it is I that rescues and sustains you. Know that there is no other. I alone am God, the Lord God Almighty, the creator and sustainer of the whole universe. There is none beside Me. I alone am HE. And, loved one, I have known you since before the foundation of the world.

Beloved, while you were in your mother's womb, I carried you. When you were born I watched over you. I rescued and protected you from the time you were an infant to this present day. I am the one who watches over you, carrying you, sustaining you, and rescuing you from the world, the flesh, and the devil.

Yes, I watch over you as a mother hen watches over her chicks. And, loved one, if I have brought you this far, will I turn My back on you now? Would I leave or forsake you now? No My child, I will not.

O beloved, I know everything about you. I even know the number of the hairs on your head. I know you better than you know yourself. So, think not that your Lord is far from you or would ever leave you. No, I dwell in you, and I sustain you, and I rescue you. Even to your old age and to the graying of the hairs on your head, I care for you.

My child, there is no other comfort. There is no other peace. There is no other joy. There is no better promise than the promise of My presence caring for My children. Yes dear one, there is no other. And beloved, I have only begun. I know the end from the beginning, and I will carry you through anything and everything.

So trust Me, child. Do not look at circumstances and say, "God has forsaken me, how shall I go through this trial"? But rejoice that I have promised to carry you, that I have promised to sustain you, that I have promised to come to your rescue all the days of your life.

Yes beloved, rejoice that I am present. Rejoice, that I fellowship with you. Rejoice, that I lead you. Rejoice, that I know the way through the wilderness. Rejoice, that I know how to bring you through the maize and confusion of a busy schedule. Rejoice, that I am your God and that there is no other. O rejoice, My child, for I carry you, sustain you, and rescue you all the days of your life, even to your old age.

April 2

I AM EXACTLY WHERE HE WANTS ME
Proverbs 20:24

My child, what may appear as disaster to you is really to serve My purpose. It is designed to advance the good news. For, dear one, I still orchestrate everything together. I know just what instrument needs to be played precisely at just the right time.

O beloved, believe Me when I tell you that I am in control. Believe that I know what I am doing in your life. For My purposes are fixed. There is order in what I do. My timing is perfect.

So child, be content where I have you. Look not at what others are doing and wish that it were you. But rather know that I have you exactly where I want you, so that My gospel will be advanced.

Beloved, all that happens to you is for a purpose. Have not I said it is a privilege to suffer for Me? So, rejoice and be glad. And receive not the negative reports. Rather use them as opportunities to share and defend the good news given to you.

Yes child, regardless the situation, no matter the condition, know that I have placed you where you are to bring praise, honor, and glory to My name. Beloved, you are where I want you, today.

April 3

NOTHING IS IMPOSSIBLE
Philippians 4:13

Beloved, I ask of you only what you are able to bear. I ask of you only what I can do through you. I ask of you only that which manifests My presence.

Child, do you not see that I can take little, something insignificant, something weak and powerless, and turn it into something great and beautiful, strong, and precious. And I can do that from nothing, yes, from that which does not exist.

So beloved, what I ask you to do, I equip you to do. For I will do the doing. I require nothing from you that I cannot perform. So, when I ask you to do certain things, when the task seems monumental and there appears no way to do it, rejoice, for I will not give you a task that I cannot perform through you.

O child, you can do anything. Nothing shall be impossible to you. So, listen to My voice and obey My command, and you will be awed at what I can do through you. Remember, beloved, that My command is to love, and that comes from a pure heart, a good conscience, and a sincere faith.

April 4

HE IS GREAT TREASURE
Matthew 6:19-24

Beloved, seek Me with your whole heart, for where your heart is there will your treasure be. O loved one, I am great treasure. In Me is everything for life and godliness. So, search for Me and you shall find Me, for I am not in hiding. I withhold not Myself from you, for it is My desire to reveal Myself fully to you and through you. It is My purpose that you be alive in spirit, soul, and body.

O child, remember, that you are spirit, that you

have a soul, and that you live in a body of flesh. Remember, that I live in you by My Spirit to reveal and manifest Myself to you and through you. So, look for Me. Seek Me diligently as you would great treasure, for the more you seek Me, the more I become real and alive to you.

Yes beloved, come and learn of Me. Come and know Me better. And the earthly will become less important, and the Spirit will become more and more your treasure.

April 5

LEARNING FROM MOSES
Exodus 33:12-17

O beloved, learn of Me through the experiences of Moses. Did not he inquire of Me? Did he not come boldly into My presence? Did not I speak to him face to face? Was not his countenance radiant from being in My presence? Did not I reveal Myself to him? Did not I manifest My power, My majesty, and My glory by signs and miracles through him? Did he not have a beautiful relationship with Me?

O My child, you have the opportunity to have that same kind of relationship. But you do not have to go to a tent outside the camp. No, the tent of My dwelling is in you, for I reside within you in all My power, glory, and splendor. You can come to Me at any moment, in any place, and be immediately in My presence. You can walk with Me and you can talk with Me, without appointment or reservation, any time of the day or night.

Beloved, the more you spend in My presence, the more radiant your life becomes. With Moses the radiance faded. With you the radiance of My presence can only increase, for I am with you and in you always. So, learn from the example of Moses. Come often into My presence, for the more you do the more I reveal Myself to you, and the more you experience My goodness, love, and compassion.

Child, I have proclaimed My name to you, over you, and in you. Come enjoy the fellowship of your Lord.

April 6

SEEK TO SERVE OTHERS
1 Corinthians 10:24

Beloved, seek good and pursue it. Seek peace and pursue it. Seek to serve others and pursue it. Forget not the sacrifice of loving others and of sharing with others from that which I have blessed you with.

O child, share yourself and share Me. Share what I have done in your life. Share what I have given you. Share with those who are hurting, with those who are going through the fire of testing and trial. Share yourself with those who need help and guidance.

Beloved, what I have given you is not meant for you to hoard or hold to yourself. Rather, it is meant to be shared, to be freely given to others. For as I freely give to you, so you are to freely give to others.

Yes child, a new command I have given, that is to love one another. So, when the phone rings or the neighbors need help, or someone needs counseling or prayer, do not hold back, but willingly and lovingly let Me minister to them through you.

O loved one, in so doing you too will be blessed. It always works this way, for this is the principle of sowing and reaping. So, continue to do good. Continue to sow seed, and you will reap a bountiful harvest.

Yes beloved, keep on loving your neighbor, that is, those around you wherever you are.

POWER WITHOUT LIMIT
Ephesians 3:20-21

Child, My power is awesome and without limit. It is incredible. It is constructive to the leveling of mountains and to the raising up of valleys. It is strong to the bringing down of strongholds and to the binding of the enemy. It is corrective to the restoration of that which has been taken away and to the renewing of the attitude of the mind.

Yes beloved, My power can transform ugly into beautiful, and bad into good. By My power the universe and the worlds were formed. By My power they all hold together. By My power I bring things into being from that which does not exist. By My power I bring resurrection to the dead. By My power I have defeated all the forces of the evil one, so that he has no claim or authority over you.

O child, this same power is in you, and it is alive and active. It is at work in you. You can never exhaust it, for it is beyond all you can ask or even think. So, tap into it. Use it. Let My power flow through your life and create blessing upon blessing, both to you and to those around you.

O beloved, turn My power loose and see things take place that you never dreamed could happen. See the lost saved. See the healing of the nations. See the sick, the lame, and the broken hearted restored. See prosperity come to those you pray for. See those you love come running to Me with praise and rejoicing on their lips.

Yes dear one, loose the power, My power that is in you, and be in awe at what I do. For, child, this power is the presence of My Spirit, the very presence of the Living God.

April 8

YOKED TOGETHER WITH CHRIST
Matthew 11:28-30

O child, we are yoked together as a team, and those yoked together share in bearing the burden. So, come to Me and take My yoke upon you, for it is My desire that you not bear the burdens alone, but that I carry them for you.

Beloved, does it not seem reasonable that a team can do far more than any single effort? Does not a team share in the load? Does not a team share in the reward? O loved one, in this team I am the strength, the power, the mighty one, and you are the vessel in which I live, move, and have My being. Yes, we are yoked together.

And child, when two are yoked and working together the resistance becomes lighter. But when one is either running ahead or dragging behind, the burden becomes twice as difficult. The beautiful thing in this relationship is that we are yoked and flowing together. I take all the burden. Have not I said that My yoke is easy and My burden is light?

O beloved, learn from the teams of animals yoked together, working in harmony. Does not the effort appear beautiful and graceful? But when there is one tugging against the other there is only room for great irritation and strife. So, come and learn of Me. Yes, yoke yourself to Me, and you shall find rest and strength to your soul.

April 9

THE ENEMY IS UNDER MY FEET
Romans 16:20

Child, know that the enemy is under your feet, he has no power or control over you, for I have broken that power. I redeemed you, I bought you, and I paid your penalty. The enemy cannot have you. He cannot violate you, for you are My child. The victory is yours.

So beloved, do not be conformed to this world, but be transformed in the renewing of your mind. And think on spiritual things. Lay up in store for yourself spiritual treasure.

My child, there is nothing that can come against you that all the resources of heaven cannot overcome, for you are Mine and I have overcome. So, let My Spirit flow. Yes, release Him. Nothing shall touch you. Loved one, the enemy is under your feet.

April 10
BLIND FAITH AND TRUST PLEASES HIM
Psalm 20:7

Child, blind faith and trust in Me pleases Me. It listens and takes Me at My Word. It brings obedience, and the end result is blessing beyond comprehension.

O beloved, listen for My voice. Quietly seek My guidance, and I will speak to you and tell you this is the way, walk in it. I will lead you and provide for you, and nothing shall be impossible to you.

My child, receive not the negative reports, but rather cast out all thoughts of failure and loss, for these are instruments of the enemy designed to defeat you. You are not to be defeated, for I have already won the victory. It is yours, so walk in it.

Beloved, My Word is true. My calling is sure. There is no room for doubt. So, get up out of the mire of depression and throw off those negative thoughts. Rejoice in your God, for I bring you great blessing. I bring you into a Promised Land. I turn everything into good.

O believe it, child. Trust Me. I keep My Word. You shall not fall or fail. These are lies of the enemy. But rather you shall go on to higher heights, to a greater revelation and knowledge of your Lord and Savior, and to blessings yet untold. Beloved, you have so much to be thankful for. I do not forget you or go back on My Word. The blessings are worth the waiting.

April 11

THE MIND OF CHRIST
Philippians 2:1-5

Beloved, I am conforming you to My image. Have not I said to let My mind be in you, and that you should have the same attitude as Me? O yes, child, know that you have My mind. Know that you can have My mind on anything and everything you do. Know that you can let My mind be your mind. Know that your thoughts and attitudes can be controlled by My mind.

Beloved, it is a matter of choosing to let My mind become your mind, and in so doing you have My thinking, My wisdom, My decision making powers, and My thought processes in everything.

Dear one, there remains no longer any reason for indecision, for My mind is your mind. There remains no longer any reason for doubt, as to who you are or whose you are. For I bring assurance, beyond a shadow of a doubt, that I am in control, and that I lead and direct.

O child, as the negative and unhealthy thoughts arise, simply give them over to My mind, and I will handle them and dismiss them. For My mind produces thoughts that are lovely and wholesome.

Beloved, I do not produce a mindset that is unproductive and destructive, but rather I build up. I set into motion. I bring thoughts of life, peace, health, gladness and victory. I bring a mindset of praise, adoration, and worship of the Heavenly Father.

So, child, let this mind be in you, the same mind as Mine. I have given it to you to safeguard you in every way.

April 12

KEEP YOURSELF PROM IDOLS
1 John 5:21

Dear one, keep yourself from idols. Keep yourself holy and pure. Let nothing come between you and Me, for anything that does is an idol. Idols are those things that become objects of worship. They become other gods. Beloved, do not put your possessions, your work, your family, even your ministry ahead of Me, for I alone am to be the object of your worship.

O dear one, I am not something abstract. I am real and personal. Your love for Me comes before anything else. So child, examine your life and see where you may have placed things or relationships above Me. And turn from those things. Put them in their proper order.

Beloved, there is nothing wrong with things, possessions, jobs and family, but they are never to be placed before Me, for if they are, they become idols. They become the center of your worship, and then I am no longer first in your life.

Child, My desire is to be first in your life at all times. So, have no other gods before you, but rather seek Me first, and all these other things shall be added unto you.

April 13

OUR GOD REIGNS
Psalm 97:1-12

Beloved, I am the Most High. I am the God of the entire universe. My name is above every name. I reign over the vastness of eternity and the presence of time. I reign over all My creation.

Child, before Me nothing can stand, for even the mountains melt in My presence. But, O dear one, I am mindful of you. And you may come boldly into My presence and walk and talk with Me. You may come boldly into My presence and experience My love.

You may come boldly into My presence and enjoy My fellowship. You may come boldly into My presence and ask My help in the time of need. You may come boldly into My presence, and I will comfort you when you need comfort.

Yes beloved, the God of all the universe, the one who reigns on high, the one who is exalted far above all gods, is the one who loves and cares for you.

O child, let all the earth rejoice.

April 14
SPEAK ONLY WHAT YOU HEAR
John 16:13-15

Child, I have heard your prayers. I know your heart. For I have placed My Spirit within you to lead you, to guide you, to teach you, to comfort you, to counsel you, and to tell you things that are to come. As I spoke only what I heard from the Father, so the Spirit speaks only what He hears from Me. And you too, child, are to speak only what you hear.

O beloved, be sensitive to My Spirit. Listen carefully, for He is a quiet voice behind you saying: "This is the way to go." My Spirit has access to all that is Mine, and He takes what is Mine and makes it known unto you. So, if you lack wisdom and understanding, ask, and He will answer with wisdom and understanding. If you need comfort, ask, and He will give you comfort.

Child, there is indeed a personal fellowship with the Holy Spirit. He is not a robot, devoid of love and compassion. No, He is My Spirit. He is moved as I am moved. So, listen to Him and know that in so doing He brings glory to My name.

POSSESSING THE LAND
Deuteronomy 6:12-19

Beloved, I am the faithful and true God. What I promise to do, I do. And dear one, I have promised to bring you into the land, a land flowing with milk and honey. It is a land full of the goodness of My presence. And I have promised to bless you and to give you an abundance. Yes, there is land to possess, cities to inhabit, fields and vineyards waiting, which are ripe and ready to harvest.

My child, you shall eat and be full. You shall not lack any good thing. I have purchased it all. It belongs to Me, and I give it to you. I share it with you. So, eat and be satisfied, for there is plenty. My resources cannot be exhausted. But beloved, these resources are not to be squandered or wasted. Rather, they are to be used to bring glory and honor to My name.

O child, I have promised you great and mighty things. So, do not despair. You shall walk in them this day. Today, you shall see just how great your inheritance is, and you shall stand in awe at the wonder of your Lord. So, as you walk in the abundance, do not forget who gave it to you. Know that it does not come from you or anyone else, but rather it comes from Me. O remember this, dear one, all the days of your life.

Yes beloved, I give you an abundance. I give you a marvelous inheritance, and I chase all your enemies out before you. Those things that seem to stand in your way, those gates of brass and bars of iron, I melt before your eyes.

O rejoice My child, for your redemption is at hand. I am faithful and true. You shall possess the land.

April 16
CHRIST IN ME THE HOPE OF GLORY
Colossians 1:27

Child, the most profound truth, yet so simple, is that I live in you, and in so doing I am your hope of Glory. Yes, I live in you. I have taken up residence. I am your invited guest. I bring with Me all that is Mine. I bring it to share.

Beloved, I bring with Me all the power of the universe. I bring with Me all the riches of glory. I bring with Me peace, joy, comfort, and freedom. I bring with Me strength to meet every weakness. I bring with Me the power of My Word. I bring with Me love and compassion.

And child, I bring with Me purity and holiness. I bring with Me victory over the world, the flesh, and the devil. I bring with Me a new nature, one that is a partaker of My divine nature. I bring with Me wisdom, guidance, and understanding. I bring with Me everything you need for life and godliness.

O beloved, I bring all this and more, for I do live in you. I am your hope of glory. Is not this beautiful? Is not this marvelous and awesome? Just think, the Almighty God, the creator of all the universe, the one who is in control of all things, lives and moves in and through you.

Child, this is truly a great thing. I live in you and in all those who receive Me. O rejoice, for there is more of Me than can ever be exhausted, yet I live in you in My entirety. Yes, I am Christ in you, your hope of glory.

April 17
THE LIGHT OF HIS PRESENCE AND HIS WORD
John 1:1-5

My child, truly the light of My presence is evident everywhere, yet My people do not see or hear Me. O loved one, do not let your light become dimmed by unbelief, doubt, or fear, for the light of My presence dispels all that. It dispels doubt and unbelief, and brings peace and comfort to your soul.

Beloved, let the light of My presence expose those areas of darkness in your life. Let My light reveal what needs to be cleansed and purified. Yes, loved one, let Me expose those areas where the clutter and cobwebs have formed.

O child, let the light of My presence and of My Word search your whole heart for anything that may hinder your walk with Me. Let the light of My Word and My presence search your mind and thoughts to cleanse and purify them. Let the light of My Word and My presence direct your path to illuminate the way, to show you what to do and when to do it.

Yes, let the light of My presence and of My Word shine through in your life, so that others may see the light and glorify your Father, which is in heaven.

April 18

RICHLY BLESSED
Psalm 40:1-5

Beloved, you are Mine, you are My inheritance. There is no difference in background or nationality, for I richly bless all those who call upon Me and place their trust in Me. For I see only My people clothed in My righteousness. In Me all the nations of the earth are blessed, for all that call upon My name I will in no way cast out.

Child, everything is wrapped up in Me. I am your salvation, and in your salvation I have included everything you need. I have included fellowship. I have included an abundance of life. I have included love and joy, peace and prosperity, health and healing, strength, comfort, and security; all in abundance.

O rejoice beloved, for I watch carefully over you. I

do not let you fall, but I hold you up and I speak instruction to you. I show you the path to take. But remember, dear one, the choice is yours.

So, choose to walk in the instruction of My Spirit and in the light of My Word, and you shall not lack any good thing. O child, I richly bless My people. So, come and walk in this marvelous principle.

April 19

GOOD GIFTS
Matthew 7:11

Child, rejoice for your Heavenly Father knows what you have need of, even before you ask. And while you are asking, the answer is on its way. O dear one, every good and perfect gift is from above, for I indeed give good gifts to My children. My gifts are always just right. They are perfect. They are the best.

Beloved, I withhold no good thing from you. I give you what is right and perfect. Sometimes I say wait, for at the moment the gift would not be properly timed. But I always give. I always bless.

O child, I lavish you and I immerse you in My provision, in My goodness, in My prosperity, in My health, and in My strength. And My presence shall go with you always, and I will give you rest on every side.

So ask, and it shall be given you. Seek, and you shall find what you are looking for. Knock, and the door will be opened to you. O rejoice, child, I give good gifts.

April 20

IN LOVE
Ephesians 1:4-5

My child, My love for you knows no bounds, and out of that love I have opened the gates of heaven to you. In love I called you. In love I chose you. In love I

94

forgave you. In love I placed you in right standing with Me. In love I made you righteous. In love I adopted you as My child. In love I seated you with Me in the heavenlies. In love I share all the riches of My glorious grace.

O beloved, in love I carry on to completion the good work I began in you. In love I surround you with My keeping power. There is nothing that can ever remove it. You may think that I do not hear you. You may think that the fiery trials will consume you, but I assure you that they will not.

Yes child, I assure you that I do hear and respond to you. Consider, how I have responded in the past. Have not I rushed to your aid, to your side? Have not I fed you, clothed you, sheltered you, protected you, and lavished you in My love? So, let not anything move you, for you are loved and cared for far more than you realize.

Beloved, it is by My grace and love that you breathe each breath you take. It is by My grace and love that your heart beats each beat. So, think positively. Do not let the negatives enter your mind, but think on Me. Think on who I am and who you are in Me. And rejoice, for I love you and ever live to make intercession for you. Child, you are secure in Me, for My love knows no bounds.

April 21

THE JOY OF THE LORD
Nehemiah 8:10

O child, I love you so. You are precious to Me, and I joy over you with songs of deliverance and with songs of joy. And I do great and mighty things that make you glad, things that make you rejoice. I fill your mouth with laughter. I restore all that has been taken away.

Yes beloved, My joy, the joy of your Lord is your strength. Without Me you would be overwhelmed, but with Me nothing shall overtake you. For the difficulties and the pressures have been conquered.

So rejoice child, and sing. Praise and shout, for I, the God of the entire universe, love you beyond a shadow of a doubt.

April 22
CONSIDER THE RESULTS OF FAITHFULNESS
Hebrews 3:2-6

My child, as I am faithful, so be you faithful. As I am holy, so, be you also holy. For consider the results of faithfulness. Did not My faithfulness result in the removal of your sin?

Did not My faithfulness result in your being in right standing with the Father? Did not My faithfulness result in your adoption as a child of God? Did not My faithfulness result in your becoming an heir? Did not My faithfulness result in bringing you a new life, life in abundance?

O beloved, this and so much more. For peace, prosperity, joy, strength, and gladness are all the results of My faithfulness. Without My faithfulness you would be lost. So child, you too are to be faithful, for out of your faithfulness I am pleased. Out of your faithfulness you shall also bring life and restoration to those around you. Out of your faithfulness I can carry on My work in bringing peace, joy, comfort, strength, and righteousness to My people.

April 23
HE HAS PROMISED TO CARE FOR HIS OWN
1 Peter 5:7

O child, there is nothing that I cannot do. There is nothing impossible for Me. There is nothing impossible for you, when you believe. For I have promised to care for you all the days of your life.

Beloved, when you became My child, I made you part of My family to share in all of the rights and privileges thereof. And I have promised to meet your every need. I have promised to give you life in abundance.

My child, worry not, for it is the Father's good pleasure to give you the kingdom. Worry not, dear one, for your Heavenly Father knows what your need is. Worry not, little one for those who put their trust in Me shall never be put to shame. Worry not, for I am the God of My Word. What I tell you is true.

So beloved, place Me first in your life. Seek Me first. Seek My righteousness. Seek My ways, walk in them, and leave your cares with Me. Cast them off. Let Me carry them for you. Your call, dear one, is to place Me first in your life, and follow wherever I lead, and I will take care of your need.

Child, simply trust Me and follow Me with your whole heart, while I abundantly supply all your need.

April 24

HE HAS SAID
Isaiah 54:10

O My child, I have given you My Word. Accept it. Listen to it. Believe it. Count on it. Act on it. Do it. For I have said that I watch over you and care for you. I have said that I give you life in the place of death. I have said that I came to give life and to give it more abundantly. I have said that I would never leave or forsake you. I have said to rejoice in the Lord always. I have said that I make all things work together for good.

Child, I have said that those who put their trust in Me would never be put to shame. I have said that I would rescue you out of all your troubles. I have said that blessed is the man who puts his trust in Me. I have said that great peace have they who love Me, and who love My Word. I have said that I shall supply all your need according to My riches in glory. I have said that the joy of the Lord is your strength.

Beloved I have said that My strength is made perfect in your weakness. I have said that My love for you fails not. I have said that you are My child and an heir. I have said to count it pure joy when you face trials and pressures, for this is My will concerning you.

Child, I have said that the tests and trials produce patience and perseverance, which lead to maturity. I have said that I have given you everything you need for life and godliness. I have said that if you lack wisdom, ask of me, and I will freely give it to you. I have said that I hear your cry and that I answer your call.

Beloved, I have said to call unto Me, and I will answer you and show you great and mighty things, that you know not. I have said that the enemy is under your feet. I have said that the battle is Mine, and the victory is yours. I have said that you will yet see the goodness of the Lord in the land of the living.

I have said that without faith it is impossible to please Me. I have said that by faith you can remove mountains. I have said that no good thing will I withhold from you. I have said that My Word is true, and that My promises are sure.

So beloved, look up. Accept the Word that I have planted in you. Listen to it. Believe it. Act on it. Yes, do it. For it is alive and active. It will change both you and the circumstance. O child, rejoice, for I have given you My Word.

April 25
BE AN IMITATOR OF HIM
Ephesians 5:1-2

Child, be an imitator of Me. Yes, in everything you do and say, imitate Me. Take on My personality. Let

My life so dominate your life that you do what ever I would do in any given circumstance or situation.

Beloved, this is part of letting Me live My life through you. So, imitate Me and you shall see the mighty workings of My Spirit in your life. O child, be an imitator of Me.

THE MASTER POTTER
Isaiah 40:31; Isaiah 64:8

Beloved, I am the master potter, and you are the work of My hand. I know precisely what to do. I put all things together, and I hold all things together. And I am the God of patience. I do not get in a hurry. I am not rushed, for I have planned long ago what I will do.

Child, I am on time. I am not ahead or behind Myself, but rather, My purposes are being accomplished on schedule. So, when it seems that time is wasting, remember: "They who wait upon the Lord shall renew their strength. They shall mount up on wings like eagles. They shall run and not be weary. They shall walk and not faint."

O beloved, waiting on Me accomplishes much. I meet the needs of those who wait. So very often, I bring My children to the place where they must wait and rest, so that they will hear My voice clearly and come to know Me better.

Child, My love is unfailing, My compassion is great, and I watch over you so tenderly. I rush to your aid. Yes, I am the potter, and you are the clay. I do all the work in shaping you after My image. So, rejoice and fret not in the waiting, for in so doing you shall reap a great reward of righteousness.

HE IS THE WORD
John 1:14-17

My child, I am the Word. I am your righteousness. I am alive and powerful. My Word gives life and power to all. For, did not I speak, and the universe was birthed? Did I not speak, and all things were created?

Yes beloved, I am the Word and I dwell within you. My Word I have planted in your heart. And in keeping My Word, in following It, in following Me, there is life and peace, prosperity and health, and long life and sufficiency.

Child, the Word became flesh, and that was I. And the Word dwells within you, and that is I. And the Word is full of grace and truth, and that is I. So, rejoice, beloved, and let My Word shine forth from you in all Its glory.

April 28

LOVING OTHERS
1 Thessalonians 3:12

Child, always extend your love and hospitality. Share your faith. Hold nothing back, but allow Me to flow through you to meet the needs of others. O beloved, do not throw up roadblocks. Do not block the flow of My love to others. For this is how I demonstrate to My people who I am and what I do.

My dear one, it is good for you to participate in this demonstration of love, for thereby you learn of My compassion, and loving-kindness to all. By it you begin to understand every good thing that you have in Me.

Child, as you bless others they receive My encouragement and joy, and you are blessed in the process. So, despise not those who need compassion and understanding. Do not withdraw from them, but freely

give of yourself. Yes, freely share your love, for in so
doing there will be refreshing on every side.

PRAYER, PATIENCE, AND OBEDIENCE
James 5:13-20

My child, learn of Me, and learn from Me. Was not I
a man of prayer? Did I not spend hours in prayer
talking to My Father? Did not I give the great pattern
of prayer?

O loved one, I set the example in prayer. I opened
up the prayer communication link for you. So, come to
Me and talk to Me. Yes, come boldly into the throne
room and commune with your Heavenly Father. For
access has been cleared. Just think, child, you may
have an immediate audience, at any time of the day or
night, with the Lord God Almighty, the creator of the
universe, your Father. Is not this a special privilege, a
special honor?

Beloved, I also learned obedience. Did not I do and
say only what I saw the Father doing? Did not I leave
heaven and all its glory to bring salvation to man? Did
not I go to the cross in obedience to the Father? O yes,
dear one, I learned obedience through the things that I
suffered. I was obedient to the will of My Father.

And child, did not I also learn patience? Did not I
exercise patience? Did not I say, when they hung Me
on the cross: "Father forgive them for they know not
what they do"? So, My loved one, you too are to learn
patience, for it is a fruit of the Spirit. Yes, let patience
have its perfect work in you.

O beloved, learn these things: patience, obedience,
and prayer. Child, to learn patience and obedience
involves prayer, and to learn prayer involves obedience
and patience.

April 30

HE IS LORD
1 Peter 3:15

Beloved, always set Me apart as Lord of your life. Let nothing else take My place; not family, home, possessions, work or play. For, indeed, I am Lord. I am the one in control. I am the one in charge.

O child, the safest, the most blessed place to be is in the center of My presence with Me in full control. This means that in everything you think, say or do, I am Lord.

May

Building Blocks

BUILDING BLOCKS
1 Peter 2:4-5

Child, I am building a spiritual house, a dwelling place for Me. I am building it block upon block, brick upon brick, and stone upon stone. I am fitting it all together. Each building block is important. Each has its place. Each has its own function. Each is a living stone, and you are one of them.

Beloved, you are one of My special, living stones. Each stone has been carefully selected by Me and prepared by Me for the purpose I intended for it. And I hold this house together by the bonding of My Spirit.

O child, you are a chosen building block. You are one of My people. You are a part of My Holy Nation. You are one of My Royal Priests. You are My dwelling place on earth today, and you will find Me in My people, for I dwell in the midst of them. Yes, I live in them, and they are being joined together for a glorious residence, a place of splendor, beauty and majesty.

So rejoice, dear one, you are a part of all this. You are My very own, and I live in you with all My glory, majesty and splendor.

May 2

GOD INTERVENES
Exodus 15:13

Beloved, I have everything in control. Did it not look impossible for the children of Israel, when they were leaving Egypt? Were they not between Pharaoh's army and the sea? Was there anywhere for them to turn? No, it looked like total disaster was about to fall upon them. But I intervened. I parted the sea so that they could cross over on dry ground. Then I closed the sea so that it totally destroyed the enemy. Was not I in control of this impossible situation?

Child, consider Daniel. Did it not look like the end, when he was thrown into the lion's den? But I intervened and closed the mouth of the lions, totally defeating the purposes of the enemy. Did it not appear impossible, when the three Hebrew children were thrown into the fiery furnace? But I intervened and walked in the furnace with them. They came out not bound or singed, not even smelling of smoke. Again, I defeated the purposes of the enemy.

Beloved, did it not look like the end of everything, when I was beaten, crucified, and buried in the tomb? Did it not seem that all hope for mankind was lost? But I intervened. I rose from the grave in newness of life, defeating the enemy once and for all. I brought hope, healing and salvation to man. For I took his punishment, crushing forever the purposes and claims of the enemy.

So child, look up. I am in control. I do the impossible. Remember, that I work all things together for good, to those that love Me and are called according to My purposes. Child, you are such a one.

May 3

LIVING AFTER THE SPIRIT
Romans 8:9-17

Child, I have made marvelous provisions for you. I have made it possible for you to live to please Me. I have made it possible for you to live not after the flesh. I have made it possible for you to live according to the Spirit. For I have given you My Spirit, and He lives in you ready and willing to help.

Beloved, My Spirit is the comforter. He is your guide. He is your instructor. He is your teacher. He shows you the way to go and what to do. He leads you only in the paths of righteousness. He directs you only according to My will. What He does, pleases Me.

Dear one, living after the Spirit will only result in

105

pleasing Me in everything you do. For My Spirit will not lead you in the ways of destruction and death, but in ways of righteousness and life.

So child, you have My Spirit. Listen and let Him control your life. Be led by Him in everything, and at all times. And even your body will be quickened and made alive, for you are under the law of the Spirit of life, who sets you free.

O rejoice beloved, you have everything going for you. What else could you want? For My Spirit, the Spirit of the living God, lives and moves in you and through you in all power, love, and compassion. So, dear one, live after the Spirit.

May 4
SET APART UNTO HIM
1 Thessalonians 5:23-24

Child, I love you with a love that knows no bounds. I have made every provision for you. I have set you apart unto Me. I have made you holy and blameless in My sight. And I live through you in all My power and glory.

O beloved, there is no way to know pure joy and happiness other than in Me. And as you allow Me, I work in your spirit, soul, and body to conform you to My image. As you let Me, I live and move and have My being in you.

Yes dear one, I conform you to My image, but this takes a choice and a commitment on your part. You must be willing, for in your willingness I can be manifested.

O child, I hear the cry of your heart, that is for Me to live My life through you and that you become like Me in every way. Beloved, I am answering that prayer. So, look up and rejoice, for I live in you, and I shall be made more and more real in your life each and every day.

HE IS STILL ON THE THRONE
Psalm 91:1-7

O My child, I am the God of My Word. I am the God of splendor and majesty, the God of beauty and holiness. I am the God of righteousness and truth. What I tell you is true.

Beloved, I am still on the throne. There is no other. Yes, I am in charge, and I orchestrate everything together in perfect harmony. So, when I say that I am your strength and your refuge, know that it is true. When I say that nothing shall harm you, then know that it is true.

Loved one, when I say that I make all things new, then believe it, for it is true. When I say that the pestilence shall not come near you, then know that it is true. And when I say that I work all things together for good, then believe it, for it is true.

O beloved, let not the circumstances rule your life. Let them not overwhelm you. Let not your heart be troubled, for I am doing a mighty work in the land and a mighty work in you. I am preparing you for My purpose, and the time is at hand. Let there be no doubt in your life at all. Let all the anxieties and fears be settled, for I, the Lord God of the entire universe, care for you.

Dear one, know that I am conforming you to My image, and that I am doing it quickly. So, let us move on to higher heights and deeper depths. For the outpouring of My Spirit is at hand, yes, even now, it has begun, and you shall walk in it. You will move in My Spirit and nothing shall hinder.

O beloved, think it not strange concerning the fiery trials, as though something strange is happening to you. But rather rejoice, for I am bringing you into maturity, so we can go on together, and so you can be that instrument of God that you always desired to be.

Yes child, rejoice, I will not let you fall. I am building you up so you can go on the highest of heights, so you can rise above the things of the earth, so you can go where I want you to go, and do what I want you to do in whatever path I lead you to do it.

Beloved, what I tell you is true.

May 6
HE CONTINUES TO REVEAL HIMSELF
Romans 1:16-17

Child, look up, for your redemption draws nigh. O dear one, you are loved. You are blessed, for your Lord watches over you with His wonders to perform. Have not I called you? Have not I chosen you to be My vessel? Have not I ordained you to be My instrument? Have not I made you a partaker of My divine nature? Have not I given you great and precious promises? Have not I placed My Spirit within you?

O beloved, all this and more. For My purpose is to manifest Myself in and through you to a world that needs Me, to help those around you. It is so that you know Me in the power of My resurrection and in the fellowship of My suffering. For in the fellowship of My suffering you learn how to put into practice the power of My resurrection.

O child, there is so much of Me to know, and I daily reveal more of Myself to you. So, be encouraged and rejoice, for your redemption is here, and you have been declared righteous. And the righteous shall live by faith. Look up and praise Me, for there is more and more of Me yet to come. And I will continue to reveal more and more of Myself, so you can attain unto that perfect day.

SOWING SEED
2 Corinthians 9:6, 10-11

Beloved, there is a time to sow and a time to reap. And those who sow generously will also reap generously. Those who sow sparingly will reap sparingly. So, sow seed My child, sow seed!

Yes beloved, sow seeds of finance. Sow seeds of hospitality. Sow seeds of time. Sow seeds of service. Sow seeds of righteousness and holiness. Sow seeds of prayer. Sow seeds of intercession. Sow seeds of your possessions.

O child, share what you have. Give graciously and generously, for whatever you sow that shall you also reap. Have not I said that you shall reap abundantly? For as seed multiplies, so shall your seed return to you even a hundred fold.

Beloved, have not I said that I will increase your store of seed and enlarge your harvest of righteousness? Have not I said that I would make you rich in every way, so you can be even more generous? O child, this is the principle of sowing and reaping, for to sow generously is to reap abundantly.

Dear one, this is sowing time, but the harvest is coming. Yes, the harvest you expect is ripening and almost ready. And you will reap bountifully. So, look to enlarging the fields where you can sow even more seed than in the past. And you will have even a greater increase and more seed to sow in more fields than you thought possible.

O child, does this not thrill you? Is not this exciting? Are not My principles and laws perfect? Yes, you shall reap abundantly, as you continue to sow abundantly. This is a promise. This is My principle, and it works, for you can see it in the natural. Does not the farmer sow in anticipation of a bountiful harvest?

So beloved, do not become wearied or distressed in sowing, for in due time you shall reap an abundance. And you shall be made rich in every way, so that you can make others rich also.

May 8

THE JUST SHALL LIVE BY FAITH
Habakkuk 2:4

Child, the righteous, those who are the just, shall live by faith. Yes, they live by faith in Me, believing in who I am and in what I do. They believe that I keep My Word.

Beloved, it is a simple thing to believe and to act on faith. For if I am the God of the universe, if I am the one who creates by speaking things into existence, is there anything that I cannot do to meet your need?

O child, believe My Word. It is true. There is nothing false about it at all. So, let not the anxieties, worries, and concerns overwhelm you, but rather rise above them in faith, believing that I am sufficient to anything and everything.

Beloved, faith is a place of dwelling. It is a way of life. It is indeed a life style. Yes dear one, be convinced, beyond a shadow of a doubt, that I am in control and care for My own. Have not I promised never to leave or forsake you? Have not I promised to supply all your need?

And loved one, have not I promised to withhold no good thing from you? Have not I promised to lead and guide you all the days of your life? Have not I promised that I give you everything you need, for both life and godliness?

O child, believe it. Act on it and praise Me for it. Know that your times are in My hands and that there is no better place to be. So, let your simplistic, child-like faith carry you over great and mighty obstacles, for the just shall live by faith.

BE HAPPY AND DO GOOD
ALL THE DAYS OF YOUR LIFE
Ecclesiastes 3:10-14

Child, I have appointed all things. And I have determined the times and the seasons for everything. I have made all things to respond to Me, for I am the authority. I am the one who put it all together. Nothing can be added to or taken from what I do. And I have great and beautiful things in store for you. I have a purpose for you to do.

Beloved, does not My Word say that there is nothing better for you to do than to be happy and do good all the days of your life? O loved one, I am the source of that happiness, for true happiness comes from knowing and serving Me.

My child, I have called you to do good all the days of your life, and I give you the strength to do it. I give you the knowledge of what is good, and I give you great joy in doing it. I have given you everlasting life, so that what you do for Me will last forever. It will not be burned up or blown away.

O beloved, I called you to serve. So, serve Me with your whole heart, for in so doing you will find great satisfaction. And I give you happiness in the midst of your service to Me. Yes loved one, it is not the task that brings the happiness, but rather it is the fact that you are serving Me, regardless the task. So, enjoy your service, no matter what it is. For I am the source of your life, godliness, and joy.

COME, LEARN OF ME
Philippians 3:7-11

Child, it is My will for you to know Me better. It is My will for you to learn of Me in all My majesty, glory, and splendor. It is My will for you to learn of Me in all of My love, kindness, and compassion. It is My will for you to learn of Me in all My power, might, and wisdom. It is My will for you to learn of My purity, holiness, and righteousness.

Yes beloved, it is My desire for you and Me to fellowship together in everything. For two cannot walk together unless they are agreed, and I desire that we walk together. I desire that you know Me, the power of My resurrection, and the fellowship of My sufferings, so that you may attain unto all the expectations, all the victory, and all the bonuses of My resurrection power.

O My child, come and learn to know Me better. Come and enjoy My presence. Let Me tell you of Myself and of My ways. Let Me share My thoughts. Let Me reveal My precepts and principles to you. For loved one, My presence goes with you everywhere, and you can learn of Me at any time, yes, even moment by moment.

So beloved, come apart for awhile and let your mind and your body rest. And I will teach you great and mighty things that you know not. I will teach you the principle of walking in the light of My revelation. Yes, I will teach you the principle of sharing in My sufferings. O dear one, I will teach you the principle of My resurrection.

Child, I will teach you the principle of My authority shared with you. I will teach you the principle of pressing on. I will teach you the principle of not growing weary in well doing. I will teach you the principle of faith. I will teach you the principle of wisdom.

O beloved, come and learn of Me, and I will reveal Myself in a measure not yet experienced by you. Yes, come and learn, and you shall be pleased. For it is My good pleasure that you know Me intimately in all that I am and in all that I do. And you will know Me personally, for I freely share Myself, My very being with you. Yes, come, My child, and learn of Me.

THINGS ARE NOT ALWAYS AS THEY APPEAR
Luke 19:1-10; Genesis 42:36

Beloved, things are not always as they appear. Know that what takes place in your life is not an accident, or just a happening. Know that I take care of My own. Know that I am the one who is in charge of everything. Know that I am the one who brings you through the tests and trials. Know that I bring you forth as fine gold.

So dear one, look to Me in everything. Look to Me even when things look just the opposite of what I tell you. Look to Me even if it seems like I have forsaken you. Look to Me and stand on My Word, for I delight to take impossibilities and turn them into blessings.

And My child, fret not about what you shall do. Just let Me do it. All I ask of you is to follow Me. Follow My leading. Follow My nudging. I will not lead you wrong.

Beloved, what looks to you as restriction, what seems to you as just the opposite of My blessing is indeed My blessing, for I specialize in things called impossible. O dear one, whether you feel it or not, I am leading you and guiding you. I am accomplishing in you what I intend to do.

So My child, rejoice, for I am in charge. I know what I am doing. Remember, things are not always as they appear, for I know the end from the beginning.

May 12

WORSHIP IS FROM THE HEART
John 4:23-24

Beloved, I am Spirit, and to worship Me is to

worship in Spirit and in truth. Child, spiritual worship comes from within. It is not based upon ritual or location, but it is from the heart. It is not lip service, but it is from a heart that is obedient and submitted to Me. It is from a heart filled with awe and wonder. It is from a heart filled with thanksgiving and praise. It is a communion of love and adoration.

Beloved, worship from the Spirit will produce acts of worship, deeds of worship, and thoughts of worship. But worship is not the act itself, but rather the motivation or the intent of the heart that produces the act of worship.

So child, worship Me in Spirit and truth. Let your worship come from a pure heart. O dear one, this pleases Me, for I delight in the worship of My people.

May 13
TOUCH THE HEM OF HIS GARMENT
Matthew 9:18-22

Child, reach out and touch the hem of My garment. Let your faith free to receive from Me all that you need. Healing, strength, and provision all come in response to faith and confidence in Me, for faith in Me will make you whole.

O beloved, how do you touch the hem of My garment? You touch it by faith in Me. You touch it by being convinced that what My Word says is true. And My Word says that with Me nothing is impossible, but that all things are possible.

So dear one, touch Me today. Reach out in faith and touch My garment, and you will not be disappointed. Rather, your faith will make you whole.

COVERED BY HIS BLOOD
Hebrews 9:11-14

Child, you are covered by the blood I shed on the cross of Calvary and this covering is your protection. It is your security, for I have entered into a blood covenant with My people. And when I see the blood, the destroyer must pass over, he cannot touch you.

O dear one, there is life in My blood. Did not I come to give life in abundance? Yes, My life was poured out, so that you could have eternal life. My body was the supreme sacrifice for all mankind, meeting all the requirements of the Father.

Beloved, My blood covers a multitude of sins. Yes, your sins, past, present, and future, have been covered by My blood. My blood is the finest cleansing agent. There is no other like it. And I have washed you in it and made you clean, even whiter than snow.

O child, the destroyer cannot have you, for all that would try to destroy you will come to no avail. Neither drought, famine, lack, illness, disease, nor poverty can penetrate the covering of My blood.

So beloved, rejoice, for you are under My blood. My covenant is with you. Simply plead My blood over each and every situation, and you shall see miracles take place.

And you shall be able to do all things through Me, for My blood is powerful and freely given. It is a covering that cannot be removed.

EVERYTHING BEGINS AND ENDS WITH HIM
Romans 11:33-36; 12:1-2

My child, everything begins and ends with Me. I raise up and I put down. Everything, dear one, is wrapped up in Me. I am before all things, in all things, and by Me all things consist. So, let the light of My presence shine forth in your life. Let the glory of your God and King be seen by all around. Let Me radiate My life through you.

O child, let not self get in the way, but allow Me to be the light of your life. And this is done by the offering of your body, your entire being to Me, as a living sacrifice. It is done by the renewing of your mind. It is done by the conforming of your thinking to My image.

Yes beloved, the best for you is to be conformed to My image in everything, to seek My mind in all matters, and to be renewed in the attitude of your mind. O dear one, this is acceptable and pleasing to Me, and it results in praise, honor, and glory to My name.

Child, the depth of the riches of My wisdom and knowledge is beyond your total comprehension, but as you are continually renewed in the attitude of your mind, you will discover more and more of Me. You shall become more and more like Me. You shall experience Me and My ways, and that will bring you great peace and joy. O beloved, everything begins, exists, and ends with Me. Indeed I planned it so.

May 16
HE HAS PROMISED TO MEET EVERY NEED
Philippians 4:19

My child, I love My children and I care for them. Have not I said that I give you everything you need for life and godliness? Have not I said to call unto Me and I will show you great and marvelous things that you know not? Have not I said that I prosper My people? Have not I said to ask anything in My name and I shall do it? Yes, loved one, I have made these statements, and My Word is true.

So beloved, come and let Me do all this in your life.

Be aware that the condition, the principle, is to ask from the Spirit and not from the flesh. It is not from a selfish want or desire, but from a desire of the heart. It is a request from the Spirit and a request from the Spirit will not be denied.

O child, I have promised prosperity. I have promised health and healing. I have promised great and mighty things in your life. I have promised to be with you always and to give you rest.

Beloved, I have promised to meet your every need: the need for riches, the need for wisdom, the need for maturity, the need for daily provision, the need for communion with your God, the need for rest, the need for peace, the need for joy, the need for strength, the need for patience, the need for perseverance, and much more.

O child, it does not end. So, call unto Me and I will show you wonderful and marvelous things. Yes, even like Daniel, for as I showed him great things that I had planned before the foundations of the earth, so with you, dear one, I reveal Myself to you and through you. O let Me do through you all these marvelous things, and you will be blessed beyond measure.

May 17

THERE IS NOTHING TO FEAR
Genesis 15:1, 6

My child, I am your shield. I am your protection. I have placed a hedge about you, and nothing can harm you. Nothing can move you, for I am your guard. I care for you and watch over you. My presence is with you always, and I give you rest.

Beloved, I give you rest from all that the world can throw against you. I give you rest in the midst of the trial, and in the midst of great difficulty and pressure. I give rest to your life and peace to your soul. I jealously watch over you.

My child, there is nothing to fear. So, fear not for your Heavenly Father watches over you. I rush to your side to defend and protect you. For whoever touches you, touches the apple of My eye.

Beloved, it is good to place your total trust and confidence in Me. It brings rest and peace in the midst of the storm. So dear one, let the waves role. Let the thunder roar. Let the lightning flash. And let the floods come, for they shall not come nigh you.

My child, with this mindset, with this attitude, nothing shall be impossible to you. Absolutely nothing shall be impossible. For I am working out My will and purpose, and none shall hinder. So, look up and rejoice, in the midst of the stretching, in the midst of the trial, and see Me as your shield. See Me as the one who allows the enemy no room to touch you.

O beloved, trust Me. Have confidence in Me, for in so doing I bring you an exceeding great reward. Yes child, I am your shield. I am your protection. I am your very life.

May 18
MY BOUNDARIES HAVE FALLEN IN PLEASANT PLACES
Psalm 16:5-6

Beloved, I have assigned unto you your portion, that which is designed only and specifically for you. I have made your lot secure. Yes, I have designed a plan for your life that is safe and secure, beautiful and pleasant. I have given you a beautiful, magnificent, and delightful inheritance.

Child, as you go through the trials and the pressures they may not seem pleasant, but they lead to pleasant places. They produce a beautiful spirit, and a radiant being filled with the power of My presence.

Beloved, My plan is to bring you into your

inheritance, for it is all planned and laid out. It is secure, and I guard it for you. O do you not see it? Do you not understand? I have seated you with Me in the heavenlies. This is your position in Me. You are seated far above all the cares of the world.

Child, you are a joint heir with Me. Your inheritance is real. It has been beautifully designed. It is pleasant, peaceful, powerful, and more than sufficient and perfect.

O beloved, you are a child of the King, and it does not yet appear to you what is in store for you, and what is ahead for you. Yes loved one, know that all your circumstances, pressures, and difficulties are only stepping stones on the boundaries of your inheritance. I have made your inheritance delightful and secure.

My child, your inheritance is pleasant because I am there, and, dear one, where My presence is there is joy forevermore.

May 19

CONSIDER ABRAHAM
Genesis 12:1-9

My child, consider Abraham. Did not he hear and recognize My voice? Did not he hear Me tell him to pick up everything and go, not knowing where he was going? Did not he listen and obey.

Beloved, he took everything he had and left the country of his father. He followed Me to a land he did not know. But it was a land that I promised to him and his offspring. There I promised to bless him and make him a great nation. There I promised that through him all the people of the earth would be blessed.

O child, he listened and then he acted on My Word. He also worshipped Me. He believed it was I who called him and gave him direction. He believed it was I telling him to leave the comfort of home and go somewhere he did not know.

Yes, he did just as I told him, and the result of that act is still being fulfilled today. Because of his act of faith, you have been made a recipient of the blessing.

Child, he believed Me, and I blessed him greatly. So, learn from him, dear one. Simply, believe Me and do what I command you to do, what I instruct you to do, and you will not be disappointed. You will find your joy and peace, and your strength and prosperity in Me, regardless of the path I have you take. O beloved, I am leading you. I am quickening you. I am bringing you to a land to possess. I give it to you. It shall be fruitful. And you shall be blessed even more than you are blessed now. My blessings are always new and ever increasing.

So rejoice child, and listen for My voice. Hear what I say and come follow Me wherever I lead, and it shall be well with you.

May 20
AND ENOCH WALKED WITH GOD
Genesis 5:22-24

Beloved, it is My desire for you to be an Enoch, that is to walk with Me in complete dedication and commitment. Yes, let your heart be so in tune with Me that our fellowship will be sweet and unbroken, that we walk and talk together.

O child, this has always been My plan for man: to have fellowship together; to walk and talk together; to share with each other. Enoch was such a man. He loved Me with all his heart. He sought Me in everything. He shared what he was doing. He spoke with Me as a friend.

Beloved, Enoch's life was totally committed to Me and to My precepts. He knew what pleased Me, and he did it. He did it out of love and devotion, not out of fear. He did it out of obedience and trust. He believed what I told him. He never doubted any of My ways.

Yes My child, Enoch walked with Me and I walked with him. For two cannot walk together unless they are agreed, and we were in agreement. O beloved, this is what I desire for you: that we walk and talk daily; that in every situation and circumstance we walk and talk together; that we share every detail with each other.

O child, come and walk with Me. Walk the paths that I walk. Come and talk with Me and learn of My ways, for there is no greater joy, and no greater experience than to be in the presence of your Lord. And beloved, I enjoy being in your presence, for I love My children so.

May 21

HIS WAYS AND HIS THOUGHTS
Colossians 1:9-10

Child, let Me make known to you the knowledge and wisdom of My ways and My purposes. For My ways are not your ways, nor are My thoughts your thoughts. But, dear one, I am renewing your mind. I am conforming you to My image, so that your ways and thoughts will be in harmony with Mine.

Beloved, My ways and My thoughts are pure and holy. They are ways and thoughts of wisdom and understanding, not of foolishness and ignorance. They are ways and thoughts of power and victory, not of weakness and defeat.

They are ways and thoughts that honor and please Me, and result in walking worthy of Me in every way. They are ways and thoughts that produce action and much fruit.

Yes child, be filled with the knowledge of My ways and My thoughts, for in so doing you will learn patience and endurance. O loved one, I have so much to share with you, so listen and learn. Walk in My ways, and you shall bring Me great joy.

May 22
IT IS IN PRAISE THAT...
Psalm 113:1-3; 114:7-8

Child, I indeed inhabit the praises of My people, for it is in praise that the impossible becomes possible. It is in praise that the dry place becomes a pool of refreshing. It is in praise that the hard rock becomes a spring of living water.

It is in praise that the blessings flow. Beloved, it is in praise that valleys are raised up and mountains are made low. It is in praise that crooked places are made straight and rough paths are made smooth. It is in praise that gates of brass and bars of iron are broken asunder.

Child, it is in praise that walls come tumbling down. It is in praise that darkness is turned to light. It is in praise that mourning is turned into gladness, and sorrow is turned into dancing. It is in praise that the power of My presence is made known. It is in praise that the enemy must flee.

Beloved, I inhabit the praises of My people. Yes, in praise My name is made known. In praise the clouds lift and the impossible becomes reality. So, praise Me and you will see mountains melt like wax before your eyes. You will see the sufficiency of your Lord.

O praise Me child, and you will never be disappointed. Yes, praise the Lord.

May 23
THE SAME SPIRIT
Ephesians 2:18

Beloved, I dwell in you by the power and presence of My Spirit. He is the same Spirit that raised Me from the dead. He is the same Spirit by whom all the miracles, signs, and wonders are performed. He is the same Spirit in you who cries: "Abba, Father." He is the same Spirit that gives you immediate and direct access to your Heavenly Father.

My child, He is My Spirit, and He dwells in you. Have not I said that greater works you would do because I would send you My Spirit, and He would be with you and in you?

Beloved, all the power, strength, and wisdom you will ever need is available by the presence of My Spirit. So, release Him today to energize your life. Release Him to do what He came to do. Release Him to be your comforter. Yes, release Him to do great signs and wonders in your life.

May 24
SECURE IN THE PROMISE OF HIS PROTECTION
1 Peter 1:3-5

Beloved, I am the Word. I am your protector. I am your holiness. I provide it all. It is My Word, My protection, and My holiness that shields you and keeps you safe. It is not your word, your strength, or your righteousness, but Mine.

My child, know that I jealously guard you from the enemy lest you be trampled underfoot. Yes, I have made provision for victory. I have already overcome.

So beloved, take delight in My Word. Take security in the promise of My protection. Rejoice, in My holiness and in My righteousness, for they are yours as a gift from Me. They do not erode, or fade, or become weak. They are as vibrant and strong as when they were first given.

Dear one, don't think it strange concerning all the trials that are coming your way. But rejoice, for I reveal Myself to you in these trials. I use them to show My Word to be true and to demonstrate My protection.

I use them to make you holy and to cause you to grow in your hope and trust in Me. I use them to manifest Myself as real and alive in and through you.

O child, trust Me. I know what I am doing. And rejoice in the hope that you have in Me, for you shall not be disappointed. You shall not be confused, but you shall see My hand in everything, for I am there. I am ever present, and I give My beloved rest.

May 25
CAST NOT AWAY YOUR CONFIDENCE
Hebrews 10:35-39

Child, as you draw near to Me, so I draw near to you. O dear one, I am already near. So, draw close to Me with bold confidence and blind faith, believing and trusting Me to be the God that I am; to be the Father that I am; to be the Savior that I am; to be the Almighty One that I am. And that I am ready, able, and willing to do what I have promised to do.

Beloved, never let your confidence in Me slip or fall, for when your confidence is in Me, when your faith is in Me nothing shall be impossible to you.

So, hold on to that hope within you, that hope which you profess. Cling to it tenaciously. Hold on to it, for that hope and trust moves mountains. It is the channel through which My blessings flow.

Child, without confidence in Me, the flow is broken. All it takes to experience the flow of prosperity in every way is the full assurance of faith in Me and in My Word. So, hold on, let it not go. Let it become stronger and stronger.

Yes beloved, confidence in Me brings great reward. So, let your faith rise. Feed it on My Word. Feed it on fellowship with Me. Watch it grow and see miracles take place before your eyes. You hold the key, My child. So, cast not away your confidence in Me.

HE GIVES GRACE TO THE HUMBLE
1 Peter 5:5

Beloved, it is My grace that strengthens you, makes you strong, restores you, settles you, and grounds you. It is My grace that makes you perfect and in right standing with Me.

O child, My grace is sufficient, for My grace is unreserved favor toward you. My grace and My love cover a multitude of sins, and I no longer see you in sin. But instead I see you perfect, strong, and holy. I see you in the light of My grace, and in My grace you will find sufficiency to meet every need.

So beloved, stand firm in My grace, for it is the center of blessing. Stand steadfast, unmoved, and unshaken in My grace. Yes, persevere in it, for everything concerning you is wrapped in it. There is nothing lacking, for in My grace there is great provision. O loved one, how I care for My people. I have opened the windows and doorways to heaven through grace.

So, come walk in My grace. Stand firm in it, for as you do, nothing can touch you.

HE HAS CHOSEN HIS DWELLING PLACE
Psalm 48:1-14

Child, your Lord, your God, the Holy one of Israel has chosen His dwelling place. He has made His dwelling place safe and secure. He has made it beautiful, and its fame reaches to the ends of the earth. Your God has so situated and fortified His dwelling that the enemy must flee in terror.

And beloved, you are that dwelling, for I tabernacle among men. I live in My dwelling by the power and presence of My Spirit. Yes, you are that dwelling. All

My children are that dwelling, and together they form My Holy City, that beautiful city, with all its splendor and glory.

So rejoice, child, you are My dwelling place. Nothing can harm or touch it. And My city, My dwelling is a place of worship, praise, joy, peace, rest, hope, strength, beauty, splendor, majesty, and glory.

O loved one, be thankful that you are My dwelling. Yes, you make up My holy city. You are a part of My holy mountain, and I shall live and reign there forever and ever.

May 28
FAITH MAKES THE IMPOSSIBLE, POSSIBLE
Proverbs 23:18

Beloved, with faith in Me, nothing is impossible. All that you need, all that you lack, all that comes against you, all that would try to overwhelm you will dissipate through the eyes of faith. For faith looks beyond the circumstance and sees the end from the beginning.

Child, faith sees and claims the victory, turning defeat into triumph. Faith moves mountains of despair. Faith takes Me at My Word and believes that I can do anything. Faith believes that My promises are true. Faith believes that I work all things together for good. Faith believes that I am to be honored in every situation.

So child, let not your heart be troubled. I am here. I am always ready to help, and though it may appear that things are hopeless, know that I am the God of hope. I do nothing by chance. I still am in control, even when things look out of control. Yes beloved, faith in Me makes the impossible, possible.

POST A LOOKOUT
Isaiah 21:6-12

O child, post a lookout. Watch carefully. Be alert, lest you fall asleep. Watch and pray. Let not the enemy, the world, the flesh or the devil come upon you unawares. But be vigilant and alert to the wiles of the enemy. Beloved, let not self rise up, but post a lookout. O dear one, My Spirit is that watchman. Listen and heed His warnings.

CONFESS HIM AS LORD
Romans 10:6-11

Beloved, My Word is near you, yes, even in your mouth and in your heart. I placed it there, and you have acknowledged it so. O child, there is so much in knowing Me, more than you can comprehend. But I make it simple for you. Yes, a simple confession by you is all that is required to know Me.

My dear one, you have confessed Me as Lord; as Lord of everything; as Lord of your life. And in confessing Me as Lord you experience all the fullness of My presence and power. Yes loved one, you experience life in abundance.

O child, it is true. Those who put their trust in Me will never be put to shame. Those who put their trust in Me shall find peace and confidence, not known by the world. So, confess Me My child. Let there be no hesitation. For indeed, I am your life. I am the very reason you exist.

TRAIN YOURSELF IN GODLINESS
1 Timothy 4:7-8

Loved one, I would have you train yourself in godliness, for godliness holds promise of great reward. Yes, hear these words: train yourself, and practice godliness. So beloved, not only pray for godliness, but conscientiously, do everything possible to be godly.

Child, it is not works that saves you, for you could never become perfect in the flesh. But in your walk it is My desire that you make every effort to please Me. You do this by practicing godliness, doing good, and being holy.

You do this, dear one, by searching out what things are godly. You search My Word daily. You talk to Me often. You let My Holy Spirit lead, guide, and instruct you in everything.

So beloved, practice godliness, for this pleases Me. Let your conversation be pure. Let the thoughts of your mind be wholesome. Let the meditation of your heart be in tune with Me. And in everything you do, do it unto Me. For this, loved one, is the beginning exercise in being godly.

So child, train yourself in godliness, for it holds promise of great reward, both now and forevermore.

June

His Word Stands the Test of Time

June 1
HIS WORD STANDS THE TEST OF TIME
2 Peter 1:19-21

Beloved, there are those that would erode My instruction, and would try to destroy My Word. But, loved one, My Word shall stand the test of time. For My Word is true. It is powerful and perfect. It cannot be destroyed.

O Child, never think that My Word is not for you today. But rejoice, that it is as current as if it were written or spoken this very moment. My Word is original, and authentic. What I say is true. Let no one convince you otherwise. All of it is profitable. Yes, it is profitable for doctrine, for reproof, correction, and instruction.

Beloved, when I tell you that I am able to deliver the godly from their trials and pressures, that Word is true. So, dear one, recognize My Word. Rejoice in it, and your joy shall be full.

June 2
IT PLEASES HIM
I Peter 1:1-2

Beloved, you are My loved one. You are My child. I redeemed you by My blood. I placed you in right standing with Me. I made you holy by the work of My Spirit. I have brought you to obedience. It pleases Me to do this.

Yes child, it pleases Me to make you holy. It pleases Me to set you apart as a child of God. It pleases Me to sprinkle you and cleanse you with My blood, and to place you under its protection.

O beloved, it pleases Me to make you a new creation. It pleases Me to bless you. It pleases Me to see you grow and mature. It pleases Me to see you seek Me with your whole heart. It pleases Me to share

My abundance with you. It pleases Me to love you. It pleases Me to receive your love and surrender in return. O loved one, it pleases Me to be your God, your Father, your redeemer, your peace, your joy, and your friend.

My child, I love you so. Do you not see it? I have done it all for you. So, My chosen one, My precious child, look up and rejoice for it pleases Me to share with you My kingdom.

June 3

SEATED WITH HIM
Ephesians 2:6-7

Beloved, by My mercy and by My grace I have brought you to a spacious place, for I have seated you with Me in the heavenlies. You are here with Me as I am there with you. And loved one, you are seated with Me, far above all principalities, powers, and rulers of darkness.

Yes child, I have lifted you up. I have freed you. I have redeemed you. I have removed the sentence of death against you. And I have placed within you the Spirit of life, so that you no longer walk after the old nature, but after the new.

O beloved, you are in the very center of My presence. Your position is secure. It is in the heavenlies. So, hold on to this truth. And when the pressures, tests, and trials come your way, simply recognize who you are, whose you are, and where your citizenship is. As you do, you will rise above the things that try to hold you down, things that would depress and discourage you, things that try to steal, kill, and destroy.

Child, in Me you are more than a conqueror, for your hope is in the living God; the one who was raised from the dead; the one who is seated at the right hand of the Father; the one who created you; the one who extends His love to you without end. O beloved, rejoice, for there is nothing too difficult for you, for you are seated with Me in the heavenlies. And all these things must bow to you, for in Me you already have overcome.

June 4
HE CAN CHANGE THE ATTITUDE OF MY ENEMIES
Ezra 6:22

Child, I am the God of the impossible. There is nothing that I cannot do, and nothing I cannot change. I can even make your enemies to be at peace with you. I can change their attitudes. I can cause them to assist you in what you do.

Beloved, there are enemies in the flesh, and there are enemies in the Spirit. Yes, there are the enemies of the world, the flesh and the devil. There are many enemies, such as: fear and doubt; lack; sickness and disease; physical limitation; blindness; waste; laziness; greed; and the enemy of opposition.

Yes child, there are many, but I have made it so they are under your feet. I conquered all when I defeated the enemy at the cross, and made it so you could have the victory over the world, the flesh and the devil.

Beloved, you are My temple, and I am building you up. I am making you strong. Yes, I make your enemies to be at peace with you, and any opposition you experience I will cause to work to your behalf.

June 5
COME BOLDLY INTO HIS PRESENCE
Ephesians 3:12

Child, I have made it possible for you to come directly into the throne room; to come without hesitation before the King of kings; to come without

132

reservation into the very presence of the God of the entire universe. And I have made it possible for you to come with boldness and confidence, knowing that your audience will be granted and your requests will be heard.

So beloved, come as often as you like. Come and live in My presence every moment of the day, for you are welcome, and I will receive you with open arms. For, dear one, I too desire your presence. Yes, I receive you with love and compassion.

Child, I am moved by what you share with Me. I listen carefully. I hear and I respond for I am a compassionate God, one you may call Father. And I speak comfort to your soul, for I care for My own. I heal your body. I meet your every need.

So come, dear one, in bold confidence, and you shall be blessed in My presence. Let Me hold you and kiss the hurt away. Let Me whisper in your ear that I love you beyond measure, and that I have only the best for you. Yes, I have made it possible for you to come without reservation into My presence where there is fullness of joy.

June 6

LIKE A STAR IN THE UNIVERSE
Philippians 2:14-16; Daniel 12:3

Child, you shine like a bright and brilliant star that lights the sky in the darkness of night. For I have called you to light, to righteousness and holiness, and to purity and blamelessness. I have called you out of darkness into My marvelous light.

Loved one, those who love righteousness, those who are wise, shine brighter and brighter unto that perfect day. And though your light was dim in the past, that no longer is so. For I have called you by My grace, and by My power you are becoming radiant and brilliant. You are becoming a light for others to see, a

133

light to follow, a light of illumination, a light to show others the paths of righteousness.

O loved one, that brightness, that beauty is the power and presence of My Spirit conforming you to My image. Have not I said that I am the light of the world? So you too, beloved, are a light shining in the darkness of this world. And that light is I in you becoming stronger and stronger every day.

Yes, I have ordered it, so that the darkness may have light, and those in darkness may see and come to the knowledge of the truth. O dear one, you shine as a star in the heavens.

Child, do not some use the stars for navigation and guidance to help find the North from the South and the East from the West? So, likewise, you are a bright shining star to help pilot those lost in the sea of darkness into the light of My presence.

O beloved, shine on. Let your light be seen. Do not hide it or let it grow dim, but let it always radiate My presence.

June 7
CHOOSE TO PLEASE HIM
Philippians 1:27

Child, find out what pleases Me and then do it. For it is I that work in you both the willing and the doing. O loved one, does this not bless you? Just think, it is I doing it all. I place within you both the desire and the ability for you to please Me.

But, beloved, I give you a choice. You can choose to follow Me or not. You can choose to obey Me or not. You can choose to follow your own desires or to follow Mine. It is only a matter of choice.

So child, choose this day whom you will serve. Will you serve the cravings of the flesh, or will you serve the desires of the Spirit. It is up to you, for I have placed the willingness and the doing within you, but the choice is yours. Beloved, choosing Me to be first in everything is the working out of your salvation. And serving Me in everything brings pleasure to My heart. O seek, dear one, to please Me in all that you do, say, or think.

NO ODDS AGAINST ME
2 Chronicles 20:15-17

Beloved, there are no odds against you when I am in control. For I am God of the impossible. I fight your battles. I give you the victories. I bring things into existence from that which does not exist. I am the resurrection and I bring life.

O child, trust Me. Have faith in Me. I will not go back on My Word to you. Those things I have promised, I will keep. The words spoken to you and over you by My Spirit are true, and you shall see them come to pass. They shall be fulfilled.

So rejoice, child, I am here to rescue you and to set your feet upon a rock. It is the rock of salvation. So, go today, knowing that I am working in your life My wonders to perform. And, go knowing that what seems impossible is only a stepping stone toward the manifestation of My power, glory, and honor.

HE IS LOVING TOWARD ALL HE HAS MADE
Psalm 145:17

Child, I am loving and compassionate toward all I have made. I am not a God of hatred or ill will, but rather, the God of love. For is it not written that I am love? And dear one, you are loved beyond measure.

Yes beloved, you are loved by the God of the entire universe. You are loved by the God of heaven and earth. You are loved by the God who is your Heavenly

Father. And He loves you with a father's heart, a heart that is united and responsive to that of His child, a heart that delights in His own.

My child, do you not know that I joy over you with singing? Do you not know that I watch over you so carefully, that I protect you and keep you from harm? Do you not know that I provide for your daily need, and I supply all you need out of the abundant riches of My glory?

Beloved, you are loved so, and I hold you to Me and whisper those precious words to you. I take your hand and tell you that I will lead you in the paths you are to go. And I tell you to fear not for I am with you always, and I will never leave or forsake you.

O child, I speak peace to your heart when it is troubled. I apply the balm of My Spirit when you are hurting. I joy over you when you are rejoicing. And I comfort you when you need comfort.

Dear one, there is nothing that can or ever will remove My love from you. So, go today rejoicing in the security of that love, a love that is without limit or condition.

June 10

FAMILY
Ephesians 2:19

My son, you are indeed a member of My family, a member of My household with all the rights and privileges thereof. You are not a stranger or an alien, but you are a son of God. I have adopted you and made you a member of My family.

Child, I am building a temple, a body in which I live. And you are part of that body built upon the foundation of who I am. I am filling that temple with My presence, for it is a temple for Me to dwell in by the power and presence of My Spirit.

Yes child, you are a member of My family; a part of

My household; a part of My temple; a part of My dwelling place. You are My house, My home, and I fill you with My presence, never to leave or forsake you

HE WILL STRIVE WITH MAN A LITTLE LONGER
Genesis 6:3; Deuteronomy 10:14-22

Beloved, My Spirit shall not always strive with man, for man is rebellious and his heart is desperately wicked. Have not I commanded that My people should fear Me, love Me, seek to please Me, to serve Me, keep My commands, and to search for Me with their whole heart?

O child, the people do not hear. Yet, I will still pour out My Spirit upon all flesh, and then they shall hear. There shall be a great awakening of My people, and they shall come from the East, the West, the North, and from the South.

O beloved, I bring great peace and comfort with Me, and they shall be comforted. I bring healing to troubled souls and health to ailing bodies, and they shall be healed. I bring love and compassion, and they shall fall in love with Me.

My child, I am the awesome and mighty one. I am King of kings and Lord of lords. I still perform signs and wonders. I shall be exalted in all the earth. I shall bring many to Me, for I will strive with man a little longer. I will strive for another day. I will offer hope a little longer. I will offer redemption a little longer.

And beloved, I will say to the people: "Come and buy food and drink without price. Come and learn of Me. Come and let Me love you. Come and seek My presence. Come and follow Me, and I will bless you and give you a great inheritance."

Yes child, I will yet do this. I will bring an outpouring of Myself, a manifestation of My presence, like has never been witnessed before. And the people shall hear and they shall cry out; "What shall we do?" And you will tell them that I am their peace, that they are to fear Me, and that they are to seek Me with their whole heart. They are to turn from their wicked ways, and come walk with Me, and enjoy the presence and blessing of their Lord.

O beloved, I will yet strive with the people a while longer. So, be ready to strive with Me and to reap the blessings of a bountiful harvest.

June 12
FAITH IS A SPIRITUAL PRINCIPLE
Hebrews 11:1-6

O beloved, faith is the one thing that pleases Me the most. Yes, believing and being fully persuaded that what I say is true, that what I say is real, pleases Me. It is credited as righteousness. And though you may not see the results immediately, what I say is so. For faith says: "If God said it I believe it."

Child, Abel brought a better sacrifice because it was done with a pure heart, and not out of obligation or formality. It was done in faith. And without faith it is impossible to please me. O loved one, My ways and My provision may not be visible to your senses, but they are real, and faith opens the doors to all that I have in store.

Beloved, faith is a spiritual principle. It is the exercise of the Spirit. So, when I say to have faith in Me, to have faith in God, then be fully persuaded and totally confident that what I say, I will do.

O child, be firmly convinced that My Word is true and does not change; that My Word is true and that I am faithful to it; that My Word is true and never fails. Be convinced that My Word is true and contains provision for every circumstance and situation in your life.

Yes, be convinced that My Word is true and holds

promise for everything you need for life and godliness. O beloved, let your faith in Me rise so that there will never be a single doubt. For if I said it, it is true. And the way to avail yourself of My provision is to believe that it is there, that it is on the way. It is to believe that your God will supply all your need according to His riches in glory.

Yes child, have faith in Me, and you will see mountains removed, valleys raised up, and crooked places made straight. You will see the mighty hand of your God at work.

GREAT AND MARVELOUS
TRUTHS IN HIS WORD
Psalm 119:18

My son, there are great and marvelous truths in My Word. In it are the keys of life. I put it all together, and I give you My Spirit so you can receive and understand it. Then I offer, yes desire, to live your life for you by the power of that same Word and the presence of My Spirit.

O child, I have done it all. Everything is available to you, and it is all included in My Word. I have made it possible for you to live an abundant life, a life free from bondage, and a life full of liberty in the Spirit.

Beloved, I have made it possible for Me to live in you and through you. I have made it possible for you to live a godly life, a life of victory and holiness. I have made it possible for you to be crucified with Me, so that your old nature be put to death. I made it possible for you to be resurrected with Me, so that you could have newness of life.

O child, these things I tell you in My Word, and there is so much more. There is My Word for every occasion, every pressure, every test, and every trial. There is My Word for joy, peace, comfort, gladness, health, healing, strength, power, love, mercy, and grace. Yes dear one, there is My Word for everything.

So beloved, let It be your delight, and come let Me live through you, and show you My great and wondrous ways. Let Me show you the majesty of your Lord and the power of My Word. Yes, there are marvelous truths in My Word.

June 14
BE CONTENT IN HIS PURPOSE AND PLAN
Jeremiah 29:11-12

Child, be content, for I have a purpose and plan for your life. And My plan is not to harm you, but to give you hope and a future. It is to prosper you in every way. So, be content, for I work all things together for good. Consider the Israelites in Egypt, and how they were reduced to slavery. Yet, even as they were oppressed, did not I multiply them? In their leaving, did not they plunder the Egyptians of their wealth?

So dear one, be content, knowing that your God is and always shall be in charge. My purpose for you shall be fulfilled. It is pure and it is perfect. And the many things that would rise up to hurt you or overwhelm you shall only result in the multiplication of your prosperity.

So rejoice child, and be content. My purpose for you is good. It shall come to fruition. You shall see it. And if you look closely, you can see that I have already prospered you. You can see that My hand has been upon you all the days of your life.

O beloved, you can see that I have come to your rescue over and over again. You can see that your God has supplied all your need. You can see great and marvelous victories, great and marvelous deliverances. You can see that My plan and purpose is being fulfilled daily in your life.

So, rejoice and give thanks, for your Heavenly

Father has only the best in store for you. Yes, I, indeed, prosper you. I provide for all your need.

BLESSED BEYOND MEASURE
Psalm 1:1-6

Beloved, you are blessed beyond measure, for you are a child of Mine, and those of My household have access to everything to meet every need.

Child, I am not a God of empty words, but I am the God of My Word, and those who take refuge in My Word find peace, joy, strength, prosperity, and comfort. All they need is found in Me. Yes dear one, you are blessed. You are blessed with every spiritual blessing. You are blessed with everything you need for life and godliness, for I have made it so. I have made provision, and you can learn of that provision from My Word.

So beloved, delight yourself in My Word. Meditate on it day and night. Let it permeate your entire being, for in so doing your life shall become fruitful and all that you do will prosper. Yes child, you are blessed.

HE LOVES AND CARES FOR HIS OWN
Psalm 4:3-8

Beloved, I hear your cry, I see your need, and I respond to your prayer. You are My very own child, and I care what happens to you. I care about everything that effects your life.

Child, I care when the tests and trials come. I care when sickness and disease attacks your body. I care when temptations arise and try to overtake you. I care when you are walking through the desert. I care when it appears that everything is against you.

Beloved, I care. Does not My Word tell you so?

Does not My Word tell you that I hear your cry and that I withhold nothing from you? Does not My Word say to cast all your care upon Me, because I care for you? Does not My Word say that I will keep him in perfect peace whose mind is fixed on Me? Does not My Word say that I comfort you?

And child, does not My Word say that I watch over you and protect you, even as a mother hen protects and gathers her chicks to herself? Does not My Word say to call unto Me and I will answer you and show you great and mighty things? Does not My Word say that I will supply all your need according to My riches in glory? Does not My Word say that I bless and prosper My people?

O beloved, I tell you over and over again that I love and care for My children. So, call unto Me and I will hear. I will listen and always answer with the very best for you. So, be patient and trust me, for I honor My Word. And rest in the assurance that what I say is true, that it is so.

Yes child, I care for My own I respond to their cry. I rescue them and I set them on paths of righteousness. So rejoice and be glad, for your Heavenly Father watches over you, His delight to care.

June 17

A NEW SELF
Ephesians 4:20-24

My child, I have placed within you a new self, a new nature, a new you. You are indeed a miracle, as each of My children are a miracle. For I have taken you from being dead in trespasses and sin, from being dead spiritually, from being dead unto Me, and I have made you alive. I have given you a new nature: created to be like Me; holy, pure, and righteous which desires only to please Me.

Beloved, I have crucified the old self. I have put it

142

to death. So, count it as such. Let it have no part of you. And put on the new self. Let it be free. Let it be you. For the new self renews the attitude of your mind. It magnifies Me and brings glory to My name. It delights in My laws and precepts. Yes, it delights in pleasing Me. It delights in My Word.

O child, let nothing hinder the flow of My holiness through you, for this is natural to the new self. Know that the old self would rebel and choose its own way, but the new self says: "Thy will be done." So, rejoice, that the old self is dead, and that it no longer has any power over your life. Let the new self be free to serve and please Me.

Rejoice, My beloved, for you have the very nature of the Heavenly Father, His pleasure to fulfill and your blessings to receive.

June 18

RELEASE FROM DEBT
Matthew 6:11-12

Child, My Word is true. It provides all the precepts and principles by which to please Me; by which you can walk in victory, your enemies under your feet.

Beloved, I am the God who answers prayer, and I know your need before you call. And while you are yet calling, I send the answer. But there are divine principles that assure you of My answer. Dear one, when I gave the pattern for prayer, I made it simple and exact. You may ask for your daily needs, and I will supply them. Yes, you may ask for freedom from debt, and I will set you free. But as I set you free so, are you to set others free from their obligations to you.

Child, do you not see it? Should not you be as forgiving as I am? If I set you free, why would you hold someone else in bondage? Does that seem fair to you? O loved one, let your heart be tender and mellow. Let My love and My ways fill it to overflowing. For your forgiveness of others is allowing Me to forgive their debts through you.

So beloved, hold not a grudge or give it a second thought, but willingly and joyfully forgive the debts of those indebted to you: those who owe you money, those who owe you time, those who owe you favors, those you have served, yes, those who owe you anything.

Just simply let it go and hold nothing against them, and extend your forgiveness of their debt. It is not difficult, and it brings freedom to both you and to your debtor. O beloved, release those who are in bondage to you, and in so doing you will experience a satisfying inner joy and peace.

June 19

REST
Hebrews 4:9-11

O beloved, enter into the joy of your Lord, and rest from your struggle and stress. Have not I said that My presence goes with you, and I give you rest?

Child, there is rest in Me. There is peace in Me. And though there may be turmoil and unrest all around, I bring rest and peace to your soul. You say: "How can this be?" But I say it is so, and the way to experience it is to believe that I provide it for you. Yes, be fully persuaded that I can do what I say.

O beloved, do you not desire to be free from your struggles and anxieties? Do you not desire a rest for your soul, a calmness in your life? Well, dear one, it is there. It is available. So, make every effort to enter that rest. And remember, that you enter by believing that I have already made every provision.

O child, as the demands come, the pressures rise, and the anxieties occur, simply say: "I rest this with you Lord. I enter your rest concerning this." And, loved one, I will give you rest. My peace, which transcends all understanding, shall flood your heart and soul, and you will experience rest in My presence.

A JOURNEY WITH JACOB
Genesis 35:1-20

My child, learn from the life of Jacob. Did not I meet him and reveal Myself to him? Was it a not a place called Bethel, meaning: "The House of God?" Did not I confirm what I had already spoken? Did not I change his name to Israel and give him great promises? Did not he go on to Ephrath, meaning: "Fruitfulness?" And later did not he go on to Edar, meaning: "A Flock?" Was not this a divine progression ordered by me?

Yes beloved, I know that these are names of locations, Bethel, Ephrath and Edar, but they provide a guide in your spiritual journey. For indeed, I meet and manifest Myself in My house, and you are that house.

And child, I have changed your name and have given you My name, which is the name that is above every name. I have given you great and precious promises, promises for life and godliness, and promises for health and prosperity. And dear one, I am producing fruitfulness in you, for have not I said to let the fruit of the Spirit be manifest in your life? So, you are growing and maturing in the Spirit.

And beloved, I am bringing you into a large flock, a great increase, for as that was My sequence with Jacob, so it is with you. Yes, from the renewal in the House of God to the revelation of Myself, from the giving of divine promises to the fruitfulness of a godly life, I bring you into a place of increase.

So, rejoice and learn from the example of Jacob. Did not I give him great increase, even though there was death of someone so near to him, his wife Rachel?

145

So, there must also be a death experience in your life, a death to self. For it is in death that life springs forth in abundance.

So rejoice, child, for you too shall be greatly increased far beyond what you have ever asked or thought.

June 21
THE LORD IS MY SHEPHERD
Psalm 23:1-6

Child, have not I said that I am the Good Shepherd? O yes, dear one, I am your shepherd and in Me there is no want. There is no lack, for, indeed, I lead you into pleasant and beautiful places, places that are bountiful with good things.

Beloved, I satisfy you, for I am your satisfaction. You need nothing else. I lead you into revelation, restoration, and renewal. I lead you into a marvelous refreshing. I am the Good Shepherd. And I watch over you to protect you from all that would harm you. I watch over you to bring peace and contentment to your life. I watch over you to bring order out of chaos. I watch over you to fill your cup to overflowing with blessings, more than you can receive.

And beloved, I lead you, guide you, and take you to safe places. I lead you on paths of righteousness and through the valley of the shadow of death, but I bring you out safely on the other side comforted and renewed.

And child, I set a table before you, and you shall feast to your heart's content on My mercy and My goodness. I shall never leave you for I am with you always, even forever. So, do not become discouraged or think you lack anything. For trust and confidence in Me brings prosperity in every way.

Yes beloved, simply believe it, for it is so. By believing, it shall be yours. I do not hold back what is

146

best for you. O no, I desire to shower you with all blessings. So, listen for the voice of your shepherd. Heed My call and come follow Me, for indeed My best, My goodness, and mercy, shall pursue you all the days of your life. And you, My child, may always dwell in the presence of your Lord forever, in all His glory, splendor, and majesty.

THE LIGHT OF THE WORLD
John 1:6-9

My child, I am indeed the delight of all men. I am the light of the world, and I shine in a dark world laden with sin, sickness, and depression. But, dear one, My light dispels the darkness, for has not the darkness been dispelled in your life?

O beloved, My light is bright. My light is pure. My light knows no guile or impurity. It is the light of My life. And dear one, I came to bring life and to bring it more abundantly.

Child, I came so that you could be changed from darkness to light. I came so that My life could become your life. I came so that you could bask in My presence, free from all cares and concerns, regardless the situation or circumstance.

Beloved, do you not see that I am the Lord God Almighty, the creator and sustainer of the entire universe? Nothing is made that has not been made by Me. I control it all. I am in charge.

And child, My light, My truth, My presence penetrates everywhere bringing to light those things that need to be revealed in your life; things that need to be dealt with and put off; things that would hinder your walk and fellowship with Me; things that would hinder and obstruct.

Beloved, there is so much blessing in our fellowship together, when your life says: "Not my will

147

but thine be done." Yes, there is so much for you to experience, so much more that I have planned for you. And I shall bring you into that experience, as you trust and obey Me more and more. O child, I have only begun. I am doing a new thing, a quick work, and you shall see it. So, arise and shine, for the light of My presence has come.

June 23

HIS FINISHED WORK
Galatians 3:13-14

Beloved, you are no longer under law, but under grace, for that which the law demands is now met in faith. Faith that I have done all that is necessary for life. Faith that I give life in abundance. Faith that everything is completed, and that all you need is Me.

O child, righteousness is not based on what you do. It is not based on service, worship, or prayers, but rather it is based on faith in Me. It is based on what I have done. Then righteousness leads you into these areas: worship, service, praise, and prayer.

Beloved, I finished what I began. All the work is done. All you need do is believe it and count on it. Then out of a heart of love and compassion follow Me and serve others. For everything was accomplished by My life, death, burial, and resurrection. I broke all claims of the enemy.

And I rose victorious giving you the victory. I share with you My resurrection power. I share with you all the blessings of heaven. I give you My Word and My name, and nothing shall be impossible to you. You have all My sufficiency, simply, by believing it and taking it for yourself.

O child, I do so much more. I fill you with My Spirit so that you, by His power, may do great signs, wonders, and miracles in My name. Yes, I have done it all, and now I move in and through you, for I have made it possible that we be one. I have broken the curse. I have freed you from bondage. I have made you one with Me.

GREATER JOY
Psalm 4:7

Child, I have chosen you, called you, and given you My Spirit, I have given you great and precious promises, so that your joy may be full. I have filled you with the oil of gladness and with songs of joy. I have given you strength and power, for indeed, My joy is your strength.

O beloved, I have filled your heart with greater joy, far more than you could ever know in the world. And My joy is without sorrow or pain. It is pure and holy. It is strength, peace, and beauty. It is like a mountain: full and majestic; strong and sturdy. So, hear My Word. Let My joy overflow in your life and praise Me in everything, for there is no greater joy found anywhere than in praising your Lord.

Beloved, there is greater joy in knowing Me better. There is greater joy in revelation. There is greater joy in walking out My Word. There is greater joy in standing on My promises. There is greater joy in the moving of My Spirit. There is greater joy in bringing a lost one to Me. O loved one, greater joy is found in the secret place of the Most High.

Yes child, I fill you with greater joy. Even when you feel it not, it is there. So, release it through praise and prayer. Release it in serving Me. Release it in feeding on My Word.

O beloved, I fill you with greater joy, and truly the joy of the Lord is your strength.

June 25

FAITH MOVES MOUNTAINS
Matthew 21:21-22

My child, faith moves mountains: mountains of lack and insufficiency; mountains of fear and doubt; mountains of opposition and oppression; mountains of depression and discouragement; mountains of bondage and captivity.

O beloved, faith makes the impossible a reality. Faith changes mourning into gladness and sorrow into joy. Faith changes things, places, and people. It is the key to unlocking the windows of heaven. For when there is faith in Me, faith in My Word, there shall be nothing impossible to you.

So child, speak to the mountain. Command it to dissipate. Command it to go and doubt not. Command in its place what you need. Speak to the mountain with authority and assurance. Speak with boldness and confidence. Speak with a mindset that anything is possible.

O beloved, tell all lack that it must go, and that there is no room for it. For lack only takes, it never replaces. Tell all the negative thoughts to go, for they only defeat. And be renewed in the attitude of your mind. Yes, speak to the mountain and believe it to be done.

My child, command what you need in My name and believe it to be so. See your God at work in a way you have never experienced before. Yes, speak to the mountain and it shall flee before you.

June 26

WHEN TWO SHALL AGREE
Matthew 18:19-20

Child, have not I said to ask and you shall receive? Have not I said that when two of you agree, concerning your request to Me, I would do it? Have not I said that you have not because you ask not? Have not I also said that you ask and receive not, because you ask out of an impure motive?

O beloved, I do not withhold from you, for I want only the best for you. You are a child of Mine, and I care for My own. But, dear one, I do know what is best. So, search your heart. Examine your motives. And come together and present your requests. I will answer them.

My child, know that when two or three gather in My name, I am there. And when two or three agree on a request, I am in the midst of that request. So, join together and pray. Join together and fellowship. And you shall find Me in the request and in the fellowship.

Beloved, there is power when two agree, and when two minister together. So, be encouraged for I hear your prayer, and I know your heart. I know before you ask and already have the answer on the way.

O dear one, let your request be pure, in accordance with My purpose. Let it come from an unselfish motive. Then agree with one another in your request, for there is strength when need is shared. There is power when you agree together, for My Word says that you shall then have what you ask. O child, let your motives be pure.

June 27

HE IS MY PEACE
John 14:27; Ephesians 2:14

Beloved, I am your peace. I am the Prince of Peace. I am the author of peace. So, let My peace rule in your heart. Have not I said: "Peace I leave with you, My peace I give unto you; not as the world gives, give I unto you. Let not your heart be troubled neither let it be afraid?"

Child, My peace is yours, and it can take you

through the storm, the wilderness, the sorrows, yes, the most difficult of circumstances. For true peace and contentment is found in Me.

And loved one, I even make your enemies to be at peace with you. Do you not see it? You want peace, then know that you already have it. You want peace, then just simply release it. You want peace, then struggle no longer, for My peace is already yours.

So child, go today resting in My peace, resting in the Prince of Peace. For true peace is not found in anything else, not in wealth, friends, family, or work. It is found only in Me.

June 28
THE TESTS AND TRIALS ARE HIS TO BEAR
2 Corinthians 1:5

Child, know that tests and trials are opportunities to fellowship in My sufferings. For the tests that come against My body, come against Me. It is My sufferings, and you share in them.

Beloved, it is part of My fellowship with you. So, realize that the tests and trials are Mine. Simply, let Me handle them. They are not intended to be placed on you, rather, they are Mine to carry, and Mine to bear.

O child, what you are going through, at the present time, I am working together for good. I will not allow more than you can withstand, for I make a way of escape. And I use these trials to bring you into a deeper and richer relationship with Me.

So beloved, rejoice in the tests and trials, for they are Mine to bear and yours to profit by.

LOVE CONQUERS ALL
1 Peter 4:8

Beloved, love covers a multitude of sins. Love covers hurts and injustice, for love is still love even when it has been wronged. Love says: "Father forgive them for they know not what they do." And love says: "Though He slay me, yet will I trust Him."

Child, love is the ingredient that keeps the world from becoming hopeless, for there is great hope in love. Love does not expect anything in return. True love manifests itself, regardless of the condition or circumstance.

O beloved, have not I said: "A new commandment I give unto you, that is to love one another, for by this shall all men know that you are My disciples, that you have love one for another?"

So child, love others. Lay aside all grudges, judgment, hatred, dislike, jealousy, contention, and envy. Let My love come through. Let it radiate in your life, for in love there is great healing and great peace.

O child, love those around you no matter who they are, or what they do, for in so doing you shall see miracles take place before your eyes. And you will say: "Surely love conquers all."

DELIVERANCE IS ON ITS WAY
2 Peter 2:9

Child, I know the end from the beginning. I see past the present. I see past the situation. I see past the circumstance and declare to you that the best is on its way. O dear one, I know how to deliver the righteous out of their trials.

Beloved, I not only know how to deliver the righteous, but I have promised to do so. Have not I said to cast all your care on Me, because I care for you? Have not I said to call unto Me, and I will deliver you out of all your trouble?

Yes child, I have given you promise after promise. I have assured you that I am for you. So, trust Me. Believe what I say. I am indeed with you in the trials, and I bring you out of them all. I use them to help you grow.

Beloved, does not My Word say to count it pure joy whenever you face trials of many kinds? This, dear one, is the testing and tempering of your faith. So, rejoice, I know what is best. I am working on your life, and you shall yet see the hand of your God manifested in and around you more than ever before.

July

Think on These Things

THINK ON THESE THINGS
Philippians 4:8-9

My child, whatsoever things are lovely, beautiful, pure, and of good report, think and meditate upon them. Have no place in your life for that which is not uplifting and encouraging, that which is negative, and that which misses the mark. For without training and practice, your godliness will be weak.

O beloved, train yourself in godliness. Commit your heart and soul to the task. For your spirit is strong, but the flesh is weak. So, begin your exercise more than ever before. For to run the race, to hike the heights, to raise valleys, and to remove mountains you must be spiritually strong and healthy.

O child, this pleases Me. Yes, godliness is a way of life. It is a mindset, and it takes discipline. And loved one, the training manual is before you. I have written all the instructions. I have given you nourishment from the meat and milk of My Word. And I have given you the Counselor, the Instructor, the great Trainer, My Spirit.

Now beloved, you have all the equipment and help you need. So, do not grow weary but continue to exercise godliness. For godliness with contentment is great gain. It is profitable for your life here and now, and it holds promise of great reward in the life to come. So My child, think on these things. Train yourself to be godly.

July 2

CRUCIFIED, YET ALIVE IN HIM
Galatians 2:20

Child, all the work is done, all the strain is removed. For I took it all with Me to the cross of Calvary. And you were crucified there with Me. Your old nature was put to death by what I did in your place. And as I rose in newness of life, so you too have newness of life, and that life is My life within you. I am alive, and I am in you. And I desire to live your life for you. Does this not take away all the stress and the strain?

O child, I have made provision to walk out all your cares and anxieties for you. Yes, I am willing to do the living through you, for I came to give life and to give it more abundantly. It is My will to live your life for you. For truly, this is the way of victory. This is the way of life at its best.

So beloved, when things happen and pressures mount, when it seems that there is too much to bear, remember that I am willing to bear it all for you. It is My will to live out the difficulties and pressures for you.

Dear child, remember, that whatever happens to you, I use to the good. I use it to bring you into a deeper and fuller relationship with Me. So, turn everything over to Me, for I care for you.

Yes beloved, you are crucified with Me, yet, you are alive, and that life is My life within you. So, lay aside all the concern and worry, and let Me do the living. O child, this is maturity. This is being conformed to My image. This is your victory. This is life in abundance.

July 3
CHOOSE BOTH THE WILLING AND THE DOING
Philippians 2:12-13

Beloved, choose to let Me have My perfect work in you. Choose to walk out your salvation. Choose to die daily to sin and its attraction. Choose to be led by My Spirit. Choose My very best for you. Choose to let Me use you for My honor and glory. Yes, choose, in awe and reverence, to let your life be pliable in My hands.

O beloved, the result of this choice provides Me the

157

opportunity to work in you both the willing and the doing of My good pleasure. I do not tell you to live for Me, and then leave you without help to do so. Neither do I demand submission based upon fear. Rather, I ask for complete surrender to Me, and then I provide everything you need to do what I ask you to do. I fully equip you with the willingness and ability to do My bidding.

O child, know that surrender to Me brings freedom from your own struggles and allows Me to do all the work. Have not I said that you are part of My body, that I am the head of the body, and that every part of the body is vital and important to the whole? So, since you are My body, should there ever be any question as to who is in control, you or I?

Beloved, is not this cause to rejoice, for I have just taken the strain out of everything. You can go your way knowing that I provide the willingness and the doing of My purpose. O dear one, it brings Me great pleasure to find one who will, without reservation, totally submit and commit their way unto Me. For, in so doing, that one will never need to question whether he or she is in My will or not.

July 4
WORRY NOT
Matthew 6:25-34

Beloved, worry not, for all that you need is found in Me. I supply all your need out of the abundant riches of My grace. Dear one, there is no benefit in worrying. There is no assistance in complaining. There is no sufficiency in grumbling. But in Me there is everything.

So child, seek Me with your whole heart. Let nothing else come between us. Let not the needs trouble you. Let not the love of money captivate you. Let nothing separate your commitment to Me, for if your mind is on other things you will not be seeking My good pleasure.

O trust Me, child, for I know your need even before you ask. Seek Me first and lay up spiritual treasures in heaven. Commit your way, yes, your every need to Me, for I have promised sufficiency for this day.

I MUST LOSE MY LIFE TO GAIN IT
Luke 9:23-25

My child, you must lose your life in order to gain it. So, turn your life over completely to Me. No longer live for self or by selfish motivation, but let Me live in and through you. Yes beloved, lose your life, count it as nothing, and count My life as everything.

HIS LEADING AND COUNSEL IS SURE
Psalm 32:8

My child, I am the one who guides you, counsels you, and watches over you to show you your way. And My leading and counsel is sure. There is nothing false about it. For My ways are righteous and perfect, and My plan for you is beyond reproach.

O beloved, I lead you in paths marked out by the presence of My Spirit. I watch over you and jealously guard you, for I want nothing to frighten or harm you. And I give you strength and power for the tasks that I have set out before you.

Yes child, I guide you, instruct you, and show you what to do. I tell you where to go and what to say. And I give you the strength and boldness to do it. O dear one, does this not encourage you? Does this not make you want to praise Me? For your God, the Almighty One, is mindful of you.

Yes beloved, I watch over you. I protect you. I guide

you. I instruct you. I counsel you. I show you the way you are to go. I strengthen you to the task. No wonder it is fitting and right that My name be praised. For I love you without end, My promises to fulfill.

July 7
WAITING IS A PART OF HIS PLAN
Genesis 17:7; Isaiah 30:18

My child, I am the God of the impossible, for nothing is too difficult for Me. Did not I tell Abraham many years before Isaac was born that he would have a son? Did not I promise him that through him all the nations of the earth would be blessed?

And beloved, was not Sarah over ninety years old when she conceived and gave birth? Yes, that was impossible for man, but with Me there is nothing impossible. For I am the God of resurrection, I am the God of life. I am the God that calls things into being from that which does not exist.

But, My child, I do things in My time. However, My timing may not be the same as your timing. Sometimes I may say wait, but I say it for a purpose. Sometimes it is to orchestrate all things together for perfect harmony. Sometimes I may say wait so you may see and recognize the manifestation of My power and glory.

Beloved, I never say wait to make you miserable, to hurt or to harm you. For those who place their trust in Me shall never be put to shame. No, dear one, it is because I know what is best. I know when the time is right for miracles. I know what is good for you.

So, take heart, My child, for waiting is part of My plan. It is part of My instruction. It is part of being conformed to My image. Remember, that after you have suffered a little while, you shall receive the promise. Yes beloved, I am the God of the impossible, and I am always on time.

160

IN HIS PRESENCE IS GREAT AND WISE COUNSEL
Psalm 16:7

Child, in My presence is everything you can or ever will need. Indeed, there are the pleasures of joy and peace at My right hand. In My presence there is great and wise counsel, and instruction for every situation.

Beloved, as you come into My presence seeking My guidance, you shall never be disappointed, for I will counsel you with love and kindness. Have not I said to trust Me with your whole heart and lean not unto your own understanding, and in all your ways acknowledge Me and I shall direct your paths?

Child, have not I said that if you lack wisdom, you should ask of Me, and I would freely give it to you? Yes, dear one, I provide wise counsel and guidance. I instruct and teach you even in the night seasons. And I whisper that this is the way you should go, come, walk in it.

O beloved, I never lead astray. I never lead amiss. I never lead out of My will. Rather I lead in paths of righteousness for My name sake. Yes, I lead you gently and peacefully in the way that is best for your life.

So, listen carefully for My counsel. Seek it constantly. Seek it from My Word. Seek it in prayer. Seek it from My Spirit, and you shall not be shaken or disappointed, for My counsel brings the pleasures of joy and peace even in the midst of great pressure.

O rejoice child, for the God of the entire universe counsels you and directs you in the way you are to go.

PLANS THAT SUCCEED
Proverbs 16:3-4

Beloved, when you commit everything to Me; all your plans, all your decisions, your work, your home, your family, your needs, and your ministry, I cause you to succeed. This is My Word. I tell you nothing false. Everything I say is true. I work everything together to accomplish My purpose, and My purpose includes great benefit and blessing for you.

O child, simply take Me at My Word. Involve Me in each and every plan, in each and every work, in each and every decision, and you will succeed. Yes, loved one, I honor My Word. And as you honor Me, I honor you. So, consult Me in everything.

Beloved, it need not be a long and drawn out consultation. It can be as simple as: "Lord, help"; or, "Thy will be done." It is an attitude. It is recognizing Me as the senior partner in your life. It is knowing that I give wise and sound counsel.

Sometimes, child, it may take a conference with Me, for you may have plans that do not fit into My purpose. So, it takes some lengthy discussion. However, the heart that says: "Regardless the outcome, regardless the conditions, I want my plans to succeed only for the glory of the Lord." Those plans shall succeed.

O beloved, include Me in your decisions, and you shall not stumble or fall, for I work out all things to the good. Yes, commit and submit your plans to Me. Consult Me in the formation and development of your plans, and you will not be disappointed. For My Word says that those plans will succeed.

So rejoice child, this is a great promise. A promise to use daily. A promise to include in all your plans, for everything you do wherever you are. O beloved, is this not good?

July 10

HE WHO CREATES WILL PROVIDE
Genesis 22:14

My child, I am Jehovah Jireh: "HE WHO CREATES

WILL PROVIDE." I am the great provider, and there is nothing impossible for Me. O dear one, I meet your every need. Every test has its provision. So, when it appears that there is lack, know that I, Jehovah Jireh, the one who creates out of nothing, will provide.

Beloved, did not I provide a ram for Abraham? O yes, for he believed what I told him. For I had promised that through his only son Isaac, his descendants would be as numerous as the stars of the heavens. Yet, when I told him to sacrifice his son, he willingly proceeded to do it. He knew that My Word is true and that I honor it. He believed that, even if Isaac was slain, I would provide. And in response to his act of faith and obedience provision was made.

So, take heart child, I am Jehovah Jireh, and that which seems as lack to you I can fill in an instant. Let there not be any doubt or fear, for you have living within you the very power and presence of that name. O loved one, I am your provider. There is nothing to withhold from you.

So, believe it beloved. Walk in it. Act upon it. Trust Me with your whole heart without a shadow of a doubt, and you will see: HE WHO CREATES, provide for your every need.

July 11

OBEDIENCE, THE KEY TO BLESSING
Psalm 119:1-2

Beloved, the key to blessing, to life in abundance, is to seek Me with your whole heart: to obey without hesitation, and to keep My Word, for My Word is life.

O child, obedience opens the windows of heaven. For obedience places no other gods before Me. It allows nothing else to come between us. Does not My Word say that those who seek Me with their whole heart, and those who walk according to My Word are blessed?

163

Yes, I bless My people. I delight in pouring out blessing upon blessing. And My children are the beneficiaries of all that My name implies.

O beloved, I have promised to go with you wherever you go. I have promised to bless your coming and your going. I have promised to bless and multiply everything you put your hand to do. I have promised abundant prosperity. I have promised all this and much more.

Child, do you not know that believing My Word is obedience? Do you not know that claiming My Word for yourself is obedience? Do you not know that My Word is forever true, and can be counted on? Do you not know that your life totally committed to Me brings great reward?

O beloved, I have made marvelous provisions. Come and walk in them. Walk in obedience, and by faith receive all that I have for you. Yes, child, I have baskets full of blessings, yours to receive.

July 12
KEEP ON KEEPING ON
2 Corinthians 4:16-18; Hebrews 12:3

My child, keep on keeping on. Do not grow weary in well doing, for what you are doing is pleasing to Me. Continue in love. Continue in a pure heart. Continue in your good motives. Continue in your most sincere faith. Yes, continue to persevere.

Beloved, I know that the enemy would try to wear you out, and that he would try to cause you to doubt. I know that he would try to lay all manner of guilt upon you. But the enemy must flee in My presence. And you, My loved one, just simply continue your trust and confidence in Me, for the only thing that counts is faith expressing itself in love.

So child, do not grow weary or say: "When will all this be over?" But rather rejoice and say: "I know that

My God is working in and through me." Rejoice that you know Me. Rejoice that you know the truth of My Word. Rejoice that you experience My presence daily.

Rejoice beloved, that all My promises, written and recorded in My book, are yea and amen. Know that these promises are real. They are true. They can be counted on. They are yours. They are like money in the bank.

Rejoice child, that you have My Spirit, the Holy Spirit, the Spirit of truth who guides you into all truth. He is the same Spirit that strengthens you and empowers you, and who gives you rest and peace. Yes, rejoice dear one, and do not grow weary, but rather offer continually the sacrifice of praise. And continue to do good to others. Continue to serve Me by helping those around you.

O beloved, with such I am pleased. So, look up and be encouraged. Know that I love you and work through you only that which is for your good.

Yes, keep your eyes fixed on Me. Just wait on Me, and you will not faint, you will not grow weary. And I will cause you to be renewed and refreshed, and to soar on wings of eagles above all that would try to bring you down.

July 13

HE ORDERS MY PATHS
Isaiah 42:16; Psalm 37:23-24

Beloved, I lay out the paths of life before you. I order your paths and I make them straight. Your paths are ordered of the Lord. Just walk in them and experience the joy of My presence. For, dear one, there is no better place to be than in My presence, walking the paths I have chosen for you.

Beloved, the paths of life are centered in Me, for I am your path. I have set the example. Have not I said that the steps of a good man are ordered of the Lord?

So child, know that I lead you. Know that I have ordered your steps. Know that the paths I have marked out for you are the same paths that I walk.

O dear one, come, walk with Me. For I take you on the pathway to heaven, the pathway to blessing, and the pathway to joy, for that pathway is in My very presence. I have laid it out for you.

So come, My child, and walk on that pathway for it is a glorious place to be. Yes, it is in My presence, and that makes it beautiful and special. And as you walk it, you will find yourself soaring on the wind, the breath of My spirit.

July 14

GIVE THANKS
Colossians 3:15-17

My child, My Word for you today is to rejoice in the Lord and give thanks. Yes, give thanks in everything. Not only in the good, but in everything else as well. Have not I said: "Give thanks in all things, for this is My will concerning you?"

So beloved, give thanks in the tests, trials, and difficulties. Give thanks in adversity and discomfort. Give thanks when your plans do not succeed. Give thanks when you are not appreciated, or understood.

Child, give thanks when you have been falsely accused and suffer for doing right. Give thanks even when there is health problems, sickness, and pain. Give thanks when the cupboard is bare and there is no bread on the table.

Give thanks when your enemies persecute you and your friends forsake you. Give thanks when your family mistreats you and uses you. Yes, give thanks even when you have given of yourself until there is no more to give and no one gives back to you.

O beloved, do not let "woe is me" overtake you. For have not I said to fret not yourself because of evil doers? Have not I said that if I care for the sparrows, surely, I would care for you? Have not I said that your God would supply all your need according to His riches in glory?

Yes child, I have said all this, and I also said to rejoice and be glad. I have said to always give thanks. I have said that I work all things together for good. So, dear one, give thanks. In all things let there be an attitude of thankfulness.

O beloved, let your thanks and praise be heard and seen. Let Me hear them, and the situations and circumstances will not become mountains, but rather they will become nothing but molehills. They will not destroy you, but you will conquer them. So child, let thanks and praise be continually on your lips, for this is pleasing to Me and it brings great peace.

ASSURANCE OF HIS GOODNESS
Psalm 34:6-10

Child, is not My Word full of assurances that I watch over you, care, protect, deliver, and provide for you in abundance? Does not My Word say to taste and see that I am good? And have you not tasted and found it so?

O beloved, there is no end to My goodness. Yes, I continue to pour out upon you blessing upon blessing. So, take Me at My Word. Trust Me with your whole heart. Let nothing or no one distract you from your relationship with Me.

Child, there is none greater. There is none that can satisfy like I do. There is no one else that loves you as I do. There is nothing that can match My protection, love, provision, deliverance, peace, and My joy. O consider what you have in Me. There is nothing else of substance. There is nothing else that will last. So,

rejoice in My goodness and in the truth that I am the
answer to every question, doubt, and anxiety.

July 16
HIS LOVE IS AWESOME AND MAJESTIC
Psalm 68:35

Child, look around you and see the mountains, the
hills, the valleys, yes, all My creation. Is it not
awesome? Do you not see strength, beauty, and
majesty? And dear one, My love for you is also
awesome, majestic, and beautiful. It knows no limit.
For, beloved, My love for you is higher than the tallest
mountain, wider than the most expansive ocean,
clearer than a cloudless day, and beautiful as a
moonlit night. There is no end to it.

O loved one, I am mindful of you at all times, and I
call you by name, for you are My child. And out of My
unlimited love, out of that awesome love, out of My
splendor and holiness, I bless you. I pour you out a
blessing so much that you are not able to receive it all.
I shower you with only the best.

Child, is not this wonderful? Is not this marvelous?
Is not this awesome? So, learn of Me and you will
continue to be amazed and awed at the goodness of
your Lord. For indeed, I am awesome and majestic.

O loved one, My love is unconditional. All you need
do is receive it. My love is not based on your merit, or
on your righteousness, but it is based on My desire to
share it. And though the mountains be shaken and
the hills be removed, My unfailing love for you cannot
and will not ever be shaken or withdrawn.

July 17
FULFILLING ALL THAT HE HAS PLANNED
Psalm 33:11

Child, My plan and My purpose are fixed. Nothing

can change what I have decreed to be. I spoke in eternity past, and I declared what was and is and is to come. And I am fulfilling all that I have planned.

O beloved, you are a part of this plan. Your life was hid in Me before I created the world. And I designed a specific plan and purpose for your life. You shall not fall short, but rather, you shall accomplish all I intended for you to accomplish.

Child, I am faithful. My loving-kindness has blotted out all that separated you from Me. I cleansed you with My blood and I seated you with Me in the heavenlies. I purposed that you would do good works; that you would follow wherever I lead; that you would be My child; that you would serve Me with your whole heart.

But you say: "Lord, I have done nothing. I've messed up my life. I haven't followed you in everything." But I tell you that I have been with you always. I taught you necessary lessons during those times, and I made up what you lacked.

Beloved, you are on time in My plan. So, seek Me diligently with your whole heart, and you shall find Me. You shall see that you are fulfilling My purpose in your life. You will see that My plan stands firm forever, and that you share in its fulfillment.

July 18

SERVICE
1 Corinthians 10:31

My child, it is good for you to serve Me with your whole heart. It is good to serve Me without reservation, for I alone am worthy of such devotion. I alone am the rewarder of those who diligently seek Me. So beloved, serve Me in everything. In your work, do it as unto Me. In your play, do it as unto Me. In your home, serve Me. In the routine of every daily activity, do it as unto Me.

169

Yes, even in what you eat or drink, do it unto Me. For in so doing, you will experience My presence in everything. You will see Me in every circumstance and in every situation.

Child, let Me be present in all that you do. Do everything as unto Me. For as you do you are seeking Me. And did not I say that I reward those who diligently seek Me?

Beloved, I want only the best for you, and the best comes from serving Me, no matter the cost. O dear one, I love you, and I call to you saying: "Serve Me with your whole heart." So, do not say: "I like to do this or I don't like to do that." But rather say: "I like serving my Lord in everything I do."

July 19
HIS WORD IS ALIVE AND POWERFUL
Hebrews 4:12

Child, My Word is indeed alive and powerful. It is overflowing with great and precious promises. It is abundantly rich in instruction, guidance, and correction. For My Word brings life, and it is life changing. It heals broken hearts and crippled bodies. It calms the most troubled sea. It is sufficient to every situation.

Yes beloved, My Word is alive and powerful. And I say to you to watch and pray, so you do not enter into temptation. I say to you to obey Me with your whole heart, for obedience has great reward. I say to you to fear not, for I am with you wherever you go.

I say to you that I am your God and that you are My child, holy and separate unto Me. I say to fix your eyes on Me, for I am the author and perfecter of your faith. Yes My child, all of this is My Word and there is so much more.

So, take heart and focus your life on Me. Let My Word work in you and through you. And be encouraged, for I have made every provision for you. I have given you My Word, and My Word is forever true. Beloved, I do not break My Word, as those in the world do, but I honor it, keep it, and give it freely to you. It is yours to receive. Yes child, My Word is alive and powerful.

FRET NOT
Psalm 37:1-7

O My child, do not fret about anything, for fretting is unbelief. It only consumes you. It causes unrest and leads to evil. It is not of Me. But My Word says to commit your way unto Me. My Word says to trust in Me, and turn everything over to Me. My Word says to rejoice in serving Me. My Word says to serve Me in everything you do.

So beloved, whatever you do, in word or deed, do all to My glory and honor. Regardless the situation, just seek Me. And though things may vex you, you can find Me in them when you praise Me, when you commit them to Me.

So, sing, praise, and rejoice, for I am on the throne and My kingdom endures forever. Do not let temporal things worry you. But rather, let your spirit be free to worship and praise My name, for in so doing you shall find rest and peace. O child, I care for My own.

HE DOES GREAT AND MIGHTY THINGS
1 Samuel 12:16-24

Child, behold I do great and mighty things. Things that are awesome and inspiring. Things that change lives. Things that change communities, nations, and the world. And I do great and marvelous things in your life.

O beloved, do you not see the miracles? Do you not

see the blessings? Yes, I know when you go through the tests that they are difficult. I know you think sometimes that everything is against you. But have not I said that if I be for you who can be against you? O dear one, nothing can stand against the test of My favor, and you are favored. You are in My grace forever, My love and kindness to know.

So, now child, stand still. Watch, for I am about to do great things before your eyes again. It is not based upon who you are or what you do, but rather, it is based upon who I am and My purpose to fulfill. I reward those who simply trust and revere My name, those who seek Me with their whole heart. So, watch and you shall see the great and mighty things I am about to do.

July 22
WALK HUMBLY WITH YOUR GOD
Micah 6:8

My child, hear what I have to say. Listen, and I will show you what is good. I will show you what is right. I will show you what pleases Me.

Beloved, it is not your deeds that please Me, for your deeds are self-righteous. Nor is it your thoughts, for your thoughts are selfish thoughts. But, My child, that which pleases Me is for you to walk humbly with Me moment by moment. And as you walk humbly with Me, your thoughts and deeds become My thoughts and deeds. Yes, as you walk humbly with Me, you will do good and love mercy.

So, keep in step with Me. Fellowship with Me. Learn of Me. Learn of My mercy. Seek it, for My mercy and grace open the doors of heaven to you. And seek to please Me by walking humbly with Me. Walk in awe and reverence. Walk in unconditional obedience. For you cannot please Me in yourself, but you do please Me when you search for Me with your whole heart. O

172

beloved, I have opened up the gates of righteousness for you to come in and to walk and talk with Me. For it pleases Me to fellowship with you. Yes dear one, I show you what is good.

FEAST ON HIS WORD
1 Peter 2:2; Psalm 119:9-16

O My child, I instruct you and feed you the sincere milk of My Word. So, crave My Word as a newborn baby craves the nourishment of its mother's milk. Yet, I would have you to know there are other forms of food to feast on, the ways of which are death and destruction. But, dear one, feasting on My Word brings nourishment and strength. So, feast on it so that you may grow and mature in the nurture and admonition of your Lord.

Beloved, growing in My Word means to eat and assimilate it and to let it do its work in you. It means to take and eat all of it. But you can not digest it all at once. You must give it time to produce growth.

And though I am doing a quick work in you, My child, it still takes time for My Word to spring forth in your life. So, let My Word have its perfect work in you, and rid yourself of all that is contrary to it and all that does not belong.

Beloved, do not let yourself be contaminated and made ill by eating forbidden fruit, but rather, crave the spiritual nourishment of My Word. For My Word is sweet as honey and it is nourishment to the soul, for it comes from My Spirit. And My Spirit is the ingredient in My Word that makes it alive, and causes it to give health and healing, life and peace. Indeed, My Word comes to life through My Spirit.

O child, My Word is bread to the eater and seed for the sower. So, eat it. Use it. Let it work. Let My Word be the only thing upon which you feast. For in so doing you will grow and become healthy in body, soul, and spirit.

July 24
HIS GOOD PLEASURE TO GIVE US THE KINGDOM
Luke 10:8-11; 12:32

My child it is My good pleasure to give you the Kingdom. For indeed, the kingdom is near. The Kingdom has come, and it is within you. It is My Kingdom, and I am its King. I am the Lord of lords.

So, let Me be your king. Let Me be the master, the ruler, and the Lord of everything in your life. In your work, in your play, in your home, in your worship, yes, in everything let Me be Lord.

O beloved, hold nothing back. Let Me be in charge of everything, for in so doing you gain everything. For when I am Lord of everything, everything in your life becomes gain. Yes, when you lose your life in Me, you find it again in abundance.

So dear one, My Kingdom is near, does not this cause you to rejoice. O it should for when I am in charge, when I am Lord, when I am lifted up your paths are made straight.

July 25
A GRAND PROCESSIONAL
Psalm 68:17, 32-35

Child, My chariots are without limit, and I send them with you as you go about your activity today. I have placed My Spirit of protection around you, and I will keep you safe. So, enjoy My presence, dear one, for I am with you all day in everything you do, and in every place you go.

O beloved, know that My chariots go before you, beside you, and behind you. Yes, I have a grand processional accompanying you, and you will say:

"Surely the Lord is with me. Surely He cares for me. Surely He is good. Surely He is merciful."

Yes child, I go before you and I prepare the way for you. So, go forth today with singing and rejoicing in your heart, for the Lord your God has sent His chariots to accompany you.

July 26

BUILD UP HIS DWELLING PLACE
Haggai 1:8; 2:6-9

Beloved, you are My habitation, My place of residence, yes, My dwelling place. Indeed, you have been fashioned for Me. And I would speak to you today about building up this house, which is the temple of the Living God.

Child, I know you have given Me your life. It is Mine. But, loved one, I have entrusted the care of My habitation to you, and it is your responsibility, with My direction, to build up My dwelling place, and not to tear it down.

So beloved, be mindful of who you are and whose you are. And zealously look after My house, for I desire that My house become more and more beautiful. I desire that My house become holy. I desire that My house become stronger and stronger. I desire that the glory of My house become greater each and every day.

Child, I am speaking of caring for My house, both spiritually and physically. So, be sensitive to My direction. And give attention to feasting on My Word, listening to My Spirit, and caring for your body. O beloved, build up My house.

July 27

A VERY PRESENT HELP IN TROUBLE
Psalm 25:1-10; 91:15

Beloved, I am faithful and true. My love is beyond

175

measure, and I hold you close to Me. I watch over you, protect you, and comfort you. I instruct you and teach you My ways. I lead you in My paths.

O child, listen. Hear what I have to say. Those who put their trust in Me can be sure of My commitment to them. Yes, you shall not be afraid, for there is no need to fear. I am ever present.

And dear one, there is no need to fret or worry about anything, for I am a very present help in trouble. There is no need to be concerned about anything or any situation, for you are My child, and I care for you. I flutter over you. I gather you to Me.

Child, I do not turn My back on you or ever forget you. So, learn to walk in this truth. Learn to rise above circumstances and see Me in them. Learn to speak My name with authority, for I am training you to do My bidding. I am instructing you in the ways of righteousness, compassion, love, and power.

O beloved, I desire that you take My Word and use it. Stand on it. Believe it. Let it work itself all the way through your entire being. So that, when the difficulty or trouble arises, you can be in complete control, simply by speaking and confessing My Word over it.

O child, rejoice, for I confide in you. I tell you marvelous things. I share with you the secret of living life to the fullest. It is simply learning to experience Me, My Word, and My Spirit in every aspect of your life. Yes dear one, rejoice, I am the God you trust. Is there anything too hard for Me?

July 28
TAKE NOT YOUR EYES OFF HIM
Matthew 14:22.32

Beloved, those who worship Me do so in spirit and in truth. Those who trust Me can do the impossible. For when your eyes are upon Me, nothing else can distract you. But if you take your eyes off Me and look at the conditions around you, then doubt creeps in, and where there is doubt there is no peace.

So child, come boldly to Me with trust and confidence in Me and My promises. Step out into the water, even as the storm rages around you. Fix your eyes, your thoughts, and your mind on Me, and nothing shall overwhelm you. Nothing shall be impossible to you, for your confidence will be in the God of the impossible.

Yes beloved, have faith in Me at all times. Doubt not that I can do anything. Doubt not that through Me you can do all things. Doubt not that I can bring life, when there is no life; healing, when there is no cure; abundance in the midst of lack; joy out of sorrow; gladness out of mourning; peace and order out of chaos; restoration out of devastation. O child, have faith in Me, and you shall walk on top of troubled waters.

July 29

FOLLOW THE PATH OF HOLINESS
I Thessalonians 4:1-11

My child, it is My will that you be holy and pure, totally set apart unto Me. Have not I said for you to be holy, as I am holy? Have not I said that I make you clean by the Word I have spoken? Have not I said that you are cleansed by the washing of My Word?

Child, it is My desire that you be pure in thought, word, and deed, and that you be holy, for holiness is godliness. It is the virtue that is above every virtue. Yes, holiness is My nature, and I want you to be a partaker of that nature. For holiness is the purest form of devotion and obedience. It is the highest form of honoring My name.

Dear one, as a child imitates his father, so be you an imitator of Me. Know that My Spirit has sanctified you to follow the path of holiness. Yes child, I have set

177

you apart, and I have declared you righteous, but I am asking you to walk in the path of holiness, to walk in the path of righteousness, for this pleases Me.

Beloved, I provide the ability, the strength, and the capability to do just that. For to walk in holiness simply means to let Me lead, guide, and direct you in everything you do. And in so doing, you will be walking in righteousness and purity.

Child, I am not asking the impossible, but rather, I am asking for your willingness to do so. Then I provide the way to do it. O rejoice, dear one, and be holy for this pleases Me.

July 30

ONE BODY, MANY PARTS
Romans 12:5-8

Beloved, there is only one body made up of many parts. But each part is vitally important, for each has it's own separate function, yet it is dependent on the other. You are an important part of My body, and it would not be complete without you.

July 31

PRAISE
Psalm 148:1-14

My child, in everything and in every situation praise your Lord and God. This is the fruit of your lips giving thanks to My name. For I love the praises of My people.

Yes beloved, I love the praises of My people. I love their adoration and worship. I love hearing My people sing their praises. I love hearing the words and sounds of high praise.

And I love hearing praises from the young to the old, from both the child and the grandparent. I love hearing praises on the instruments, for I designed musical instruments for the purpose of praising Me. Child, I love hearing your praise.

So, let praise be in your heart and on your lips at all times, for praising is to the spirit as breathing is to the body. Yes, your praise is to be constant and spontaneous. It should never cease.

Beloved, I meet you in praise, for I inhabit the praises of My people. Praise strikes a responsive chord in Me, and I rush to your side, to the aide of My praisers. Did not I send My praisers out first ahead of the army to confuse the enemy? Indeed, I honor My praisers.

So child, praise Me for who I am. Praise Me for whose you are. Praise Me in your coming and in your going. Praise Me in your joy and in your sorrow. Praise Me in your sickness and in your health. Praise Me in your weakness and in your strength. Praise Me in your lack and in your abundance.

O beloved, praise Me in everything. In so doing, darkness will turn to light, sorrow will turn to joy, mourning will turn to dancing, night will turn into day, and the wilderness will turn into a garden of good things. Praise Me and see the mountains melt and the valleys rise up. Yes, praise Me My child, for it is to your good, and it pleases Me.

August

Part of His Body

PART OF HIS BODY
Ephesians 4:11-16

Child, you are part of My body, and each member is vital to the whole. Each member has its own function. Each member helps to strengthen and build up My body.

Beloved, I have placed within each member, gifts and abilities to bless each other. I have placed within each member My Spirit, who takes the gifts and talents and uses them to My honor. It is My Spirit that generates within each one the desire, the will, and the doing of My purpose.

O child, you have been given so much. You have Me, the very power and presence of the living God, dwelling within you. You have the leading of My Spirit. You have a new nature, a new self that is totally righteous and pure. You have My Word, and it changes not.

Beloved, you have My mind, My peace, My joy, and My strength. You have My resurrection power. You have spiritual eyes and ears to see and hear great and mighty things. And you are surrounded by My angels, who watch over you.

O child, you should be rejoicing constantly. There is no need ever to walk in depression. Because of My great love for you, walking in victory is a reality. So, rejoice, I have given you great and wonderful gifts, life in abundance. All of these are to share and help build up My people. All are to strengthen My body.

HE CAME TO BRING LIFE
Philippians 3:12-16

Beloved, I am the way, the truth, and the life. It is only by Me that you have access to the Father. O child, I am the vine, you are a branch. And I bring life to the branches. Did not I say that I came to bring life in abundance? Did not I say that to those who believe in Me I would give eternal life? Did not I say that I was the resurrection and the life? Could the grave hold Me?

Beloved, I rose from the grave in newness of life, and that is what I bring to you. I bring a living hope, an eternal hope, and an expectation of life today. So dear one, look to Me. Let My life flow freely within you, and let My Spirit pour out of you, life to those around you.

O child, I have infused you with life. So receive it, even as you receive your salvation, your healing, and all My promises. Receive all by faith. This is the promise: I give you life, and I do it in abundance. You shall lack nothing.

Tap into it, dear one. Live up to what you have attained in Me. For I am the God of the here and the now. I am your life.

August 3
HIS PURPOSE IS FIXED
Isaiah 46:10-11

My child, My purpose stands fixed. What I determine to do, I will do. What I have planned shall come to pass. For I alone am the God of the universe. There is none beside Me. Who else brought all things into existence? Surely it was not an idol of gold, silver, wood, or clay. No loved one, it was I who did it.

O beloved, I am the Lord God Almighty, the all powerful, all knowing, and all present one. It was My purpose to make you My own. I did that even before you were born. And I have carried and sustained you all the days of your life. I have always watched over you and protected you.

Dear child, this is your God, the one who loves and

cares, who knows the end from the beginning, who keeps His Word and His promises, and brings you into new and greater things. I am the one who brings you into a richer and deeper fellowship with Me. Child, I share all of Me, and it pleases Me to do so.

Yes loved one, My purpose is fixed. My plans for you shall be accomplished, and none can hinder. So, remain always close to Me, even in the very center of My presence, for that is My plan for you, and it is the safest, most secure place in all the universe.

STRAY SHEEP
Psalm 119:176

My child, you are sheep of My pasture. You are Mine, and that will always remain the same. It never changes. My faithfulness is great and endures forever. Nothing can separate you from the love of your Heavenly Father.

Beloved, you are My sheep: a sheep that sometimes goes astray; one that goes astray in your thinking and attitude; one that wants your own way; one that pouts if things don't always work out like you want. But I know your heart. I know it is perfect. I know its desire is to please Me, for I planted that desire within you.

So My child, yield not to the flesh. Let not self surface to rule, but continue to die to self. Let not selfish motives and selfish things be manifested in your life, for you are dead and your life is hid in Me. And the life you are to live now is to be lived by faith in Me through the power and presence of My Spirit.

Yes beloved, you are My sheep and I care for My sheep. I even gave My life for My sheep. So, let not self lead you astray. Watch and be alert. Do not rebel, but recognize the thoughts and intents of the heart for what they are. Let them be pure and holy. And fret not, but let My peace rule your heart and mind.

O child, My beloved sheep, I am full of love and compassion for you, and I am always near to lead, guide, and protect you. I am ever near to bring you back, and to keep you from going astray. So, stray not, My dear one, for it is to your good to stay ever close to Me, listening, watching, and obeying My instruction.

August 5

THE KING'S BUSINESS
Nehemiah 4:6; Jeremiah 48:10

Beloved, My work is not taken up with playing games. No My work is serious. It is life changing. It has to do with things eternal, things that last. It is not something secondary. It is the most important thing in all the universe. For it is My work. Child it rescues those from the gates of hell and provides for an abundance of life.

O loved one, My work is not to be approached lightly or insincerely, for it is the King's business. All else does not matter. Only what I want accomplished, only what I call you to do is what counts.

Beloved, there is no room for laziness or neglect in My work. For it all relates to the rule of life, My life. It all requires diligence, wisdom, commitment, and dedication. It calls for perseverance, even in the midst of adversity. It calls for action, even when the results seem futile, and even when it seems impossible.

But, My fellow worker, I will accomplish My purpose, and you shall be a part of the King's business. So, learn a lesson today. Do not only hear what I have to say, but do what I say. Be a doer of My Word.

Dear child, do not say: "Lord I cannot do what you ask. I am not able. I don't know how. I am not prepared, or, Lord, what if...?" But rather be willing to do what I ask and I will provide the strength, the ability, and the capability to do it all.

Yes beloved, even if the task seems awesome and

184

distasteful to you, perform it wholeheartedly, and you shall find blessing in it. For I honor My work, and I bless My faithful workers.

LOVE MY PEOPLE
Romans 14:1

My child, there are many things for you to learn. Yes, I would have you learn to love My people with purity, kindness, compassion, and patience. For many of My people are weak and in need of My strength, yet, they do not know how to find it, or how to possess it.

So beloved, love My people and do not become impatient with them. Learn to hear what I have to say to them through you, for this is how many hear Me. Hear what I say and share with them what I tell you. Yes, even when it sounds firm, for if done in love, it produces good fruit.

O child, do not look down upon My people. Do not judge them, but have compassion on them. Have not I said to help bear the infirmities of the weak? Remember, dear one, that the spirit is willing, but the flesh is weak. Yes, remember that weakness is human. But also remember that where there is weakness, there is opportunity for Me to demonstrate My strength.

Beloved, there is no other like Me, for I am the Almighty one, the deliverer, the God of joy, strength, peace, happiness, compassion and love. See, I too have emotions, so I know and I understand My people.

O child, love your brother and sister in pure godly love and despise them not. For when your heart is pure, I can minister to them through you to their benefit and to My praise, honor, and glory. So, teach them to hear Me, teach them to search for Me with their whole heart. Beloved, love My people and despise not those who are weak.

185

IT IS TIME
Hosea 10:12

Child, I am coming back for a strong, beautiful, and radiant Bride: a live, vibrant, and healthy Body. Beloved, signs and wonders accompany Me wherever I go, so it is time to get ready. It is time for My people to cleanse themselves of all that would hinder and slow them down. For when it is time, I will do a swift work.

Child, I am preparing My people. The lessons are being taught, and it is time for My people to receive what I have in store for them. Have not I said that I would announce My work, and My plan before hand? Have not I said that I will do a new thing?

O beloved, prepare yourself for I am beginning something the Church has never yet seen. This is a new thing, a new day. And loved one, the results of this will be the adorning of My dwelling place with beauty, splendor, and holiness.

O My child, rejoice for I do a quick work. So, be ready. It is time to go. It is time to move out, and I shall lead you in paths prepared long ago. Yes beloved, it is My time. It is the hour. So, awake O soul. Awake O sleeper. Do not slumber any longer. It is morning, and the new day is dawning. It is time to arise and shine, for My glory rests upon you, and there are things to do.

So beloved, rise and go forth in song and praise. Go forth to build. Go forth to restore. Go forth to work in My vineyard. Go forth to heal the broken hearted and cause the blind to see and the lame to walk. Go forth to heal all the diseases known and unknown to mankind.

Yes child, go forth and proclaim the day of the Lord. Go forth and share the good news that I have made provision for all to be placed in right standing with the Father. O go forth in confidence and strength, rejoicing that your God lives, and that He saves to the uttermost those who come to the Father through Me. O beloved, it is time.

PUREST OF MOTIVES
2 Samuel 22:26-27

My child, I love, care, and heal you to bring praise, honor, and glory to My name. I do it out of the purest motives in existence. I do it for My sake. Yet, in doing it for My sake, all the blessings of heaven becomes yours. Yes, out of My goodness comes great benefit to you.

Beloved, I am good; there is nothing bad or evil in Me. I am holy and pure, without blemish or tarnish. There is nothing false or impure about Me. And I am faithful and true. I keep My Word. I cannot lie.

O child, think not of Me in the way the world and its system thinks, for things done in the world are done out of impure and selfish motives. But what I do has no guile in it. I am honest, just, and fair. And I am full of love and compassion. And beloved, I have made you My inheritance, and you are precious and honored in My sight. O child, you are loved with the purest love there is, My love.

HE CAUSES ME TO GROW
AND BEAR MUCH FRUIT
Isaiah 27:6

My child, I tenderly care and watch over you day and night. I jealously guard and protect you. And I cause you to grow, to bud, and to blossom. I nurture you and bring you to maturity, so that you may bear much fruit.

Beloved, you are part of My vineyard, and I am the

husbandman. I am the one who planted you, and who placed the germ of life within you. I am the one who causes you to yearn for Me both day and night.

Child, I gently watch over you by My Spirit, and I tenderly prune and care for you. I do this so that you may bear beautiful fruit, and bring forth a bountiful harvest.

So, rejoice dear one, for I am bringing the increase. Only be faithful where you are and grow in the nurture and admonition of your Lord.

August 10
FEAR NOT, MY CHILD
Isaiah 41:10

Fear not, My child, for I am with you. O loved one, there is nothing to fear, for am not I the God of the universe? Am not I your shield, your fortress, and the mighty rock? Am not I the God that speaks peace and comfort to your soul?

O beloved, there is nothing to fear, for indeed I am with you, My presence to be made known. So, reach out and touch others with My love. Reach out and touch others with My peace, for they too need to know Me in a way that brings strength and joy to their lives.

My child, learn and grow from each and every circumstance. Learn to know Me and My ways better. Learn to follow My leading. Learn to hear My voice and to respond to it no matter the turmoil around you. I will not lead you astray, but I will always lead you in paths of righteousness.

So, fear not for the victory is already won. Lift up your head and go forth rejoicing in your God. He is the one who makes the impossible, possible.

Yes, He is the one who says: "I will be glorified in all the earth." He is the one who says: "Fear not for I am with you." He is the one who says: "You are my child and I love you so."

HIS BLOOD
Exodus 12:2-13

My son, as the Israelites were protected by blood of the Passover lamb, so I protect and comfort you by the precious blood I shed for you. I have applied the blood to you. On the door post of your heart has been applied the blood of the Lamb slain before the foundation of the world. Yes, My blood covers you. My blood has washed you, for without the shedding of blood there is no remission of sin.

O child, My precious blood was freely poured out for you, and all life is in that blood. Eternal life, eternal protection, and eternal love are all part of the blood I shed on the cross of Calvary. O dear one, there is great power in that blood.

So beloved, claim the blood, yes, plead the blood, My blood over your life. For it is life, protection, health, peace, comfort, and security. And it is yours, for I shed it for you. Apply it daily, as a fresh and new reminder of what it has done and what it can do. Yes, child, I protect and rescue you with My blood.

HE KNOWS ME BETTER
THAN I KNOW MYSELF
Ephesians 1:11-12

My child, I know you better than you know yourself. Before you were in your mother's womb, I knew you. I have been with you all the days of your life, and I shall remain with you and in you forever.

Beloved, I know your every need, your every hurt, your every joy, your every sorrow, your every anxiety, your every motive, and your every thought. I know you when you are asleep and when you are awake.

O dear one, you are My creation, My handiwork. I

have breathed into you the breath of life, yes, life eternal. And I know your coming and your going. I know when you are thirsty and dry, and I refresh you with My Word and with My Spirit. Yes beloved, I pour out upon you, and upon all My people, rivers of living water to cause desert places to bloom, meadows to produce good things, and gardens to teem with fruit of the vine.

O child, I know you, for as the potter fashions the vessel, so I fashion and shape you. I am conforming you to My image. I am bringing forth a beautiful vessel designed specifically for My purpose, and it is to be used to bring honor to My name.

So beloved, rejoice in that I know you, and that I know where you are. Rejoice that I rush to your rescue with a fresh out-pouring of My presence. Yes, rejoice, for there is no other like Me. Rejoice that I know what I am doing in and through you.

August 13
HE IS EVER READY TO SHARE HIMSELF
Amos 4:13

Child, I am ever ready to hear your call. I am ever ready to fellowship with you. I am ever ready to share with you all that I am. I am ever ready to share with you great and mighty things. I am ever ready to reveal new revelation, things that you know not.

O beloved, I share with you wisdom and knowledge. I share with you discernment and good judgment. I reveal truths that you have passed over. I share with you the mighty power of My name. I share with you the majesty and wonder of My presence.

Dear one, I visit with you as a friend. I love you as a child. I have placed My Spirit within you to lead, guide, and instruct. I have given My angels charge over you to watch over and protect you. And I have given you My Word which is true, for I cannot lie.

Yes beloved, I show you great and mighty things. So, come often; come daily; come as a friend; come as a child; come as an intercessor; come as a servant. Yes, come as you want, and I shall reveal Myself as sufficient to meet every need. For I am able to do exceeding abundantly above all you ask or think.

August 14

ASK AND IT WILL BE GIVEN
Matthew 7:7-8

Beloved, there is so much to share with you. Do you not see it as you read and meditate on My Word? O child, there is no end to My Word, to My instruction, and to My truth. For My truth is endless, and it goes on forever. My truth endures, for it is the same today as it was yesterday. My truth is strong and powerful.

Child, when I say to ask and you will receive, it shall be done. This is My Word. This is My commitment to you. And if I said it, it is true. If I spoke it, you can count on it. If I breathed the words, then they are real, and there is no changing or shadow of turning.

Yet beloved, the conditions are that of motive. I do not answer to impure and unholy motives. I know the thoughts and intent of the heart. But, I know that your motive is to please Me, and to place Me first.

So, call child, and I will fulfill My Word. Ask without doubt. Ask and believe what I say and what I tell you. And when I say to delight yourself in Me, and I will give you the desires of your heart, believe it, for it is true. When I say that I will withhold no good thing from those who love Me, believe it, for it is so.

O beloved, simply believe and trust Me. Take Me at My Word, and you shall be amazed at what takes place in and around you. Yes, rejoice in Me and in the purity of My Word.

August 15
THE PATH TO HIS BEST
Psalm 51:17-19

My child, let Mount Zion rejoice, for I am prospering My people. I, indeed, make them glad, for I live and
dwell in and among them, with My power and My
presence to reveal. And I give them joy and gladness,
not sorrow and sighing. I do not put heavy burdens on
My people, but rather, I take the difficulties and the
pressures and turn them into good.

Beloved, I do not remove Myself from you. I ascend
not into the heavens without you. I do not take My
presence from you, for you are My dwelling place. And
I desire, daily, a moment by moment fellowship with
you, which is one that exalts My name. It is one from a
pure and contrite heart.

O child, the path to My best is one of brokenness
and death to self. It is one of complete surrender to
Me. It is one that rejoices in everything. It is one that
gives thanks in all things. It is one that looks for Me in
every situation.

So beloved, rejoice, for I return unto you the joy of
your salvation. I make it new and fresh every day. O
loved one. I am building steadiness and stability in
your life. I am indeed building up the walls of Jerusalem. I am prospering My people.

August 16
HE IS LOVING, KIND AND GOOD
Psalm 85:8-13; 86:15

Child, I am loving, kind, and good. Do not I watch
over you day and night? Do not I jealously guard and
protect you? Do not I perform signs and wonders
before your very own eyes? Do not I supply all your
need? Do not I have everything in control?

Beloved, do not I abound unto you in love, mercy,

192

and grace? Do not I bless you with My presence? Do not I speak to you daily and whisper to you that this is the way, walk in it? Do not I teach you My ways? Do not I promise peace and prosperity?

O child, I love you so much, and that love is beyond your comprehension. So, would not I care for My own? Would not I care for you? Yes, I care for you, and I know the concerns, the difficulties, and the situations that arise in your life.

So, peace to you beloved, and fret not, for I am in charge, I know what I am doing. Simply trust Me to be Me. Trust Me to honor My Word. Trust Me to bring you safely through the difficulty. And trust Me to bear each burden and to answer each question. For indeed, I have promised to do so.

Child, let all concern and all worry go. Release it, and let Me do the orchestrating. For I blend everything together for good. O rejoice, dear one, for I know what I am doing. Yes, leave the piloting through troubled waters to Me, and you will see again My hand at work. You will experience great benefit, both for you and those around you. You will see My name honored and lifted up.

August 17

FELLOWSHIP IS SHARING
EACH OTHERS PRESENCE
1 John 1:3; 2 Corinthians 13:14

Beloved, come soar with Me on the wings of My Spirit, for I am bringing you to new heights, even to heavenly places. There is fellowship there with Me. There is fellowship with the Father, and fellowship with the Spirit. O child, fellowship with Me is the act of sharing. It is walking, talking, and visiting with each other. It is enjoying each other's presence. It is communion with each other. It is not one sided, but mutual. So, come and let us fellowship together.

193

Beloved, there is sweet communion in the presence of your Lord. In My presence there is no pretense, for My fellowship is pure. There is no hidden motive or deviation. And, dear one, if our fellowship is to be meaningful, there must be a purity of heart and a childlike attitude of trust on your part.

So child, let us fellowship. Let us share together, for I created you and called you to this relationship. And I have met all the requirements necessary, so we can flow together. O come, beloved, into My presence, and let us share with each other. I will take you to the heavenlies on the wings of My spirit

August 18
BE NOT UNEQUALLY YOKED TOGETHER WITH UNBELIEVERS
2 Corinthians 6:14-18

O child, be alert. Watch and pray, for your adversary, the devil, goes about seeking whom he may devour. And you, dear one, are to resist him, and he will flee from you.

Beloved, do not form relationships with those who are not ethical, whose ways are wicked and disobedient, and whose lives are dominated by the enemy. For those who seek to gratify their own passions will only use you to that end.

So child, watch and do not form unhealthy and unwholesome relationships with anyone. Yet, I would have you love them and pray for them, for I am not willing that any should perish. But you are not to be unequally yoked with them.

O hear the Word of the Lord. Do not form relationships with the enemy or his representatives, for when you seek these associations, you become like them. But when you seek to associate with Me and My people, you become like Me.

So beloved, seek Me in everything, and I will lead

and guide you, even in the establishment of relationships. O child, consult Me in all things, for unholy relationships will destroy you. But wholesome relationships will build you up.

ALL HIS FOUNTAINS ARE IN YOU
Psalm 87:5-7; John 7:38

Beloved, lift up your head and let the fountains of My abundance flow today. For all that I am, and all that I have are fountains flowing within you.

Yes, all My fountains, all My blessings, all My refreshings are within you. They are full to overflowing. They are full to the brim and spilling over. O loved one, have not I said that I would open the floodgates of heaven and pour you out a blessing?

So My child, believe it. Act on it. Practice it. Step out on faith and believe what I tell you. For what I tell you is true. When I tell you that peace is flowing like a river, know that peace comes from My fountain within.

Do you not see the fountains? There are fountains everywhere you look. They are beautiful and ornate, bubbling and overflowing all over. They are well placed and graciously designed. They adorn the very presence of your God.

O beloved, see them. Look! There are these: the fountain of My Word, the fountain of My Spirit, the fountain of praise, the fountain of worship, the fountain of peace, the fountain of sufficiency, and the fountain of joy.

And there are these: the fountain of health and healing, the fountain of comfort, the fountain of love, the fountain of strength, the fountain of confidence, the fountain of faith, the fountain of trust, and the fountain of wisdom.

And there are these: the fountain of service, the fountain of obedience, the fountain of patience, the

195

fountain of godliness, the fountain of goodness, the fountain of rest, the fountain of kindness, and the fountain of compassion.

And there are these: the fountain of boldness, the fountain of temperance, the fountain of meekness, the fountain of power, the fountain of victory, and the fountain of life in abundance.

My child, all these and more I have placed within you. You are My dwelling, and I share them with you, for I love you more than anything. Did not I lay down My life for you? Yes, all My fountains are in you. So, let them flow. Let them fill you to overflowing. Let them bring a continuous refreshing to your soul.

O loved one; there is no lack in My fountains. All provision has been made. So, come and enjoy, for all My fountains are in you, and they never cease. They do not stagnate. I continually fill them with living water from the river of mercy and grace, the wells of My presence. They are refreshing and free.

August 20
PARTAKERS OF HIS DIVINE NATURE
2 Peter 1:3-4; Hebrews 1:3

My child, I have given you everything you need, and I have made every provision for you to know Me better. I have provided the means for you to partake of My divine nature. For I am in you, your hope of glory. You are My dwelling place. And as such, you may participate in everything that I am.

O beloved, does this not thrill you to know that there is no stone unturned? Does it not thrill you to know that I go before you? Does it not thrill you to know that I care for you? Does it not thrill you to know that I am faithful over God's house? Does it not thrill you to know that you are that house, the residence of the Father?

So, fix your thoughts on Me and add to your faith

My virtues. For the more you associate with Me the more you will become like Me. And My radiance will fill your life, and it will be seen by those around you. O beloved, rejoice, for have not I done it all? Yes, all you need do is to commit and submit to Me.

HIS PLAN INCLUDES DISCIPLINE
Hebrews 12:5-6

Beloved, My ways are pure, holy, and just, and I will accomplish what I intend to do. I will bring praise, honor, and glory to My name. O dear one, I am the one who created the universe and all that is in it. I made the earth and its inhabitants by My great power, and I will do with them as I please. Nothing can deter Me from My purpose and plan.

Child, I discipline, exhort, correct, and chasten to bring restoration, for My heart is always inclined unto My people. I do not destroy those I love. But instead, I mold and shape, bend and break to bring My children into the fullness of My presence and to the place of blessing.

Beloved, you can see it in the natural. Discipline is necessary for raising children. So likewise, discipline is necessary to bring you to spiritual maturity. O loved one, I do not forget you, but rather, I am working with you, and loving you all the time. Afterward comes a bountiful harvest of righteousness.

So child, rejoice and be glad, for I am accomplishing My purpose in the earth. And I am accomplishing My purpose and plan in your life, and it is good. Beloved, My plan includes discipline.

August 22
AS A SHEPHERD CARRIES A LITTLE LAMB
Psalm 28:8-9

Beloved, I bless My people, and I tenderly watch over them. I gently carry them forever as a shepherd carries a little lamb.

So, rest in the arms of your God, your Heavenly Father, your shepherd, for He will carry you and sustain you. He will strengthen you with the joy of the Lord. He will refresh you with the power of His Spirit. He will renew you with the presence of His love. For indeed you are precious to Him.

O beloved, there is nothing you need that I cannot meet. There is no mountain that I cannot remove. There is no valley that I cannot raise. There is no path that I cannot straighten. There is no gate of brass, or bar of iron that I cannot crush. There is no ocean that I cannot calm. There is no storm that I cannot still.

And child, there is no enemy that I cannot defeat. There is no lack that I cannot supply. There is no question that I cannot answer. There is no problem that I cannot solve. There is no burden that I cannot bear. There is no thirst that I cannot quench. There is no famine that I cannot satisfy. There is no turmoil that I cannot soothe.

O beloved, there is nothing I cannot do. So, rejoice and be glad. Let your heart give thanks and leap for joy, for I am your strength. I am your salvation. I am your Father. I am your shepherd, who will carry you forever.

August 23
OBEDIENCE UNLOCKS
THE STOREHOUSE OF BLESSING
Deuteronomy 28:1-14

Child, there is great benefit in serving Me in total

obedience, and in serving Me with an undivided heart. This is a heart that is fixed on pleasing Me. For out of obedience, with no deviation, there are blessings beyond measure.

Beloved, obedience is the key to unlocking the storehouse of blessing, for obedience pleases Me and seeks My will in everything. Obedience should be the natural response of My children: a response without reservation or hesitation; a response because of who I am; a response because of whose they are; and a response of a child to his loving Heavenly Father.

Child, obedience should be by choice because of the desire and longing to do so, rather than from forced compliance. It should come from a thankful and grateful heart. It should come because you want to obey, rather than from an attitude that you have to obey. I have given you the power of choice. Have not I said for you to choose this day whom you will serve?

So beloved, the choice is yours, but O the benefits and blessings entered into when you choose to be fully obedient to My Word and to the leading of My Spirit. For a life of obedience, following My precepts and principles, is a life without guile or malice, and it is in the very center of My presence receiving all that I have in store. So rejoice, dear one, obedience is not distasteful, but rather, it produces great benefit.

August 24
ABUNDANCE
1 Kings 17:13-16; John 10:10

My child, think not of Me as small or unable to come to your rescue. Think not of Me as one who withholds Himself from you. Think not that I do not care for you. Think not that you are insignificant, and that I pass you by. Think not that I have left you when problems, pressures, and lack seem to be about to overwhelm or devour you. Think not that your

199

faithfulness is in vain. Think not that I am not healing you when you are ill. Think not that I will not provide for your every need, yes, even when there is no flour and oil in the pantry. O think not that I sit idly by with no thought for your situation.

Beloved, do not think so little of your God and Father. For I am your Heavenly Father. You are My child, and I care for My children. I provide for them. I shower them with all spiritual and material blessings, for I did not come to take life away, but rather, I came to give life, life to enjoy, and blessings to share.

Yes My child, I came to give life in abundance. And I am able to do far more than you could ever ask or think. I am able to meet all your needs and more. I am able to provide everything, so that you are fully equipped and prepared to do every good work that I have in store for you.

O beloved, My grace is sufficient and it abounds to you. You are in My favor and that does not change. So, believe what I tell you. Believe that you have all sufficiency in Me. Believe that I supply all you need. Believe that I do not withhold any good thing from you. Believe that I care. Believe that I walk and talk with you and deliver you from all that would oppress you. O loved one, believe that you are My child and that I am your Heavenly Father. Believe that you are an heir. Believe that I am your friend. Believe that I abound to you in love and compassion, joy and prosperity, and health and healing.

My child, I came to give life, so receive your full portion. Receive the fullness of your God and Savior, for it is yours. I hold nothing back. Simply believe it. Count on it.

Yes beloved, I want only the best for you, and that is what you shall have. So, come and reach out and receive a touch from Me today.

DO NOT THINK MORE HIGHLY OF YOURSELF THAN YOU OUGHT
Romans 12:3; I Peter 5:6

My child, humble yourself. Put to death the self life and become alive unto Me. Let your faith flow. Let it strongly influence your life, for faith is a gift from Me, while exaggeration and ego are of self.

So beloved, die to the exaltation of self and become alive through the faith measured to you. For the just shall live by faith, that is, by their trust and confidence in Me. This is not in themselves, for self will fail. But faith in Me will take you through the impossible, and it will bring things into being from that which does not exist.

So child, do no think more highly of yourself than you ought. This does not mean that you are any less special to Me. No, you are a child of God with all the rights and privileges thereof. But you are to remember that you did not attain this position in and of yourself, for it was given to you without merit on your part. Remember, dear one, that this privilege is not based on your self-righteousness, but on faith and trust in the grace and mercy of the Lord your God.

HE DOES GREAT THINGS TO MAKE ME GLAD
Psalm 126:3

Beloved, I bring great joy, for I do great and mighty things that make you glad. I call you to rejoice in Me, to joy in the God of your salvation. I do not call you to make you sad. Rather, I call you to share with Me in all that I am, and in all that I have.

Yes child, I do great things, and I am attentive to every detail of your life. I do not hold back any good thing from you. So, wander not off on your own, but stay ever close to Me, and you will see your fortunes restored, miracles take place and a harvest in abundance.

O beloved, listen carefully. Hear what I have to say. You are blessed, and I have only good in store for you. Do not I take that which is not good and turn it into your benefit? Remember that you are not alone to live your life by yourself, but I am with you to live for you and through you.

O child, is this not a wonder? Your Heavenly Father lives in you and through you. Yes, you have so much going for you. So, rejoice with songs of joy, for your God showers you with abundance. He fills your life with good things. He gives only the best.

Yes, I do great things to make you glad.

August 27
THE SPIRIT AND THE WORD
Ephesians 5:18; 6:17

Beloved, I have given you everything you need to please Me and to know Me better. I have given you My Word, and It speaks truth and It imparts life. And I have given you My Spirit, and He endues you with power and revelation.

So, heed My Word, child, and be filled with My Spirit, for in so doing you will please Me and come to know Me better.

August 28
HE COMFORTS ME AS A LITTLE CHILD
Isaiah 66:13

Beloved, I comfort you as a mother comforts her little child. Yes, as a mother comforts her child: as she holds her child to her; as she sings lullabies to her child; as she whispers her love to her child; as she nurses her child from her breast; as she bounces her child on her knee; as she protects her child from all that would come against it; as she clothes her child to keep it warm from the cold; as she shields her child from the heat of the day; as she responds to her child's every cry; so, My dear one, am I attentive unto you.

O dear one, I am the Father of mercies and the God of all comfort. I care for you because you are My child. So, be assured that I allow nothing to harm you. I protect you. I shield you. I fight for you. I hold you to Me and whisper that I love you.

Beloved, I delight in you, for you are My precious child, and I allow nothing to come near you. No harm shall befall you, for I will never leave or forsake you. Child, this is My promise to you, and I keep My promises. I honor My Word.

August 29
UNLESS THE LORD BUILD THE HOUSE
Psalm 127:1-2

My child, unless I build the house the labor to build it is meaningless, for without Me there is no purpose. There is only chaos. This simply means that you are to let Me do the doing.

Beloved, it means not to run ahead of Me or behind Me. It means that My involvement makes everything around you successful. It means that whatever is done in the flesh will fail, but whatever is done in and by My Spirit will succeed. It means that My will and purpose are accomplished.

Child, doing things in the flesh, doing things by yourself, is futile, for without My presence there is only emptiness and no purpose. But in My presence there is great success, for I provide for My own. I build them up. I watch over them. I meet all their need.

O beloved, let this truth sink deep into your soul, that is, unless I am involved totally in your life, everything you do is in vain. It is meaningless. But, O, when I do the doing, when you turn everything over to Me there is life and godliness, health and healing, peace and prosperity, joy and gladness, food and clothing, shelter and security, all in abundance.

August 30
USE THE GIFTS GOD HAS GIVEN YOU
1 Peter 4:10-11

Child, I am the God of sufficiency, the one who cares. I am the Lord of the harvest, and I give the increase. I make no investment without the assurance of an abundant return. And I have invested in you.

Beloved, I have called you. I have anointed you. I have given you My Spirit. I have blessed all that you have put your hand to do. And I have given you marvelous gifts. Gifts to share with others.

I have given you the gifts of love, joy, peace, and prosperity. I have given you gifts of the Spirit to minister by. They are yours to be used, and not to be hidden. They are yours to bless others, and not just to bless yourself.

So child, use what I have given you to bless those around you. Recognize what you have. Recognize what I have given you, for everything you have: material, physical, or spiritual comes from Me to be used for My glory. And loved one, your talents, those attributes and skills you excel in, are also gifts from Me. So, channel them, by the Spirit, into full time commitment to Me. They are to be used to serve others.

O beloved, stir them up. Let them become refined, and use them to minister to Me and to bless those around you. Let My investment in you reap a hundred fold dividend. Yes child, let My investment bear much fruit, both in and through you.

HIS KINGDOM STANDS FIRM
Matthew 16:13-19

Beloved, My kingdom stands, and it cannot be shaken. What I say is true, for I cannot lie, and My Word does not return void. My church, My body, and My kingdom are built on the foundation that I am the Son of the Living God. I have established it and nothing can tear it down. It is forever.

Child, though I am the King of kings and the Lord of lords, the enemy still tries to annihilate My Kingdom. But the enemy is defeated, and My Kingdom is getting stronger and stronger. It is becoming a mighty army, and nothing shall prevail against it, for I have overcome.

Loved one, as I have overcome, so you shall overcome the world, the flesh, and the devil. For all My promises and provisions are true. All that I have said is real. There is no diversity or shadow of turning in My Word.

Beloved, you are a part of My Kingdom, for you have made Me Lord. So, take heart, nothing can touch My Kingdom without My permission. You are more than a conqueror in My name.

O child, I make the weak strong and I give strength to the weary. I bring with Me the joy of the Lord, which is your strength, for My Kingdom is not of flesh and blood. Rather, it is of the Spirit, which is far more powerful than what you can see, hear, taste, or touch.

Beloved, My Kingdom is established, firm, and fixed. So, go forth in My name. The enemy is defeated, and you are the victor. The spoils are yours. O rejoice, My child, for I am ever present to battle for you and to give you the victory. Yes, My Kingdom is established and nothing can shake or remove it.

September

*Patience and Endurance
Under Trial*

PATIENCE AND ENDURANCE UNDER TRIAL
James 1:12

Child, I am the one who leads and directs your life. I am the one who marked out the paths of your life. I am the one who is in control of your circumstances, who cares for you, who heals you, and who allows nothing to touch you without permission.

O beloved, I am conforming you to My image, and I am producing the fruit of the Spirit in your life. I am developing love, joy, peace, patience, kindness, godliness, goodness, faithfulness, and self-control.

So child, look not at the circumstances as though they would overwhelm you, as though they were bigger than you, or as though they were bigger than Me. No, fear not, for I am bigger than all your problems. Yes, I am bigger than any mountain in your life. And I assure you that, in Me, patience and endurance under trial is not only possible, but also has its reward.

O beloved, I have only the best ahead for you, and nothing can take it away. So, come, lean on Me. Be not afraid. Wait on Me, for those who wait patiently on Me shall renew their strength.

My child, did not I come to give an abundance of life? I did not come to steal, kill, or destroy, for that is what the enemy does. But I came to give life and to give it abundantly. So, enter into that security today. Let your mind be at rest. Let your emotions become settled, for I speak life to you. I speak peace to you. I speak rest to your soul.

HOLY SPIRIT AND FIRE
Matthew 3:11

Child, I baptize you in the Holy Spirit and in Fire. I do the baptizing. I am the one who places My Spirit, the Spirit of the Living God, within you. And I am the one who places you in the Holy Spirit.

Beloved, My Spirit and My Word are a consuming fire. It is My intention that you be totally overwhelmed by My Spirit; that all of self be put to death by My Spirit; that My Spirit totally possess and consume you; that My Spirit live and move in your being; and that nothing else matters other than living for Me, doing what I would have you to do.

Child, I give you My Spirit, and I immerse you in Him.

September 3

CHILDLIKE
Mark 10:13-16

Beloved, become childlike in your faith and trust in Me. For as a small child trusts his parents, so, My child, trust Me.

Yes, look to Me in all the simplicity of childlike trust. Trust that believes that I am Father God, and that Father God can do anything. Trust, beloved, that results in obedience. Trust that has a desire to please. Trust that looks in awe and wonder at who I am and at what I do. Trust that knows the sense of total security and protection. Dear one, let your childlike trust in Me come forth and scatter all the hard knocks, scrapes, scratches, difficulties, and hurts. For Father can make them all better.

Beloved, let your childlike confidence in Me break through all the veneer of disappointment, hardships, tragedy, and heart break. Let Me kiss the hurt away. Let Me apply the salve of My Spirit. Let me hold you to Myself and tell you all is well, for Father is here. I will never leave or forsake you. I am with you always. I watch over you like a mother hen. I cover you with My wings.

Beloved, you are Mine, and you are loved. So, let

the child in you be free. Let that childlike trust become strong. For I made children with a simplicity of trust. I placed it there. I never intended it to be any different at age two or ninety two.

O come to Me, child, and I will give you rest. For I love My children, and it pleases Me to see them walk in faith, in childlike trust. Yes, it pleases Me to see them play, to see them grow, to see them obey, to see them serve, and to see them bring praise, honor, and glory to their Heavenly Father.

O beloved, take My hand and be the child you really are, the child you've always wanted to be.

September 4

A VESSEL OF THE LORD
Isaiah 52:11-12

Child, you are a vessel of the Lord. You belong to Me, and you are to be clean and pure as a vessel that touches no unclean thing. I have chosen you and have called you to be holy and pure, to be separate from the world. For you are in the world, but you are not to be a part of it.

Yes beloved, you are My vessel, a vessel of honor. A vessel ornate and beautiful, one without flaw. A vessel designed for a specific purpose, dedicated to serve Me. A vessel I have filled with My presence. One I have filled with the anointing oil of My Spirit. Yes, you are a vessel of the Living God filled to overflowing with good things.

O child, you are one of My precious and priceless vessels. And as you let Me keep you filled with My presence, My Word, My Spirit, and My power, you shall never become unclean or contaminated. But rather, you shall remain pure and holy; consecrated solely and entirely unto Me and My service. You shall always serve in the anointing. So rejoice, beloved, you are a vessel of the Lord.

THE BEST IS ON ITS WAY
Isaiah 48:17-18

Beloved, I know what is best. I know what is best for you. I know what is best for your family. I know what is best for your work. I know what is best for your ministry. I know what is best for your community. I know what is best for your nation. I know what is best for the world. Did not I give My best so that the world might be saved?

Yes child, I am the best. There is no other like Me. I am the one who leads, guides, and directs in paths of righteousness. I am the one who makes peace flow like a river. I am the one who brings hope and salvation. I am the one who brings splendor and glory. I am the one who brings power and majesty. I am the one who brings purpose. I am the one who brings order out of chaos.

O beloved, I show you what is best. I tell you new things. I announce them ahead of time. I give you time to prepare for them, for I want only the best for you.

My child, have not I said that I will carry you and sustain you all the days of your life? Have not I said that I teach you what is best for you? Have not I said that My purpose is fixed, and that I do what I have planned?

Beloved, I do all this so that My name will be honored and praised. I will not yield My glory to another. So rejoice, loved one, the best is on its way, far greater than you now perceive.

September 6
FILLED WITH THE RADIANCE
OF THE SPIRIT
2 Corinthians 3:15-18

Child, I am Spirit. I am wholly Spirit, and they that

worship Me must worship Me in Spirit and in Truth. O beloved, I am at work transforming you into My image, taking you from glory to glory. And as you grow, the more you become like Me. I am filling you full of My radiance, which is the resting of My glory upon your life.

So rejoice, child, in what you have, and in what you know. For you are one of My very own, and I am filling you full and running over with My presence and My Spirit. And the freedom you experience in the Spirit takes you above the things of the earth and raises you to the heavenlies, free from all that would hinder or hold you down.

Yes rejoice, for you are free, and you are receiving an ever increasing portion of My radiance, the glory of My Spirit.

September 7

CONSUMED BY HIS WORD
Psalm 119:20: John 1:14

Child, I am the Word, and in Me you shall find great delight, for I am everything you need. I am your life. Nothing else matters, save living only for Me. Indeed, there is no other worthy of such devotion.

Beloved, do you not see it? I am the Word. I am your peace. I am your comforter. Your life is meaningless without Me. I bring purpose and balance to you through My Word.

O dear one, I delight in you. I joy over you, and it pleases Me that you return that love. So, let yourself be engrossed in My precepts, in My Word, for in It you shall find Me in ways you never imagined.

Child, you shall be awed and totally consumed by My Word, and you shall be conformed to It. For indeed, It is alive and powerful. It is new and refreshing. It is totally impregnated with My love, for I am the Word. So, fall in love with Me and My Word all over again. Each day let It consume you. Yes, passionately, read It and absorb what I have to say.

O beloved, I change not. I am the same yesterday, today, and forever. My principles and precepts do not change. So, devour My Word. Listen for My voice. Hear My call. Follow My leading, and let My Word accomplish Its life changing work.

Child, just think, My Word is as fresh and new as the day I gave It. It is as life changing as the day I first spoke It. It is as healing as It was when I walked here on earth. It is as powerful as It was when I spoke and the universe was put into place. Nothing can stand above It. Nothing can rise up against It. Nothing can be hidden from It.

Yes beloved, remember that I am the God of My Word. What I have spoken and written, is so. So, let It consume you, and in so doing you will find hope and purpose.

September 8
NEVER LEAVE OR FORSAKE ME
Hebrews 13:1-6

Child, I never leave you or forsake you. No peril, hardship, principality, or power can separate you from Me, for in Me you are more than a conqueror.

O beloved, see it, and know it. Know that I am your sufficiency. Know that I am your everything. Know that it is My grace that brought you into right standing with the Father, and that it is My grace that keeps you there. Know that out of love and compassion I care for you. Know that it was My divine order that made you one of the family, a child of the living God.

Child, know that I work all things together for good. O, see it and flow in it. Know that which seems as adversity, that which seems as disaster, and that which appears as hopeless is part of My plan for you. I take all this and mix it together with My purpose to

212

bring My best to you, to provide opportunities for your growth, and to manifest Myself to you. So, loved one, think not that I have forgotten you, or that I don't care what happens to you. But rather, know that I will supply all your needs.

Know that you are more than a conqueror. Know that no weapon formed against you can prosper. Know that if I be for you, and I am, absolutely nothing can be against you. And, know that I have not given you over to fear, but I have given you power, love, and a sound mind.

O rejoice, beloved, for I will never leave or forsake you. Nothing can separate you from My love.

September 9

HE FILLS THE WHOLE UNIVERSE WITH HIS PRESENCE
Psalm 24:1; 139:7-10

My child, I am indeed majestic, high, and lifted up. I fill the whole universe with My presence. There is nowhere that I am not. O, do you not see it? Yes, the universe is a part of Me, for it resides in My bosom. It is My heartbeat. It is totally engulfed in Me. And as such, you are in Me and I am in you.

O, see it child. See the universe in My chest. See My heart. See that it is springing forth from Me. See that there is no distance in Me. See it all together as one. See it delighting in its creator.

Child, do you not hear the heavens rejoicing? Do you not hear My voice thundering in its midst? It is the voice of power and authority, the voice of the creator. It is the voice of love and compassion.

Beloved, do you not know that what I created is good? Do you not know that everything that has breath is to praise Me in the splendor of My holiness? Do you not know that I am powerful and mighty? Do you not know that I alone am worthy of glory? Do you not know that I speak to you day and night? Do you not rejoice in the knowledge that I bless you and strengthen you daily?

Yes child, I am majestic and mighty. The entire universe is hid in Me, yet, I am mindful of you. I know where you are. I know your needs, and I have made every provision to meet them. So, praise and worship Me, for I show you great and mighty things. And I hold you close to Me and tell you that you are Mine. I whisper My love to you and give you peace.

September 10
SEEK HIM AND HE WILL BE FOUND
Jeremiah 29:13

Beloved, seek righteousness and pursue it. Seek Me, My child, and you will find Me, when you search for Me with your whole heart. For I do not withhold Myself from those who seek Me, from those who desire to know Me, or from those who hunger for truth. And, loved one, you shall know the truth and the truth will set you free.

So My child, seek Me with your whole heart. Open your heart, and I will give you understanding. Open your mouth and I will fill it. I will pour you out a blessing so great that there will not be room enough to receive it. For I give Myself to you. I reveal Myself to you.

Beloved, I have ordered your steps. Before you were born I knew you, and I called you by name. I am the one that placed within you the desire to know Me, that longing to know who I am, that prayer to know Me better.

So My child, look not at what may be different, but rather look at who I am. Look beyond, where you have never been before. Look at Me, knowing that I am taking you to new heights of My Spirit. I am bringing you to Me. I have brought you into My salvation. I have brought you into My righteousness. Beloved, these never fade. They do not erode away. They last forever, yes, throughout eternity. And they are yours now.

O My child, I have heard your call. I have heard your cry. I have seen the longing of your soul. And I have responded. So, let Me be your comfort. Let Me speak peace and rest to your life. For you are My child, My people, and nothing can separate you from My love.

I am bringing you into a fuller knowledge of Me. I am conforming you to My image. O, let go, and let Me do it, and you will know who I am and what I do in a way you never thought possible.

September 11
EVERYTHING COMES FROM GOD
I Chronicles 29:10-14

Child, I am the one who provides for your every need. I am the one who blesses you with abundance. I am the one who has blessed you with everything you have. I blessed you with all your earthly possessions and with all your spiritual possessions. I have given you everything.

Beloved, you indeed know that everything comes from Me, but there are those who think that they accomplish their own prosperity. Yet, without Me, without My providing the ability to make wealth they would be paupers. They still do not recognize that it comes from Me.

O child, I have entrusted to you everything you own. I receive it back from you as you dedicate it to Me. As you give it to Me, as you lay it at My feet, I multiply it. For it was given in trust to be used to bring honor and glory to My name.

So loved one, fret not, for I have promised a sufficient supply to meet your every need. But as you return to Me what I have given you, I in turn trust you with more, so that My purposes may be fulfilled. So, turn it all over and watch what I do through you. You will be amazed and awed at your Lord.

Beloved, make what you have count. Do not squander it upon yourself. Do not be frivolous, but rather, be frugal. Be wise and honor Me. Do what I tell you to do, and you shall be glad and abundantly blessed.

O child, look around and count your blessings. Indeed, it all has come from Me. Have not I said many times that I would share with you of everything I have? And I do just that. I have entrusted you with blessing upon blessing. So, sow your seed back to Me, and you will see increase, and your harvest will be bountiful.

Yes beloved, give willingly, not grudgingly, for this pleases Me and you will be doubly blessed. Child, you cannot out give your God. You cannot out give your Heavenly Father.

September 12
LOVE BUILDS UP
1 Corinthians 13:13

My child, true love knows no bounds. It knows no end. It never fails. It is the better way. It leaves no room for bitterness or hate. It leaves no room for malice, anger or pride. O beloved, love builds up, it does not tear down. So, learn to love. Decide to love, and you will see things change in your life. For when love governs your life, all other motives flee. So, My child, pursue the way of love.

September 13
GREAT THINGS TOOK PLACE
ON THE CROSS OF CALVARY
John 19:16-18

O beloved, there was so much that took place on

the cross of Calvary. The cross was not an accident. It was not just something that happened, or an unavoidable tragedy. It was not just personal death and mutilation of My body. But it was the end of sin and the beginning of that which is new.

For child, on the cross I bore the sins of the world to bring forgiveness to a lost people. I took sin and its consequence upon Myself and paid the penalty for it all. And I left it buried in the grave when I rose in newness of life.

Beloved, the enemy thought he had triumphed, but he was defeated. Yes, the bleakest day in the history of the world, the darkest day of My life was in fact a new beginning. For it met all the requirements of the Father, and it opened for you the doors of the heavenlies, even into the most Holy Place. It restored fellowship with the Father and placed you in right standing with Him. O loved one, your salvation and all that goes with it: your healing, your strength, your joy, your peace, your sufficiency, and your protection was all purchased on the cross.

As I told Pilate that he had no power over Me, but only that which was granted from above, so, I tell you that nothing can touch you, but only as I permit it. Child, did it not look like the total end of everything, and that the enemy had succeeded? But he had not. He did not win.

So with you, loved one, when it looks like there is no way out and that you are being completely destroyed, know that it is the beginning of a better and brighter day. Know that it is the dawning of new and greater things. Know that it is not the end, but a commencement.

O beloved, My work on the cross ended every requirement necessary to enter into My rest. So, cast all your cares on Me, and the power of My blood, shed on the cross, will sustain, strengthen, and settle you. It will give you peace. Yes child, take heart. Look up and rejoice, for in Me you shall overcome. Indeed, great things took place on the cross of Calvary.

September 14
A HEAVENLY WARDROBE
Isaiah 61:10

Child, you are clothed in My righteousness. You are arrayed in a heavenly wardrobe. There are no other garments like them. Indeed, My righteousness is beautiful. O loved one, you are adorned in My beauty and majesty. You are adorned from the top of your head to the bottom of your feet with beauty and grace. You are adorned in splendor with the garments of My righteousness.

Child, there are many garments that make up the wardrobe of My splendor. There are the garments of praise, worship, holiness, joy, peace, love, and the garment of loveliness. And there is so much more.

O beloved, I provide you a complete wardrobe full of splendid apparel. The garments are beautiful and exquisite. I have made them especially for you. They are tailor made. They are made for royalty, and I share them freely with you.

Child, there is a garment for every occasion, for every activity, for every circumstance, for every work, for every difficulty, for every trial, for every field to plow, for every race to run, and for every walk there is to walk. But dear one, there is a choice. There is a selection process. You can choose to wear, or you can choose not to wear the garments of My wardrobe. But I urge you to put them on, for there is no other like them. They do not fade or wear out, but rather, become more beautiful with use. And they last forever.

Beloved, they are all there. O, wear them with dignity, for you are a king and a priest. Yes child, I clothe you in the garments of My splendor, and in the beauty of My righteousness. So, wear and enjoy.

FORGET THE FORMER THINGS
Isaiah 43:18-19

Beloved, forget the former things. Remember them no more. Do not let the past pursue you, for today is a new day. Today I begin something new. Today I bring you good news. Today I tell you that I love you, and I call you by name. And I choose for you to know Me better than ever before.

O child, I make a way in the wilderness. I care for My own. So, do not let your heart be troubled. Do not let it be afraid. I have not brought you into the desert to leave you there to die of thirst, or to forsake you. No, I have brought you into this place so you could learn many things. I will not leave you there alone, for I am your instructor. I am right there with you.

O loved one, know that this is a new day. Know that you are learning. Know that this lesson is not for ever. Know that there are blessings in the wilderness. So, look for them, because they are there.

Child, learn to praise Me regardless the circumstance. Learn to be thankful no matter the situation. Learn to rejoice in all things. For I make all things work together to good for you. Yes, I make all things new. O beloved, see it. Believe it. Trust Me no matter what anyone says or does, no matter the magnitude of the problem. Just simply, in childlike trust, say: "My God loves me and cares for me. I will trust Him completely, for I am more than a conqueror through Him who loves me so." Yes, today is a new day.

HELP IS ON THE WAY
Jeremiah 20:11-13

Child, I am for you, and if I am for you, who or what can be against you. So, do not be discouraged, but hope in Me. Have not I rescued you many times? Have not you seen My hand of deliverance over and over again? Would I leave you alone now?

O beloved, help is on the way. This is not the time to give up, but it is the time to trust Me without hesitation, or doubt. Surely, I will come to your aid. I will arrive right on time. None shall be harmed. My name shall be exalted, and you shall see the hand of the Lord at work performing miracle after miracle.

Child, this is a test, a time of inactivity, before the floodwaters come, and just before I open the windows of heaven and rain down blessing upon blessing. This is the time to praise Me for things not seen. This is the time for faith to be exercised and be put into action. This is the time of waiting upon your God.

So dear one, withdraw not from your confidence in Me, but rather rejoice, for you shall yet see the salvation of the Lord. You shall see needs fulfilled. You shall see lack flee and prosperity take its place. Yes beloved, rejoice and continue to do good. For your work shall be rewarded, and you shall see the fruit of your labor.

September 17
FAITH IN ACTION
Matthew 17:20

O child, turn your faith loose. Let it rise within you. Let it work for you, for faith is an active substance capable of the impossible. So, put your faith into action. Let it not lie dormant and inactive, but turn it loose. Stir it up. Use it.

Beloved, where is your faith to be placed, but only in the creator of the entire universe. It is to be placed in the one who keeps His Word, in the one who cannot lie.

So, trust Me, child. Believe My Word and act upon It. For there is no greater key to unlocking the power of My Spirit than faith acting upon My Word, and standing upon My Word whispered to you by My Spirit.

Yes beloved, act on your faith. Tell the mountain to be removed. Tell the flood to recede. Tell the lack to flee. Believe it. Child, do not stagger at the overwhelming circumstance, but firmly hold onto Me and My sufficiency.

And, by faith, lay hold of what you need, and you shall see it take place. It shall be so, for in Me you can do all things. Have not I said that I will supply all your need from the riches of My glory?

So child, faint not. There is no reason for any situation to master you, for by faith you can overcome that which would appear to surround and overtake you. Yes dear one, put your faith into action. Turn it loose, so miracles can take place.

September 18

PRAISE AND THANKSGIVING
Psalm 30:4-12

My child, I love a thankful heart. I love hearing the praises of My people. Have not I said that I inhabit the praises of My people? Yes, the sacrifice of praise stirs My heart. So, bring your sacrifices. Bring the sacrifices of praise and thanksgiving. Bring the sacrifices of joy and gladness. Bring the sacrifices of singing and dancing before Me.

Yes My child, bring to Me the praise and thanksgiving of your heart, and you will experience a peace that transcends all understanding. For, loved one, in praising, your faith is released. Yes, it becomes active, for you are praising and thanking the God and Father of the impossible.

Beloved, as you turn your faith loose in praise, you will begin to see things happen around you. Circumstances will not seem as difficult. Time will seem more manageable. Needs and wants will dissipate. And you will be awed at My presence, power, and peace made strong and evident in your life.

Child, you will not be confused or discouraged, but you will soar on wings of eagles. You will rise above the things of earth, for you will reach the heavenlies in praise. Nothing shall be impossible to My praisers.

September 19
HE IS MY DELIVERER
Exodus 15:1-2

My child, I go before you and behind you. I surround you and protect you from anything that would try to attack you or come against you. For I am your shield. I am your deliverer. I rush to your side and lift you up out of every pressure, difficulty, and circumstance.

Beloved, I am God, there is no other. I am your God, the living one who sees and hears you. And I bring deliverance. I bring hope when there is no hope. I bring protection when there is no protection.

O child, it is My work to consume the offering. It is your work and spiritual responsibility to place yourself on the altar. It is My responsibility to light the fire. So, believe what I say, do what I ask, and rest in My promises, for I keep My Word.

Yes beloved, simply take Me at My Word. Don't turn to the left, or to the right, but press ahead believing what I say is true. Believe that I am your shield. Believe that I am your rear guard. Believe that I give you great reward. Believe that I am the Lord thy God that healeth thee. Believe that by My stripes you are already healed.

Child, believe that no weapon formed against you will prosper. Believe that I supply all your need. Believe that I give you increase. Believe that you are favored, that you are in right standing with Me.

Believe that you are Mine and that I love you without limit. Believe that if I be for you no one can be against you.

Dear one, believe that the enemy is under your feet, and that he is a defeated foe. Believe that the battles are Mine and that the victories are yours. Believe that regardless the situation or circumstance, I work all things together for good.

Yes, believe and rejoice, for I am your deliverer. I go before you. I surround you with My presence. I am your everything, and nothing is too difficult for Me. For I am the God of My Word.

September 20

TROUBLES
Psalm 34:19

Beloved, in the world you shall have many troubles, but be of good cheer, I have overcome them all. O loved one, there is so much to be thankful for. For I have placed within you My precious Holy Spirit, who is with you always. And when the pressures mount and it seems all is despair, and that there is no end or any way out, My Spirit knows and makes a way.

Child, it is granted unto you the privilege of participating in My sufferings, for suffering provides strength to My body. It brings My body into conformity. O, know that pressures are the molds that shape you into My image and bring you to maturity. Yes, troubles are opportunities for Me to do miracles in your life. And they result in great blessing.

So rejoice, beloved, and grow up in your faith. Resist not the difficulty, but rise above it in faith and see the end from the beginning. For, dear one, I have begun a good work in you, and I shall complete it.

September 21

LOOK UP
Psalm 34:4-5

My child, look up, for your redemption draws nigh. Yes, look up, for your help comes from Me. Look up, for I am manifesting Myself to you. Look up, for there are great and mighty things taking place around you.

Beloved, look up, for there are signs and wonders in abundance. Look up, for miracles are taking place. Look up, for there is nothing to hinder for I am your God. Look up, and see what I am doing, and what I am about to do.

O child, there is so much to rejoice in. Yes, even during the trials you can rejoice, for they are not your trials, but rather, they are Mine to bear. Remember, loved one, that I have said to cast all your care on Me because I care for you.

So beloved, look up and look past the pressures. Look past the tests. Look past the trials. Look past the temptations and see Me. See My purpose. See the blessings. See that I turn all things into good for you. O child, see that I am your sufficiency.

Yes, look up and see Me high and lifted up, and see yourself seated there with Me. Yes, rise with Me above that which seems to be smothering you, that which seems to have you cornered, and come up with Me into the heavenlies. O beloved, look up.

September 22

A CALL TO SERVE EVEN IN WEAKNESS
2 Corinthians 13:3-4

Child, in your weakness I have called you to serve, for when you are weak then I am strong. O dear one, I live in you with all My power and majesty. So, fret not concerning your weaknesses, but count on Me to fill them with My strength and presence.

Beloved, you have a call to serve, a call to love those around you, and a call to respond to their need. And you have a call to help build, encourage, lift up, and comfort others. You have a call to minister to those in need of ministry.

So child, listen and be sensitive to My Spirit, for I will use you to do My will. I will speak through you to accomplish My purpose, and you shall know that it is I doing it all. O loved one, I am looking for willing vessels. I am looking for submitted and committed servants and friends who will faithfully do My bidding. For the world needs Me, and I shall reveal Myself to them through My people.

Beloved, taste and see that your Lord is good: that I operate totally out of love and compassion; that My motive is pure and holy; that I want only the best for My people. So, come willingly in your weakness, and I will strengthen you and use you to bring joy to My heart.

September 23
SINGLENESS OF PURPOSE
Deuteronomy 10:12-13

Child, know that I work in you both the willingness and the ability to do My will. It is I, who gives you the desire to do My bidding. It is I, who gives you the strength to do it.

O beloved, it is My purpose that you follow Me wholeheartedly, that you imitate Me and that there be singleness of purpose in your life. This purpose is to follow Me unconditionally no matter the cost, and no matter where it leads.

Child, it is My purpose that you become mature. It is My purpose that your life be lived to please Me. It is My purpose that the desires of the flesh and self be denied and put to death, and that the Spirit rise to control.

O beloved, lay aside everything that would distract from My purpose and consider what I did. Consider the price I paid to please the Father. Was not this singleness of purpose? Did not I come that you and all mankind could have life?

So child, imitate Me. Do not exalt yourself, but rejoice in serving Me. Rejoice in My working through you to do My will. Rejoice in ministering Me to the need of others.

O rejoice, dear one, for I work in you both the willing and the doing, My purpose to fulfill.

September 24
HIS GLORIOUS INHERITANCE IN THE SAINTS
Ephesians 1:18

Child, you have made Me rich. For did not I redeem you at great price? Did not I consider you worthy of redemption? O loved one, I was not willing for you to perish, for you are My creation.

Beloved, you were created in the image of your God, and you were created for a purpose. You were created for fellowship with Me and to bring praise, honor, and glory to My name. And My investment in you shall reap a bountiful harvest. I shall reap a harvest of righteousness, a harvest of holiness, and a harvest of praise and worship.

Yes child, you are a glorious inheritance. So, rejoice that you are a part of making Me rich in My glorious inheritance in the saints, and that I made it all possible.

September 25
TODAY
Job 42:10-16

Beloved, have not I said that I am doing a new thing? Yes, I am doing a new thing in your life. O child, consider Job. Did not I bring him into a new beginning? Did not I make his latter years greater than his former years? Did not I bring him out of his calamity and make him twice as prosperous as before? O loved one, I am doing a new thing. It is My time.

Beloved, look not at where you have been, or at what you have or have not done. For yesterday is gone, and today is at hand. Today is the day of salvation. Today is the day of new things. Today is the day of restoration. Today is the day of new beginning.

And though there may be giants in the land, I have overcome them. O look, loved one, and see only the good things. Know that you are right where I want you to be. So, move with Me. Go forward in My name, for I take you into a new day and into new dimensions of My Spirit.

O beloved, you have only begun. The best is yet to come. And your latter days shall be greater than your former ones, for I have begun a new thing. I have ordained it so.

September 26
THE GOD OF DETAIL
Genesis 1:1

Child, I care about every detail in your life. I speak to you about great and small things. I speak to you of things you think are insignificant. I speak to you of things you think are far beyond the possibility of your experience. Beloved, it is the detail that, when put together, becomes a beautiful picture. Do you not see it in creation? All that you see, feel, touch, and even the air that you breathe, is made up of detail that you cannot see without powerful magnification. It is held together by My power forming the universe in all its splendor and majesty.

So child, in My Word there is great detail, and that detail fulfills the purposes of your God. All of the detail of My Word amplifies Me. It points to the redemption of man and the glory of his God.

So beloved, do not neglect or despise detail, for it is in detail that everything is built and held together. So, look for the detail in My Word. Look for the detail in our relationship. Look for the detail in your work. Look for the detail in your ministry. For by it all things are made manifest, and in it you shall experience more and more of Me. Yes child, I am a God of the intricate, the God of detail.

September 27
HE HAS PROMISED
Leviticus 26:3-13

O child, if I be for you who can be against you, for have not I promised to be with you always? Have not I promised to watch over you, sustain you, and care for you all the days of your life? Have not I promised that you shall find Me when you search for Me with your whole heart?

Beloved, have not I placed within you the desire to follow Me, to do My will, and to be obedient to My plan and purpose? Have not I promised to be your God and that you would be My child? Have not I promised to dwell in you and that My presence would be always with you?

Child, have not I promised that I make even your enemies to be at peace with you? Have not I given you My Holy Spirit to lead and guide you, and to show you where to go? Have not I promised to abundantly supply your need?

O dear one, I have not only promised all this and more, but I do all that I promise. Only believe it and take Me at My Word. Have you not seen My hand of blessing and deliverance around you? Would I stop now? Would I take you part way on the journey and then forsake you to the savage beasts? Would I go back on My Word? No, never My child. My Word is true. You can count on It.

So rejoice, for I am your God, and you are My people. And I shall always zealously love and care for My own. So shall you walk in victory all the days of your life.

VESTED AUTHORITY
Ephesians 1:22-23

My child, all power and authority has been given to Me, and I delegate that authority to you, for you are My representative. You are My ambassador. You are an agent of heavenly things.

Beloved, I have vested in you My authority. It is backed up by all of heaven itself, for all things have been placed under My feet. I am the victorious one. I am the one who defeated the enemy. My power is awesome, and My strength is immeasurable. My might is beyond compare, and My authority is total.

So child, I endue you with that same power and authority, and that authority is in My name. You are a representative of that name. You are a representative of My kingdom. You are a representative of the Lord God of all the universe.

Beloved, in this authority you can do the impossible. At your command valleys will be raised up, mountains will be brought low, and crooked places will be made straight. At your command healing and health will be made manifest. At your command the blind shall see and the lame shall walk. At your command the floods of anxiety and fear will recede and dissipate. At your command the enemy must flee, and nothing shall be impossible to you, for I have given you authority over the world, the flesh, and the devil.

O child, rejoice in the midst of difficulty and

pressure, for I have given you authority to see miracles take place before your very own eyes. And when adversity comes, look at it as an opportunity for you to exercise your authority. Look at it as an opportunity for your Lord to demonstrate again His mighty power. Yes, look at it as an opportunity to see the enemy defeated, regardless the problem or circumstance.

O beloved, this is victorious living, for I have defeated the enemy. He is a defeated foe, and you have the authority to proclaim it so. So, walk in that victory with all the authority I have vested in you.

September 29

ANOINTED
2 Kings 2:9, 11-15

My child, as the prophets Elijah and Elisha had an anointing, and as the apostle Paul had a calling, an anointing for a specific purpose, so have you. Yes, I have called you to fulfill My purposes in your life. For beloved, I have work for you to do, a plan for you to fulfill, and I have anointed you for the tasks set out before you.

So loved one, do not fear, do not be reluctant, do not hesitate, but move out in that anointing. Respond to My leading and nudging, for what I tell you is true.

Beloved, My work, My plan is not something deigned or planned by man. No, I designed it. It is original and genuine. It has My seal upon it, the seal of My Spirit.

So My child, know that I am using you. Know that I am showing you what to do. Know that I have anointed you with the power and capability to do what I ask you to do. O beloved, you have a calling, you have an anointing.

DISCIPLINE
Hebrews 12:1-12

Beloved, your good is what I always have in mind for you. It is what I always have in store. For I am not a mean and angry god, a god of hate and vengeance, a god of wanton destruction, a god to be afraid of, or a god to hide from.

No, My child, I am the God of love and compassion. I am the God of kindness. I am the God of patience. I am the God of holiness. I am the God of perfection. I am the God who cares about His children.

And, dear one, you are My child and as a father corrects, instructs, and disciplines His children, so I disciple and correct My children. I do it for the best. I do it so that you may benefit. I do it so that you will produce a harvest of righteousness. I do it so that you will bring forth fruit that is eternal.

O beloved, I love you so, and I desire only the ultimate good for you. And out of that love, I correct you. I discipline you. I chasten you. Not because it pleases Me to discipline you, but because discipline is for your good.

Child, I know that no discipline is pleasant, but when you are trained by it you will rejoice, for it reaps a bountiful harvest of righteousness and holiness. So, in the midst of discipline, think not of Me as stern and mean, but rather, think of Me as the one who loves you more than you can ever know. Think that the discipline is for your good. Remember, you are My child and I love you always.

October

Spiritual Warfare

SPIRITUAL WARFARE
2 Corinthians 10:3-6

My child, you do not wrestle against flesh and blood, but against principalities, powers, and rulers of darkness. Know that your warfare is a spiritual one fought against the enemy and the desires of the flesh. But rest assured that in your battle, in this warfare, I have overcome the evil one, and through Me you too are an overcomer. The victory is already yours.

Beloved, the beginning of this is found in Me. Truly, your trust in Me is the beginning of your victory. For the more you trust Me, the more of My power and strength you are able to employ, even to the removing of mountains. And you will demolish strongholds of the enemy, destroy every argument against the knowledge of Me, and bring into captivity every thought and make it obedient to Me.

O dear one, I am compassionate and full of mercy, and My love for you endures forever. That is why I have given you all the equipment you need for life and holiness. Yes, I love you always. So, take heart, I am there in the midst of you providing everything you need, even to fighting your battles for you.

A FAITHFUL MESSENGER
John 13:3, 20

Beloved, all power in heaven and earth has been given unto Me. I am before all things, and by Me all things were created, and by Me all things exist. But I never exalted Myself above the Father. Rather, I came as a servant and as a messenger. I humbled Myself and became obedient to death, even death upon a cross.

O child, the messenger is not greater than the one

who sent him. Did not I always acknowledge that it was the Father who sent Me, who told Me what to do, and that I did nothing of My own volition. I did only the will of the Father?

So, you too, beloved, have the same mind, which is to do only what I would have you to do. For I have called you, commissioned you, and I have given you authority to use My name. I have promised to lead and guide you in the paths you are to go.

O child, I have given you your instructions. They are all in My Word. And I have given you My Spirit, and He resides within you to bring praise and honor to My name. But, dear one, never let self puff up and take the credit for what I do. For I am the one who works in you both the willing and the doing of My good pleasure. Simply be My faithful messenger, and you will be blessed in so doing.

October 3
A VESSEL OF HONOR
Jeremiah 18:1-6

My child, I am doing a new thing. I am doing the impossible. I am taking vessels cracked and flawed, and I am putting them again on My potter's wheel. I am remolding and reshaping them so they may come forth as beautiful vessels, more beautiful than ever before.

I do this not only for you, but also for Me. I am making you a vessel of honor and attraction to others. And dear one, I am filling that vessel. I am filling it with living water, the water of My Spirit, so that out of it can flow refreshing and healing to those around you.

Child, I make the old flaws disappear, for I have made you a new creation. In a clay vessel I mold, bend, and shape, and then place it in the fire. In a silver vessel I heat the silver and remove the dross, so out of the refined silver comes forth a vessel for the finer. But it is the fire that makes My work perfect. The fire is necessary, dear one, to make My work beautiful.

Beloved, I am the craftsman and you are the material. I am the one who molds and shapes to make beautiful vessels for My kingdom. And you are beautiful, for I make you so. I give you everything. You have My Spirit, My Word, and you are My heir.

Child, all I have is yours, and all that is yours is Mine. We are in this together. For I live and move through My people My best to perform. O there is much to do, and I will do it. You are a part of it.

Yes beloved, I am doing a new thing.

October 4
CALLED TO PURITY AND HOLINESS
1 Thessalonians 3:13; 4:3-8

My child, My call to you is that of purity and holiness. So, do not be disturbed by what is going on around you, for in all of it I have an opportunity to manifest Myself.

O beloved, know that circumstances and pressures are used to bring you to holiness, to bring you into a denial of self, and to bring you to the place where My life is manifested always through you.

O child, know that I am the one who strengthens you. I am the one who brings you through the trials. I am the one who brings you into purity. So dear one, be pure, even as I am pure. Be holy, as I am holy.

Beloved, all purity and holiness is already within you. All you need do is release it. Exercise it. Let My purity be your purity. And as you do, you will see, and so will others: the manifestation of My holiness, the manifestation of My presence, and the manifestation of My peace.

Child, holiness is walking with Me in control of everything in your life. So rejoice, I am strengthening

your heart. I am manifesting Myself. I am bringing you
into holiness. I am bringing you into contentment.

October 5

SEE HIM IN EVERYTHING
Exodus 2:1-25

Child, do you not see My hand in everything? Do
you not see Me in all things? O dear one, everything
that goes on around you is not just a happening.
There is a purpose, and that purpose is to bring
praise, honor, and glory to My name.

Beloved, I do not leave you without hope. I do not
begin something and then not finish it. So, loved one,
know that I am still working on you. I have much
refining to do, for you are My workmanship, created to
do good works.

O child, I know the prayer of your heart, which is a
desire to know Me better. And that desire is pure and
holy, for indeed, I placed it there. So, do not despair.
Have not I said that I would give you the desire of your
heart?

Beloved, consider everything that happens to you
as though it were divinely permitted by Me to accomplish My work in you, and to bring forth the best
through you.

O child, you are being conformed to My image. You
are being molded, shaped, bent, and broken to My will
and plan for your life. So, when all the trials, tests and
disappointments come, know that they are refining
experiences to bring forth a vessel pure and holy. They
bring you more and more into the likeness of your God
and Savior. They bring you into a closer relationship
with Me.

So beloved, rejoice in the pressures, for they are My
way of bringing miraculous change in your life, which
change is for the better.

MUCH WORK TO DO
John 6:29; 1 Corinthians 15:58

Dear one, there is much work to do, for My heart beats to the needs of My people. And I have many yet to bring in. But their hearts have not turned to Me. They are rebellious, and they seek after their own pleasures. They lust after the things of the flesh, the world, and the devil.

Yet child, I paid the penalty for them. Freedom from their bondage has been purchased. But they need someone to care, someone to seek them out, someone to tell them that there is hope, and someone to bring them to Me.

Beloved, let My compassion flow through you and touch those around you. Pray for the multitudes. Pray for the land, for I will yet drive out the wickedness from it. I will separate the sheep from the goats. But not one of Mine shall I lose, for I will draw them to Me.

So, let the vision, let the burden for your neighbor, country, and the world ignite and catch fire in your life. And go where I say to go. Speak what I say to speak. Do what I tell you to do.

O hear Me child, and listen. I have already given the commission to go. So, be alert. Be ready. There is enough waiting. Move out and share Me to the world.

THE PROVING GROUND
1 Peter 1:6.7

Beloved, I give you words today of assurance, encouragement, and hope, for I do not just let things happen. I do not just let you go through tests for no reason. I do not allow things to take place just for the sake of allowing them.

But, My child, I take what happens: the difficulties,

the trials, the hardships, the sufferings, and I turn them into instruments of blessing. I take the trials, and I use them to prove and temper your faith. I use them to strengthen your faith. I use them to prove your faith genuine. I use them so I can remove the impurities of self. I use them so that out of the proving of your faith will come forth a vessel worth far more than fine gold.

O loved one, do not look at the circumstances and say: "Woe is me." But look at the test and say: "Here is an opportunity to grow. Here is an opportunity to die to self. Here is an opportunity to trust my God. Here is an opportunity for my Lord to manifest Himself."

Beloved, remember, you are not the only one going through the proving ground. There are others. So, comfort one another and know that I am your fortress. Know that I am your strength. Know that you will not fall, for I rescue you.

Yes, let the tests and trials have their perfect work, and in so doing your faith will become strong and beautiful. For out of fire comes proven beauty. 0 dear one, know that there is no difficulty so great that I cannot rescue you from it, for I will not allow more than you can bear.

So, rejoice and look for Me in each trial, and you will find Me. And your faith will soar, for it is being made pure and genuine, steadfast and sure.

October 8
BUILT UPON THE CHIEF CORNERSTONE
1 Peter 2:6-7

Beloved, I was rejected, but I became the Chief Cornerstone, the stone upon which all the building is being built. And, dear one, you are a stone, a building block in My residence.

Child, I choose carefully each block, each stone, and then chisel and shape it to fit into the place I have assigned for it. And that place is important. It is a place only to be filled by you. It is filled as you let My Spirit do the shaping and the placing.

You are not a dead stone, but a living stone. You are one who lives, moves, and has their being in Me. The building is to My honor and glory, and each stone and each building block, shares in that glory.

So dear one, rejoice. I am shaping you. I am fitting you into My plan. And, O, the splendor of that plan. That plan was designed before the foundations of the world. And you were there, yes, even then you were made a part of the plan's fulfillment.

So child, enter each day, with its disappointments, stresses, joys, and sorrows, knowing, that you are in My plan. You are in My building, and I am so proud and pleased with you. We are bonded by the breath of My Spirit, and I make you beautiful. I have pierced the enemy, and he has no authority over you. Beloved, you are built upon Me, the Chief Cornerstone.

October 9
HEAR WHAT HE HAS TO SAY AND DO IT
1 Peter 5:8-9

My child, I tell you today to be faithful, steadfast, and firm in your walk with Me. Let not the enemy try to cause you to turn from one side to the other. Let him not cause you to walk after the flesh, but let Me instruct you, lead you, and walk with you. And I will restore you, strengthen you, and settle you.

So beloved, hear what I have to say and do it, for I desire obedience and faithfulness. Listen carefully, for I do not speak idle words. My words are true and life giving. Yes, heed My instruction. Believe My Word. Trust what I am telling you. And follow Me, even when it does not make any sense to you to do so. O child, hear what I tell you and do it. Hear My instruction and follow it.

October 10
CONSIDER PAUL AND SILAS
Acts 16:16-34

Child, consider Paul and Silas. Were they not beaten, falsely arrested, and thrown into prison? Yet did not they pray and sing in the darkest hour? Did not they rejoice and give thanks in all things?

Beloved, this is My will for you. This is what pleases Me; that is, giving thanks and praise in all things. O know, loved one, that I am your sufficiency. You will find all you need in Me. And when the darkness seems about to overtake you, look up and rejoice in Me. I will take you through the difficult and the impossible, because nothing is too difficult or impossible for Me.

My child, as you trust Me, as you look to Me, as you give thanks in everything, you will see My hand upon you. You will see My presence in everything. And you will see great things take place before your eyes. O loved one, did not I shake the very foundations of that prison?

So, likewise, My beloved, no situation, bondage, circumstance, or pressure can lock you in when you praise, rejoice, and give thanks. Yes, remember Paul and Silas praying and singing when you go through the tests and the trials, for My power was demonstrated in their praise. And remember, child, the end result was the salvation of the jailer and his whole household.

O beloved, let not your heart be troubled, but rejoice and praise Me no matter the situation or circumstance.

HE HAS GIVEN ME THE VICTORY
Psalm 60:12; 1 Corinthians 15:57

Child, I am loving and forgiving, and I am the God of restoration. I am the God of the impossible. I am the God that can take an overwhelming situation, an out numbered army, and give them the victory. And that is what I have done for you.

Beloved, I have given you the victory in all things: your relationships, your health, your work, and your finances. I have dispelled the odds, and have given you victory in every area. All you need do is to walk in it, believing it to be so.

O child, let not the toothless roars of the enemy frighten you, for there is nothing that shall harm you. I have already pulled all the teeth from the lion's mouth and all the claws from his paws. He is no longer a threat to you.

Yes beloved, believe that I have given you the victory. Know that My name is exalted, for I have defeated the enemy. So, come, walk in that victory. Walk in confidence with Me. Walk in total and complete trust. Walk in the leading and counsel of My Spirit. Walk with Me hand in hand.

O rejoice child, for the victory is yours, and I restore unto you all that was ravaged by the enemy. He cannot touch the apple of My eye. So, look up and give thanks, for your deliverance has come to pass. And though the odds appear greater than you, know that I am greater than any odds.

October 12

WORKING IN ME THE MANIFESTATION
OF HIS PRESENCE
Isaiah 26:8-9

Child, this day is the day I have made, a day for

241

you to rejoice and be glad. It is a day of victory, a day of joy, a day of renewal, a day of direction, and a day of peace. For when the meditation of the heart and the words of the mouth please Me, all the joy of My presence comes rushing forth.

O beloved, I give you the desires of your heart. I give you the desire to please Me in every way: the desire to place Me first in everything; the desire for Me to be Lord of your life; the desire for Me to be in control; the desire for Me to lead and guide you; and the desire to know My ways.

Dear child, I give you the desire to learn of Me; the desire to seek Me with your whole heart; the desire to have My mind in everything you do; the desire to minister as I would minister; the desire to judge fairly; the desire to be what I want you to be; yes, the desire to be like Me.

Beloved, I give you all these desires. But first there must be a learning process. It does not happen over night. I am working in you My glory and honor to fulfill. And I will show you the dross and the unclean things, and I will cleanse you of them as you recognize them.

Yes child, I will work in you the manifestation of My presence. So, rejoice and let the words of your mouth and the meditation of your heart be fixed on Me. For this will please Me. And I shall work in you a good work, that which is pleasing and acceptable to the Father.

October 13
SING UNTO THE LORD
Psalm 66:1-4

Beloved, I am the God of My Word. When I tell you something, it is true. I do not say one thing and do another. When I tell you that I provide for you, and that I meet all your need, then I do just that. O loved one, there is no shadow of turning in Me. You can count on what I say.

So child, rejoice. Sing unto your Lord. Sing your praises. Let there always be a melody in your heart. Let it be known that your God reigns. Yes, let it be known that the Lord God, the creator and sustainer of all things, is in charge and cares for His people. No good thing will He withhold from those who love Him.

O beloved, I indeed, bless My people. I turn their mourning into gladness, their darkness into light, and their anxieties into rejoicing. Yes, I care for My children. It pleases Me to do so. It brings Me joy to give them life in abundance.

Child, it pleases Me to hear My people rejoice. It pleases Me to hear My people giving thanks and praise. It pleases Me for My people to sing their adoration. And it pleases Me to give them the kingdom. It pleases Me to share with them from the storehouse of heaven.

O beloved, I pour out for you blessings daily. Do not I sustain you? Do not I give you life, food, clothing, and shelter? Yes, I love My children. And I love you and delight to make you glad. I fill you with the joy of My presence.

October 14

AN AMBASSADOR
2 Corinthians 5:20

My child, be faithful and steadfast in your relationship with Me. For you are My representative, you are My ambassador. O loved one, this is an honor and a privilege.

Beloved, strengthen your relationship with Me. Let it become closer than that of two lovers, for you are loved beyond measure. My love is total and unconditional. It is limitless and knows no end.

So dear one, come and learn to walk in My love. Let

Me become alive in your life and in everything you do. For you are My representative in all things.

O child, grasp this truth. Know, that in whatever you do, you are a divinely appointed representative of My kingdom. You are an ambassador, personally appointed by Me. And in everything you do, in everything you say, and in every thought you think, you are My representative. So dear one, be a representative true to your appointment.

Beloved, ambassadors do not represent themselves, but they represent the interest of those who appoint them, even to the point of death. And an ambassador is an ambassador twenty four hours a day, for at no time is an ambassador not a representative of the one who made the appointment. So, be My representative in all of its dignity, authority, and honor, for indeed, it is a privilege to be My ambassador.

October 15
BUILDING UP JERUSALEM
Isaiah 66:10-12

O My child, I am building up Jerusalem. I am building up My people. I am strengthening My dwelling place. I am building up a strong generation, and you are part of it. Yes, I am building you up.

Beloved, I am strengthening and fortifying you with My Word and with My Spirit. I am instructing you and teaching you what is best for you. I am showing you the right paths to take.

So child, despair not, but simply believe that I am accomplishing in your life that which pleases Me. Only believe that you are being instructed and led. Simply, follow My Word. Yes, follow My direction, and peace will flow like a river.

Beloved, think not of what could be or what might have been, but rather be renewed in the attitude of your mind and follow Me wherever I lead you. Let Me nurse and care for you as a mother comforts and cares for her child. I will not lead you astray. I will not allow anything to take place in your life that I cannot handle.

O child, you are Mine, and I love you and will care for you all the days of your life. Indeed, loved one, I am building up My people. I am building up My city. I am building up Jerusalem.

October 16
SHINING AS BRIGHT AS THE NOONDAY SUN
Isaiah 60:1-2

Beloved, you shall shine as bright as the noonday sun, for My righteousness is brilliant, and you are clothed in it. Yes, you shall shine, and those around you shall know that it is the Lord. They shall see Me in you. They will recognize the Lord God in your presence, for I have clothed you in My righteousness.

O child, I am high and lifted up, and My train fills the universe. And you, loved one, are under the mantle of My holiness and righteousness. So, let My righteousness radiate through you.

Beloved, seek Me in all things. Seek what I would do in every situation. Seek Me in what you eat, in what you wear, in what you say, in what you do, and in where you go. For, dear one, I am in charge of your life only as you let Me.

So My child, rejoice and let the light of My Spirit flood your soul. Let your strength be renewed. Let the glory of My presence radiate through you. Let your countenance shine as the stars of the heavens. Yes, loved one, you shall shine as bright as the noonday sun.

HE IS EVER PRESENT
Jeremiah 23:24

Beloved, do not be concerned about anything. Just know that I am with you and am working in you. Know that I am caring for you every minute of the day. Know that I am ever present. Is not this beautiful? Does it not cause you to rejoice that I counsel you, that I speak to you, that I direct you, and that there is nowhere that I am not?

O child, just listen. Hear Me. Release the clutter from your life, which are those things that do not matter. Let My Spirit rise from within. Let Him salve the emotions. Let Him control your entire being.

Beloved, you are loved. So, do not let yourself become discouraged, or let your life sink in despair. But reach out and touch Me. Touch Me by faith. Listen for Me. Hear My voice. It is a whisper. Only be still and know that I am there. Be still and know that I am your God.

My child, do not doubt Me. Do not doubt that I speak and talk to you. Do not fear that you will not hear My voice, for I am more willing to talk to you than you are to listen.

So, be quiet, dear one, and let your soul come to rest. Let not what you see and hear distract you. Let it not move or shake you. But rejoice and praise your God.

O beloved, I am here. I am present. Is not My salvation great? Yes, it is beyond description, and throughout eternity you will learn more and more of Me, but you will never exhaust My love and My grace. So, let your life soar. Turn loose of the dross. Let it float free.

And My child, let My Spirit be free to speak to you and instruct you. For I love you and do not hold back any good thing from you.

CARRIED ON WINGS OF EAGLES
Exodus 19:4

My child, daily I tell you of My love for you. Daily I provide for your spiritual nourishment and growth through My Word and My Spirit. Yes, I am your strength. I am the one who leads you in every place you are to go. I am there in the darkness and in the light.

Beloved, I am the one who abounds in love to you. Does not My Word tell you that I am your everything? So, when you sin, My child, tell Me about it. I forgive and represent you to the Father, and He sees you clothed only in My righteousness.

But, My child, I also tell you that obeying My Word and loving others is evidence that you love Me. And when you let Me, I am the one who does it all. I am the one who lives a godly and pure life through you.

O dear one, you can abound in every good work. You can abound in purity. You can abound in plenty, and you can abound in My grace, even when in want. For if I am in each and every moment of your day, nothing can come your way that I cannot handle.

So child, let Me live My life in and through you, and as you do your life will become content and at peace, no matter the circumstance. Let go of all things that could or do hinder. Yes, sometimes, even when those things, in and of themselves, are good.

Remember, that all good things come from Me, but you are not to look at the things, or at the circumstances. Rather, look to Me in everything, every moment of every day. And as you do, your life will be complete.

I love you, dear one, and I carry you on wings of eagles. I set you free. And I let you soar on the wind, the breath of My Spirit.

October 19
DEVOTE YOURSELF TO DOING GOOD
Titus 3:8

Child, it is a good thing to praise Me for who I am and what I do. Loved one, it is a good thing to devote yourself wholly to doing good, for goodness is of Me. It comes from Me. It originates with Me. Indeed, I am good.

Beloved, I would have you imitate Me, emulate the things I do, seek and follow Me with your whole heart, and do the things that I show you to do.

O dear one, doing good pleases Me. It brings joy to My heart to see goodness and love in My people, for I have placed that goodness in their hearts. And I receive great pleasure in seeing My children releasing that goodness and practicing it on others.

Child, does not the expansion of My name, God, become Good? Yes, I am good, and all goodness comes from Me, and by it you share with others of My divine nature. You do this when you help others, when you pray for others, and when you meet other's needs.

Dear one, do you not do such things in your work? Is it not My work? Yes beloved, My goodness is known throughout the universe. And My people have this mark about them: they are good, and they devote themselves to doing whatever is good. So child, be eager to do what is good, for this brings Me joy and great pleasure.

October 20
THE LAW OF THE SPIRIT OF LIFE
Romans 8:1-2

O beloved, am not I the mighty God? Am not I the good God? Am not I the God of love and compassion? Am not I the God of understanding? Do not I know the limitations of man? Do not I know the boundaries of human frailty and weakness? And have not I made provision to meet every one of those needs?

O child, have not I given you life, eternal life: life that did not generate with you, but out of My Spirit; life that flows from the very heart of the Father? Yes, I have given you the law of the Spirit of life.

Beloved, the law of the Spirit of life has indeed set you free from the law of sin and death. The law of life, the law of My Spirit and My Word, brings no condemnation, but rather, it brings freedom. It brings freedom from self. It brings freedom to worship and serve Me. It brings freedom from the sinful nature. It brings freedom to live.

O child, do you not see? Do you not understand? Do you not comprehend the magnitude of what I am telling you, of what I have done? For I have done it all, and it does not end. Not only have I done it all, but when you let Me, I live through you, so that it is no longer you that lives, but it is I that lives through you.

Beloved, I tell you the truth. The law of the Spirit of life has indeed set you free from the law of sin and death. O child, there is no better place to be than in the very center of My presence walking in the law of the Spirit of life.

October 21
HIS WORD BRINGS GREAT DELIGHT
Psalm 112:1

O child, there is great delight in experiencing My Word. There is great joy in living out My principles. There is great pleasure in understanding My precepts, for My Word brings life. It is powerful and active.

Beloved, My Word brings satisfaction to the inner man, for I am the Word, and as you become more and more immersed in My Word the more you shall come to know Me. As you read My Word, as you meditate on It, and as you let It consume you, you will see great and wonderful things. Yes, you will receive wisdom and understanding, which revelation is life giving and soul changing.

Child, My Word is not hidden, for I have spoken It freely. It is before you. It is near you, even in your mouth. So, open your mouth, and I will fill it with My Word.

O beloved, know that your peace and joy are found in Me, in My Word. So, neglect not My Word. Neglect not My presence. Neglect not My commands, for in them you have everything you need for every situation.

O child, come feast on My Word, and you shall be satisfied.

October 22
GOD ORCHESTRATES IT ALL
Psalm 77:13-14

Child, I am the one who is in control. I hold all things together, and though there may be quaking and trembling around you, you will not be shaken. For I, the Lord God Almighty, hold everything in place. I let nothing touch you without My permission.

Beloved, I am the one who orchestrates it all. I am the one who lifts up and puts down. I am the one who judges rightly. I am the one who exalts a man, and not the man himself. I raise up one for a purpose, and I put down another for a purpose. And I surround you with My unfailing love. I draw you near to Me and whisper love songs in your ear. You are the apple of My eye.

O rejoice, beloved, for My Name is near you, even on your lips, and that Name is powerful. It is the Name that is above every name. It is the Name of authority. It is the Name of power. It is the Name of love and compassion. And I have given you that Name. I share it with you.

So, child, rejoice, for in My Name you shall do great

things. In My Name, marvelous deeds take place. Yes, loved one, give thanks and rejoice, for your God is great and wonderful and He loves you with all of His heart.

O beloved, return that love in praise, adoration, worship, and service.

October 23

GREAT THINGS IN STORE
Malachi 3:10

My child, I care for My own. There is no need that I cannot meet. There is no problem that I cannot solve. There is no pressure that I cannot relieve. There is no lack that I cannot fill. There is nothing impossible for Me.

Beloved, when I tell you that I am faithful, and when I tell you that I will open the floodgates of heaven and pour you out a blessing, then I will do just that. And though I have already blessed you, I am sending more. I am sending the rain of My Spirit, and it will fall on you. You shall receive power, and you shall rejoice and be glad.

Child, I shall send My anointing so that you will always be aware of My presence. I shall open the windows of heaven and shower you with all that you desire of Me. And you will receive more of Me than you ever thought possible. For this, dear one, is in response to a heart that seeks Me, and to a life that chooses to follow Me without hesitation.

O child, great things are in store, so search My Word and you shall find provision for all your need.

October 24

WISDOM
James 1:5; Job 28:12, 28

My child, to know and trust Me is the beginning of

wisdom. Yes, wisdom is seeking Me with your whole heart. Wisdom is acknowledging Me in all things, and seeking My counsel in everything.

So beloved, as you seek My counsel I shall make you wise in all your judgments and decisions. As you seek Me I shall bring understanding. And loved one, to shun wickedness is good understanding.

Child, I am righteous, holy, and pure. There is no deceit or malice in Me. I alone am worthy to receive glory, honor, and praise. Anything else is foolishness, false, and full of folly.

Yes beloved, pursue wisdom, and let nothing stand in the way. Seek it and follow it. Ask Me for it and you shall receive it. I will not withhold it from you. I am the beginning of wisdom.

October 25
EXPECT A MIRACLE
Mark 6:35-44

My child, that which looks impossible to man is possible with Me, for I am God of the impossible. Nothing is too difficult for Me.

Yes dear one, when there appears to be no answer, and no way out of the dilemma or circumstance, remember, that I am God of the impossible. And when there seems to be only lack, and when it seems that the end has come and gone, remember, that I am God of the impossible.

O beloved, I always arrive on time for My timing is perfect. So, despise not the small loaves and fishes, for I make them sufficient. Is not My name: The All Sufficient One? So, expect a miracle. Yes, live on the miracle edge of faith, for this is a place of trust, a place of expectation and anticipation, a place of dependency, and a place of excitement.

O beloved, is it not thrilling to see Me arrive and do that which is impossible for you to do? So, do not become discouraged. Do not let what you see deter your faith in Me, for I shall prevail. I shall care for My people, and I will multiply the loaves and the fishes.

And child, when I pour out the blessings, and when I multiply what is available, there is always more than enough. Yes, there are baskets full and left over. So, go forth and do what I have called you to do, and trust Me to make up what you lack, for I am God of the impossible.

October 26

HE IS REAL
John 14:15-21; 15:16

Beloved, I love you and I reveal Myself to you. I make My presence known. Child, I am real. I am not a figment of your imagination. I am not some wild dream, but I am real, and I choose you to be My very own. Yes, I am as real as the air you breathe and the water you drink. I am food for the soul and a well of refreshing for your spirit.

Child, you did not choose Me, but I chose you. I am the one who called you. I am the one who changed you. I am the one who made you a new creation. I am the one who placed My Spirit within you. I am the one who empowers you and endues you with strength.

Beloved, I am the one who has made everything new. I am the one who makes old things pass away. I am the one who brought you out of darkness into marvelous light. O loved one, I am the one who is your life, for I live in you and reveal Myself through you. So, come and learn to know Me better. Come sit at My feet and become My disciple. And I will instruct you and teach you in the way you are to go. I will guide you with My eye.

Child, as you come to know Me better, the more others will see Me through you. For I, indeed, reveal Myself through My children.

October 27
DRAW FROM THE WELLS OF YOUR SALVATION
Isaiah 12:1-6

Child, I do great and mighty things. Should you not rejoice and be exceedingly glad? The things I do are marvelous and special. Yes, they are wonderful and beautiful. They are designed to honor My name and bless My people.

O beloved, I do not hide My presence from you. I do not seclude Myself in the heavens. I do not take off on a journey to the outreaches of the universe. No, I am ever present, and I am ever near, My wonders to perform.

So rejoice child, and draw daily from the wells of My handiwork. Draw from the depths of your salvation. And I shall rise up within you as a spring of living water. I shall refresh you and abundantly supply all your need.

O dear one, I shall bless you with blessings beyond your wildest imagination, for I do great things. I am the great God, loving and compassionate. And I favor My people. Have not I made you a member of My family? Would I spurn you or leave you out? No, child. Rather, I seat you at My banqueting table and tell you to feast, enjoy, and indulge in My provision to your heart's content.

O beloved, I love you so. There is nothing that I would not do for you. There is nothing that I cannot work together for your good. So, rejoice and drink from the wells of your salvation. There is an abundant supply. You shall not exhaust it. Indeed, dear one, I do great and glorious things and I share them with you.

LOVE IS THE BETTER WAY
1 Corinthians 12:31

Beloved, have not I said that love is the better way? Have not I said that My love is shed abroad in your heart? Have not I said that true love is My love in you manifesting itself through you?

O child, My love is unconditional. It is without reservation or limit. My love has no room for retribution, rejection, or condition, for it is perfect, complete, satisfying, and peaceful. And, dear one, My love is boundless and full, and it brings contentment and joy.

So beloved, let My love be free. Turn it loose: so that it permeates every part of your life, so that it becomes your life, so it is manifested in your life, so that it can reach out and touch others. Turn it loose, loved one, so that it reaches around the world to those who do not know Me, so they too can come to know My love, even as you know it.

O child, you have My love, and My love shares itself. And in sharing My love, it multiplies and grows, and brings blessing to all.

AN AWE INSPIRING GOD
Job 25:2

Beloved, I alone am God. There is no other. I am the awe inspiring God, for I am the God of light, and in Me there is no darkness. I am the Most High, Faithful, and True. I am the Lord God, the Almighty One, who does great and mighty things. I am the one who cares for My people, and one who reaches out and draws them to Me. I am the one who shows My children a better way, the way of truth and life.

O child, I am the Lord, and I am filled with compassion for My people. I know the limitations of their flesh. So, I have placed within them My Spirit. I have made them alive. I have quickened and empowered them by the same Spirit that raised Me from the dead.

Yes beloved, that same power that watched over all My people in ages past, that was present on the mountain with Moses, that divided the Red Sea, that manifested itself in a cloud by day and a pillar of fire by night, that has rescued you even when you did not know it, is alive and active in you today.

Child, I live in you in all of My power, majesty, and light. So, remember the greatness and majesty of your Lord, for in remembering comes praise, and in such praise I am found. O beloved, rejoice, for I am. I walk with you, talk with you, and provide for you. Yes dear one, I am the Holy One of Israel, who displays miracles and power in and through you.

O child, My majesty and splendor is clothed in the light of My righteousness, greatness, and goodness, with My wonders to perform.

October 30

WALK IN FAITH
Romans 14:16-23

My child, have not I spoken? Have not I said that which does not come from faith is sin? Do you not know that My kingdom is of faith, not of unbelief? It is of righteousness, peace, and joy in the Holy Spirit.

Yes beloved, My kingdom is that of trusting Me. It is of being clothed in My righteousness. It is of radiating My joy. It is of resting in My peace. It is of My strength being made perfect in your weakness.

O child, let My peace and My joy settle your life. Let Me be your life. Let go of the control in everything, and let Me come forth in power and great glory. Let Me come forth loud, clear, and strong.

Yes My loved one, this is where it all begins and

this is where it all ends. It is in Me. So, in whatever you do, I desire that you do it unto My praise, honor, and glory.

Beloved, unbelief is sin. So, in everything, your work, your finances, your shelter, your activities, your friends, your eating, your transportation, your ministry, and in everything else, let it be done in faith, trusting Me completely.

Dear child, hold nothing back to yourself, but turn everything over to Me and learn what it means to walk by faith. Learn what it means to walk in belief and trust. For you have not been called to walk in unbelief, but you have been called to walk in faith. Yes loved one, walk in it, for it turns mountains into molehills and causes the desert places to bloom.

So beloved, in whatever you say or do, do all in faith, believing and trusting Me to accomplish My best in you and through you.

October 31
SHOWING US GOOD THINGS TO COME
Zechariah 4:6

Child, I have shown you things to come. They are good things. They are things that I am accomplishing in the earth, even today. My redemptive work shall not go unheeded. I will call My own to Me. I shall remove the wickedness from the land, for there is no place in My kingdom for it. All unrighteousness and all evil shall be brought down and banned from My holy place.

Beloved, you shall see it take place. You shall see the wicked flee. You shall see the morality of My people become pure and clean. You shall see My righteousness reach out to the lowest pits of hell, and you shall see it ascend to the highest heights within the land.

For, dear one, I am the God of holiness, and I

desire to live in the midst of a people who are whole and clean. It will be My righteousness that you will see. It is the righteousness of God, for man cannot be righteous in his own flesh.

And My righteousness shall invade every stronghold of the enemy. The youth of the land shall have a new heart and a new song. The music of the land will be made pure. The leaders will no longer seek selfish interest. Crime and corruption will be pushed back as My Spirit floods the land.

O rejoice, child, for you shall see it take place. So, let My Spirit invade every part of your being to cleanse and purify you. Then watch what I do before your eyes. You shall take part in it.

O beloved, I do great and mighty things that you never dreamed of. So, prepare yourself and watch. Speak out the words I tell you to speak, and be silent when I tell you to be silent. For I am orchestrating a mighty work in the land. It already has begun.

November

Turn Your Faith Loose

November 1
TURN YOUR FAITH LOOSE
Romans 4:3, 18-25; 2 Corinthians 5:7

My child, exercise your faith and turn it loose, for faith is the substance, the ingredient that moves the hand of God. O loved one, faith pleases Me.

Beloved, faith is believing, trusting and hoping in Me. Faith is taking Me at My Word. Faith is believing what I say is true. Faith simply says: "My God can do anything. He loves Me and will supply all my needs. He cares for me always."

Faith says: "My God never leaves or forsakes me, for He is the God of the impossible. He is the God of miracles, not just for yesterday, but for today. He is compassionate, and full of love." Faith says: "I believe you Lord, and I am confident, I am sure, I am convinced that you are here and that you will meet every need of my life."

And faith says: "I know that in all things, no matter what they are, no matter the degree of difficulty, no matter the length of time it takes, my God is at work in my life. My God is doing what is best for me, and in so doing His name is honored and glorified."

Child, faith simply believes and accepts that I am blessing and manifesting Myself in everything. Faith believes that, though you cannot see what is happening, I am real and always with you. Faith believes that I call things into being from that which exists not. Faith believes that I work everything together for good.

Beloved, faith is a shield that protects from all that the enemy can throw at you. So, turn your faith loose and let it live. For by it you can conquer the world and anything in it. Child, does not this cause you to rejoice? O turn your faith loose and watch what happens.

WHAT HE SAYS IS TRUE
Psalm 119:160

My child, I am faithful to My Word. What I say is true. I do not say one thing and do another. I do not tell you something and then go back on My Word. No, what I tell you is true. It is real. There is no question about it. There is no maybe. My Word stands firm, true and fixed. It never changes. It is always consistent.

So My beloved, when I say I am faithful to provide a way out of testing and temptation, I provide that way out. When I say that I strengthen you, make you steadfast, grounded in faith, then that is exactly what I do. When I say that out of My abundance I make you super abundant, I do just that.

My dear child, I left all the glory, honor, and riches of heaven and became totally stripped and shamed before the world. I hung on the cross of Calvary and died for you. I did this so you could receive an abundance of life, share with Me all the wealth of the heavenlies, and become rich in all I am and in all that I possess.

Beloved, My promises are like pure gold. They are rich. They are eternal and they are life giving. So, search out these nuggets. Believe My promises. Trust Me to perform what I said I would do. For there is no better way to live, grow, and mature than by feasting on the promises of My Word.

Yes child, find My promises and claim them for yourself. For they are true and they are yours to claim, yours to inherit. They are yours today. O rejoice, for what I say is true.

November 3

AT HIS FEET
Psalm 95:6

Child, I am with you, for indeed, that is what My name means, and that is where I am. So, come before Me. Come and kneel at My feet, for your God is here. But, loved one, I do not force you. I have given you a choice, and O, the joy, peace and blessing when you choose to come before Me and learn of Me. Yes, there is great benefit when you sit at My feet and let Me instruct you and teach you in the way you are to go.

Beloved, there is power given as you kneel at My feet, for I anoint you and I commission you to go and bear much fruit. There is peace at My feet, for I give you peace, not as the world gives, but I give the kind of peace that transcends all understanding.

And child, there is joy at My feet, for the joy of the Lord is your strength. There is victory at My feet, for I have overcome, and you share in that victory. There is rest at My feet, for My Word brings rest to your soul.

O loved one, there is no better place to be than in My presence, kneeling before Me with My arms reaching out to you and My heart blessing you with love. So come before Me. Fall on your knees and worship Me, and your life will be energized with My presence. You will go out with joy and be led forth with peace.

November 4

HIDDEN TRUTHS
Matthew 13:11

Child, I share with you things that can only be known in the Spirit. I share with you the secrets of the kingdom. I share with you truths hidden from the world. The world does not know or comprehend them, for My truths can only be spiritually discerned. The world does not know Me.

But you know Me, for I reveal Myself to you. Yes, to all My children I make Myself and My ways known. You once were in darkness, and My Word meant nothing. But now you are in marvelous light, and My Word is alive, and you see things that you never saw before.

O beloved, continue to walk in My ways, for the more you walk with Me, and the more you seek understanding, the more I reveal Myself to you. So, take what you know and stand on it.

And receive My Word with gladness. Let nothing turn you from It, for in receiving My Word you receive Me. In standing firm and fast upon My Word you shall see marvelous things take place. My Word produces fruit in abundance.

Child, you shall reap bountifully of My provision. You shall see that your God is able and willing to do anything that brings you into a deeper and more rewarding walk with Him. O praise the Lord, for He is good, there is no other like Him.

November 5
SO LIVE THAT OTHERS WILL SEE JESUS
John 14:9

Child, I am the way, the truth, and the life, and those who seek Me must seek Me in Spirit and in truth. O dear one, when I came I solely represented the Father and His purpose. My life was so lived that the Father was seen in Me. My life was so in tune with the Father that those who saw Me saw the Father.

Beloved, My desire for your life is that I am allowed to so live through you that others may see Me in you, glorifying the Father which is in heaven. This comes through a commitment and devotion to Me, to My Word and to My Spirit. So, rejoice and let Me be Me through you. Live by My strength and power. Use My mind and so fulfill the will of your Lord. Yes, live as a representative of Me in the very image of My presence.

SET FREE
Galatians 5:1

Child, I have done great things. I have set you free. Freedom is yours, for I have purchased it for you. I bought you at great price and set you free. You need no longer be in bondage to yourself, to your sinful nature, which is the old man. For I have given you a new man. I have given you a spirit man that sets you free. Everything you need to experience your freedom, you have already received. So, know, dear one, that you are free. There is no condemnation. There is no bondage.

O beloved, the freedom I have given you brings joy. For I have promised to be with you always, to supply all your needs, and never to leave you or forsake you. But you have a choice, for I have given you a free will. You can choose freedom, or you can choose to remain in bondage. You can choose to live your own life, or you can choose Me to live it for you. You can choose freedom in Me or bondage to yourself. Yes, you can choose to be under My complete control, and in so doing you will have chosen every thing I have for you and lose nothing, but your life hid in Me.

I love you My child, and the freedom I give you is free. My desire is that you in turn give Me freedom in your life. O the power, the strength, and the possibilities that can be yours, as you allow My complete control. It is beyond measure and human comprehension. So, rejoice in Me, for everything you need is in Me. Yes dear one, I am in you the hope of Glory. I have set you free.

WALK IN OBEDIENCE
Deuteronomy 6:3

O My child, have not I said that obedience brings prosperity, and that to obey is better than sacrifice. Yes dear one, obedience brings blessing. Obedience brings favor. It brings wisdom and knowledge.

Beloved, the obedient walk in My precepts and principles. The obedient know the joy of complete surrender. The obedient know the results of being at peace with their God.

O child, come walk in obedience. Walk in faithfulness. Walk in My ways and you will experience a deluge of blessing, for I will open the floodgates of heaven and pour out so much that you will not be able to contain it all.

HE LOVES US ALL THE SAME
James 1:17

Yes, My child, all good and perfect gifts come from Me in whom there is no shadow of turning. I am always the same. I love all My children the same. I do not respond to one differently than to another, for My principles are the same for everyone. But I do have different plans for each one, and each is called to do that which I have ordained for them to do. Yet the reward is the same.

Beloved, faithfulness is what I have called each to do, and it is the key to My good pleasure. A heart sold out to Me is what I am looking for. So, think not that others are better than you, or that I have passed you by. But know that faithfulness is what brings great reward.

Child, there is no shifting or changing in Me. I am the same yesterday, today, and forever. And I lay out

My principles for each to walk in. I lay out My promises for each to share. I give gifts of ministry for each to use for My glory. I bless all based on the same principles and conditions.

O beloved, seek to please Me, but remember always that I love you and care for you. That will never change. You are family. So, be encouraged, for I treat you as a child who shares in all that the Father is and has. Yes, loved one, all good and perfect gifts come from Me.

November 9
DO NOT GIVE INTO THE DEMANDS
OF THE FLESH
Romans 6:10-14

O child, My redemptive work brings with it healing and health to your body. Have not I said to present your body to Me as a living sacrifice? Have not I said to bring your body into subjection to the Spirit? Have not I said to put to death the deeds of the flesh? Have not I said to be alive unto Me?

Yes beloved, do not give way to the rule, to the demands of the flesh, but rather choose to make it a slave to the Spirit. And seek Me in all things. For when anything becomes an obsession to the body it interferes with the natural order of things. It deters discipline, and then the body becomes a slave to that excess.

Child, there is to be no bondage to you, for I have set you free. There are to be no other gods before you, and that includes the cravings of the flesh. Loved one, I provide sufficient for you. So, choose not to indulge yourself in the flesh, but rather choose that I be Lord of everything, yes, of every detail concerning you.

O beloved, in a simple and childlike manner, consult Me in all things and I will bring wisdom, victory, and peace to your life. Count yourself dead unto sin and self. And count yourself alive unto Me. For My way is the way of love and trust, the way of a pure heart and good conscience, and a sincere faith.

So child, follow My way, and you will not live to fulfill the desires of the flesh. But rather, you will live to please Me, and the desires of your heart will be to bring praise, honor, and glory to My name. Yes, submit your body to Me. Let it be Mine to live in and to use for My glory.

November 10
HE BECAME POOR SO I COULD BECOME RICH
2 Corinthians 8:9

Child, trust Me in everything, and whatever you do in word or deed do it all unto Me. Do it for the glory of your Heavenly Father.

O beloved, did not I become poor for your sake, so that, by partaking of Me, you would become rich? And loved one, those riches cover a multitude of need. They cover all your spiritual need. They cover all your physical need. They cover all your emotional needs. They cover all your financial need.

My child, these riches are your prosperity in every way. Did not I come to give life and to give it more abundantly? O dear one, I have given you so much. I have given you everything you need to meet every occasion.

Beloved, I have given you spiritual weapons that can demolish all strongholds that resist and set themselves against the knowledge of Me. And I have given you the weapons to bring every thought into captivity and to make them obedient to Me.

Yes child, I have made you rich. I have made you prosperous. I have made you a victor. So, trust Me always and believe it to be so.

267

November 11
MOVED WITH COMPASSION
Psalm 103:13-14

Beloved, I am the Father of mercies, the God of all comfort, and I am moved with compassion for My own. I know their pain and sorrow, for indeed I too suffered and was acquainted with grief.

O child, was not I moved with compassion when I raised Lazarus from the dead? Was not I filled with compassion when I healed the sick? Was not I moved with compassion when I fed the multitudes? Was not I so stirred in My heart over the sin of mankind, that I gave up My very own life so that man could have direct access to Me?

Beloved, was not I moved with compassion for Job in all his trouble? Was not I moved with compassion to feed and care for the children of Israel in the wilderness? O loved one, I did not create man to make him miserable. I created him for fellowship with Me, and in so doing I became mindful of all his needs.

So rejoice child, I care for you, and I am moved with compassion to comfort you in all your needs. Yes, I comfort you as a mother comforts her little one, for I am moved and consumed with love and compassion for you.

November 12
HE IS THE RESURRECTION AND THE LIFE
John 11:25

Child, I am the resurrection and the life. I am your hope of glory, for I reside within you to make you alive. I dwell within you to give you new life and new hope, hope for today and hope for tomorrow.

O beloved, I am the King of Glory. I am the Almighty One, and I conquered death and its grave. I give you the victory, for death shall never hold My people. I defeated the grave and its hold by the power of My resurrection. Death is only a beautiful home-coming.

Child, I have brought hope to all. The physical death of My loved ones is only a transition from one place to another. It is from one glory to another. It is from mortality to immortality.

Yes beloved, there is hope and there is victory. There is eternal life, resurrection life for both now and forever. So, stand firm. Let nothing move or shake you, for great and powerful is your God. He ever lives to care for His own.

November 13
CALLED TO A LIFE OF LOVE
Song of Solomon 1:1-4

Beloved, I call you to a life of love. Have not I said that a new command I give you, which is to love one another? Have not I said to live a life of love, which is to love one another deeply? Have not I said that I am love?

Yes child, love pleases Me. Love is the response of My Spirit that lives within you. Love is the manifestation of Me in and through you. The greatest attribute of all is love, for without love there is nothing. Beloved, without love there is only sounding brass and tinkling cymbals.

Child, love is the life I call you to live. I call you to share in My love: to be the beneficiary of it, and to be lavished in it. Then I send you forth radiating that same love to others. So, live a life of love. Love one another freely, for indeed love covers a multitude of sins.

Beloved, did not My love cover your sins? Did not love take Me to the cross? Does not My love bring blessing upon blessing? Does not My love reveal My Word so you can be instructed by it? Did not My love

269

give you the gift of the Holy Spirit so you could be endued with power, so you could hear My voice, so you could be counseled moment by moment, and so you could have wisdom? Does not My love compel Me to care for My own?

O child, pure love is endless and without limit or reservation. Love does not seek its own self-interest, but the interest and well being of others. So, live a life of love, and you will be blessed in the process. For love generates love, and it returns fifty, yes, even a hundred fold.

November 14
FIX YOUR THOUGHTS
Hebrews 3:1

My child, fix your thoughts daily on Me. Yes, moment by moment fix your mind on Me, for I have given you the mind of Christ. Let Me fill your thoughts with the glory of My presence and with the awe of My majesty. In so doing you shall become a doer of the Word and not a hearer only.

Beloved, as you fix your thoughts on Me, My redemptive plan will become clearer and clearer. You will begin to understand things you have not understood in the past. You will become infused with thoughts and ways that are divinely ordered.

O dear one, I love you so very much, and I lavish you in My love. You are My very own and I desire only the best for you. And the best is My perfect will for your life. So, fix your thoughts on Me. Let Me increase, and let the flesh decrease, and only the best for you will result. Yes, fix your thoughts on Me, and I will carry you to realms you have never dreamed, where blessings abound on every side.

THE DAY OF THE LORD
Zechariah 14:6-9

Child, the day of your Lord is at hand. It is the day of His visitation. It is the day that I be high and lifted up. It is the day that I am made Lord of everything.

O beloved, let everything that has breath praise My name, for My kingdom has come. It is in you. Out of you, out of My body, I cause rivers of living waters to flow, and those waters bring healing to the nations.

So child, rejoice with Me for all of heaven and earth sing in My presence. There is no other name above My name. There is no other God beside Me, and I shall accomplish My purpose in you and throughout the whole earth.

O beloved, let everything, every thought, every deed, and every motive be separated unto Me. Let them be made holy and pure. Let all things be sanctified. For I am the most high God, and you shall see the goodness of your Lord in everything. So, praise Me child, and watch what takes place, for I am doing a great and mighty thing. Yes, awesome and majestic are My works, and they are My joy to perform.

TURNING TRAGEDY INTO TRIUMPH
Galatians 4:12-14

Beloved, I turn tragedy and opposition into triumph and opportunity. I restore where there is only ashes. I build where it is impossible to build. I take all situations and circumstances and turn them into good.

Rejoice child, even in the illnesses you experience, for I can make them opportunities to advance My name. Consider Paul. Did not he write that it was because of an illness that he first preached the gospel to the Galatians? Can not I do the same today?

So beloved, fret not at that which has struck you, but rather rejoice in the fact that I can use it to minister to others. And rest, dear one, in the confidence that your healing is on the way.

O child, I am the good God. The God of miracles, signs, and wonders. I still turn darkness into light, and bad into good.

November 17
ADD TO YOUR FAITH
2 Peter 1:5-8

Beloved, My desire is that you abound in your knowledge of Me. For as you come to know Me better your life becomes at peace, settled, and fruitful. O child, add to your faith those things that honor Me. Add in ever increasing measure: love, kindness, godliness, brotherly love, self-control, patience, knowledge, and goodness. Yes, think on these things. Meditate on these virtues. Choose to add them. Choose to experience them. Choose to let them be productive in your life. And in so doing, you shall enhance your daily walk with Me.

November 18
A FAMILY RELATIONSHIP
Ephesians 2:22; Hebrews 3:6

My child, I love My family, and I long to fellowship with them. I call My children to respond to My love. I encourage them to come into My presence, for there is a relationship far greater than any earthly one. I have made you family. I call you My child.

Beloved, all the warmth and coziness that you can imagine of home, love, peace, contentment, and happiness is found in Me. And I desire to share such a family relationship with you. This is a relationship that is spontaneous, peaceful, exciting, awesome, beautiful, warm and secure. O child, this is what I want to share with you.

So, My dear one, be happy, for you are at home. I have come to live with you as Father God. And I fill My home with thoughts of love, sharing, joy, happiness and with all the goodness of family. O beloved, it is better than you think, for being at home with Me is far more than any earthly family relationship. It is good.

So, My loved one, My beautiful child, come and walk with Me. Come and fellowship with Me. Come and enjoy My presence, for I desire to walk and talk with you, and to share with you all that I am, all that I have. For you are part of My precious family, and I love you so.

November 19

A PURE HEART AND A CLEAN MIND
Psalm 51:10-12

Beloved, I have created in you a clean heart, one that is pure, one that seeks after Me. I have created a heart that longs for Me and My ways, a heart that desires to please Me. I have placed My Spirit in your heart to bring you peace and victory.

Beloved, My Spirit creates a right spirit within you. He reveals the attitude of your mind. He brings to light that which does not please Me. He cleanses and purifies your mind and restores the joy of your salvation.

O child, it is My good pleasure to prosper you in spirit and in truth. It is My good pleasure to prosper you in the cleansing of your mind. It is My good pleasure to prosper you in the renewing of your spirit. It is My good pleasure to prosper your relationship with Me.

Yes child, it is My good pleasure to prosper you in every way, for I want nothing but the best for you. So, rejoice and be glad. I am still working on you to bless you always in all things. O loved one, I see your heart and I know it is pure. It is undivided. I know its desire is for Me.

November 20
REVEALED THROUGH HIS WORD
1 Samuel 3:19-21

Child, I am the Word. Let It not go unnoticed. Let It not fall to the ground, for I reveal Myself through My Word. My Word is pure and trustworthy. It can be counted on to change lives. It can change circumstances. It gives power to withstand anything the enemy brings against you, no matter the hurt or disappointment.

So beloved, rightly divide My Word. Study It. Meditate on It. Use It as a tool, for It is a battering ram to bring down strongholds. It is a hammer to build. It is a sword to conquer. It is ointment to heal. It is a treasury to prosperity. It is bread to feed the hungry and water to quench a thirsty soul.

Child, I reveal Myself through My Word. Despise It not. Believe It all. Reject none of It. But hold It up, for It is the light of the world. It is a lamp to guide. It is a shield to protect. It is comfort to a troubled soul.

So, listen and let Me speak to you through My Word marvelous truths, truths that will change your life. Yes beloved, I reveal Myself through My Word.

November 21
CONSULT HIM IN EVERYTHING
Ephesians 6:5-7; 1 Corinthians 10:31

Child, if your body, soul, and spirit are Mine; if in fact, you have given Me complete control of your life; if in fact you have released My Spirit for power in your life; if in fact you have said from your heart: Jesus be Lord of My life, should not I then be involved in making your life decisions?

274

Yes loved one, should not I be consulted in everything: what you do, the places you go, the people you see, the words you say, the clothes you wear, the car you drive, the work you do, and even the food you eat? O Beloved, should not everything you do, say, and think be in consultation with Me?

November 22

THE SPIRIT'S WORK
Acts 1:8; 2:1-2

My child, you are in the very presence of My Spirit, for I have placed My Spirit within you. And My Spirit is greater than he that is in the world.

Dear one, the working of My Spirit is to bring you into a deeper relationship with Me, for He leads, guides, instructs, corrects, and comforts My people. He does not speak on His own, but He speaks that which glorifies Me.

Beloved, My Spirit is your friend. He guards you jealously. He shields and protects you aggressively. He defends you, and when the enemy comes at you, like a flood He raises up a standard against him. My Spirit's work is to equip you with everything you need for service, for battle, and for godliness.

Child, He fills you full with My nature. He anoints you and touches others through you. He opens your eyes to truth, and He always directs the praise, honor, and glory to Me. And loved one, I am about to pour out blessings of My Spirit, greater than has ever been seen before. I am ready to move and renew My body. I will do this through the power and presence of My Spirit.

O beloved, I endue you with power and boldness. I anoint you and commission you to share Me, and the power of My presence, and the fellowship of My Spirit with those around you.

Yes child, enter into the joy and fellowship of My Spirit. Grieve Him not, for He is your friend. He is your protector. He is your instructor. He is the bearer of good news. He is the energizer of your life. He also intercedes on your behalf. So, become His friend, and you will see great and marvelous things take place in and around you all the days of your life.

November 23
RIGHTEOUSNESS AND FAITH
Galatians 3:6-11

My child, I have made you righteous. I have made you acceptable in My sight, and I receive you into My presence. You are in right standing with Me, for I have met all the requirements for you. And I have begun a good work in you, and I will carry it on to completion.

Yes, you are clothed in My righteousness, and it is credited to you by your faith in Me. O loved one, this standing is a favor experienced only as you believe it and receive it.

So My child, come and enter into My presence with thanksgiving in your heart, for I have made you a new creation. I have removed the old and I have made all things new.

Beloved, righteousness is My gift to you. As you live and move in My righteousness, I take you from faith to faith. So, learn to walk in righteousness by exercising your faith. Learn to live by faith. For this is how the righteous shall live. This is how the righteous please Me. Yes, they please Me by their complete trust and confidence in Me.

O child, look not at what you see, but look to Me as the author and perfecter of your faith. For the righteous live by faith, not by what they see. So, keep your faith keenly honed. Let your faith always be on the cutting edge, for faith is the way of victory. It is the way of life. It is the way of the righteous.

HIS GRACE ABOUNDS
2 Corinthians 9:8

My child, indeed My grace abounds to you, and by that grace and divine power I provide everything you need. O loved one, I give you great and precious promises, so you can partake of My divine nature. I give you My Word so that you can share in everything that I am, so that you may know the sufficiency of your Lord, so that you may come to know Me better, so that your joy may be full, and that you may abound in every good work.

Beloved, there are no shadows with Me. My Word is clear. My truths are simple, yet they confound the wise. Dear one, the simple truth is that I care for My own. There is nothing in all the universe that can change that. Yes, I know that the enemy tries to tell you differently. I know your emotions lie to you. But loved one, the simple, profound, and irreversible truth is that I care for My children.

Child, I have given you everything you need. It is already done. All you need was purchased on the cross of Calvary. When you invited Me into your life, I came with all that I am. So, you have your sufficiency in Me. You have My favor. You have My promises of life in abundance, health and healing, joy and comfort, peace and prosperity, and love and compassion.

Beloved, you have Me, and there is need for nothing else. For everything you need is found in Me. So, rejoice for I abound to you and care for you. O loved one, release all of Me to flow through you so others may share in what you have. Yes beloved, I fulfill all your need both now and forever.

November 25

HE DELIGHTS IN ME
Isaiah 62:1-5

Beloved, I rejoice over My own with singing, for I take delight in them. They give Me great pleasure. Yes, dear one, I care for My own. I watch over them to protect them and to deliver them out of all their difficulties.

O child, take Me at My Word. Trust Me. Believe what I say is true. I would not say it if it were not so. I cannot lie. I do not give you false hope. So, rejoice for I am with you. I will rescue you. I will deliver you from the snare of the fowler. I will supply all your need. I make up what you lack.

Yes beloved, rejoice for I delight in you. I love you without measure, and I care for you in every way.

November 26

SHEEP OF HIS PASTURE
Isaiah 40:10-11

Dear one, you are sheep of My pasture, and I am the one who tenderly cares for you. I am your God, and you are My people. You are Mine, and I lovingly watch over you. Yes, I lead you, guide you, protect you, and care for you with an abundance of love and compassion.

O child, I jealously tend over My flock, and you are one of them. I know you by name. I know everything about you. I know your personality. I know your likes and dislikes. I know your wants and your desires. I know your weaknesses, and I know your strengths. I know that your heart is pure and that it seeks after Me.

Yes beloved, I know My sheep, and they know Me. Do you not recognize My voice? Do you not recognize My Word? Does it not become alive to you? Do you not recognize My Spirit? Do you not recognize My leading? O dear one, you know Me and I know you.

So, rejoice in that you are My sheep and that I am your shepherd. I will never lead you astray, but will always lead you safely in the paths of righteousness. I will take you to green pasture where you can prosper in every way. O child, there is nothing I would not do for My sheep.

HE GIVES WISDOM
Proverbs 2:3-6

Beloved, the wisdom that comes from Me is the highest wisdom there is. And you can share in that wisdom, for I have said that if any man lack wisdom let him ask of Me, and I will freely give it. It is not hidden. It is in full view.

Child, My wisdom goes beyond human comprehension, yet it is so simple. All you need is to take Me at My Word and believe that it is so. Yes, My wisdom is so profound that it confounds the scholars, yet is so simple that a child may possess it.

O dear one, I give you wisdom. I give you discernment. I give you sound judgment. I included it in My salvation plan. It is for you. And those who put their trust in Me shall never be ashamed. They shall never lack for any good thing, for I love them and call them by name. I impart to them My wisdom. I make known My ways unto them.

A WORD OF ENCOURAGEMENT
2 Chronicles 20:15-22

My child, I have a Word of encouragement for you. It is a Word of peace, confidence, and faith. It is a Word of victory. It is a Word of praise. It is a Word of miracles. O loved one, look not at what is going on around you, or at what you are going through, but look beyond what you see. Yes, see the end from the beginning. See the victory already won.

Beloved, speak life into every situation. Speak My presence and breathe My Spirit into everything. When the enemy and his army come against you, do not loose heart. He has no authority over you. I have promised to care for My own. I have already defeated the enemy. He and his subjects have no control over you. They cannot touch you.

Dear child, sing your praises in the midst of difficulty, and in the midst of the pressure. For the battle is Mine, it is already won. And I give you the victory. So stand firm and steadfast, trusting Me without wavering and without doubt. Know that I, the Lord your God, go before you. I am with you always. I fight the battles for you, and I give you the victories. I have everything under control.

So beloved, praise Me even when you have not yet seen the manifestation of My visitation, for it is on its way. Know that I watch over the righteous in all their ways to bring them into victory. O loved one, act on what I say, and on what you know, not on what you see. For the battle is Mine, and the victory is yours.

Child, is not this a Word of encouragement?

November 29
A SHIELD ABOUT ME
Psalm 5:12; 7:10

My child, I am a shield about you. You have many of My shields surrounding you. They are the shields of My grace and favor, My glory and honor, My salvation, My righteousness, My peace, My prosperity, and My protection.

O beloved, I am your shield, and nothing can touch you, for I guard you jealously. And I hear your cry and

I answer your call. I know your concerns and I know your cares. Just cast them all at My feet, and let Me bear them.

My child, I indeed bless the righteous. I protect them. I favor them. I watch over them. So, be encouraged. Let nothing sway or move you. Trust Me, for there is nothing that can hinder your God from doing anything. I am the God of miracles, the God of the impossible.

O My beloved, rejoice, for I hear and receive your call. I know where you are. I know and understand the situation and the circumstance. So, turn your faith loose, and you will see miracles take place before your very own eyes. And great peace will dwell within your land.

Child, there is so much to share with you, but for today I speak hope, peace, and assurance to your heart. Be assured that I hear your cry for help and that My heart responds to the call of My children. So, peace to you My child, I am here to rescue and to help you.

Yes beloved, I am the shield about you.

November 30
SURROUNDED WITH HIS UNFAILING LOVE
Psalm 32:10; 33:4-5

O child, I surround you with My unfailing love, a love that knows no limit, and a love that is pure and real. It is not fake or self-serving. It fails not. My love will never let you down, for have not I said that I would never leave or forsake you? Have not I said that those who put their trust in Me shall never be ashamed?

O child, My love for you is an active love. I watch over you as a mother watches over her young. I rush to your aide. I rescue and deliver you from all your troubles. I instruct you in the way that you are to go. I protect you from the enemy. I care for you with all the caring of a loving Heavenly Father.

O beloved, My love is something to be desired, for it is forgiving and guiltless. It accepts you as you are. It is never removed, for I take it not away. It is without measure. It has not been parceled out to you. You have it all.

Child, as you come to know Me better you will learn to experience more and more of that love. So, rejoice, I have lavished you in My love. I have surrounded you with songs of deliverance. I have promised to love and care for you always.

December

Blessings More Than Can Be Numbered

December 1
BLESSINGS MORE THAN CAN BE NUMBERED
Deuteronomy 7:13-14

My child, I bless you far beyond what you ever could ask or think. Have not I said that the things I have planned for you are more than can be numbered? If you were to speak of them could you declare them all?

So dear one, look around you. Do you not see what I have done, and what I am doing? Look at the things you take for granted. Look at your relationships. Look at your work. Look at your family. Look at your ministry. Do not I bless you beyond measure? And look at your daily needs, are they not met? Do not I clothe, feed and shelter you?

Beloved, do not I talk with you, speak to you, give you instruction, protect you, answer your prayers, and tell you that I love you? Do not I give you favor? Have not I said that you are the head, not the tail?

Have not I given you new life? Have not I come to dwell within you? Have not I paid the penalty of sin for you? Have not I given you healing, joy, peace, gladness, and prosperity?

O child, when you face the pressures, the stretching, the exhaustion, the tiredness, and the weariness, know that your God blesses you. Do not loose heart but know that your God is working to bring another blessing to your life.

December 2
HE SETS THE TIME
Ecclesiastes 3:1

My child, let your heart not be troubled for I have brought you peace and prosperity. I have opened for you a path lined with My presence and goodness. So, forget the former things. Do not dwell on them any longer for today is a new day and I am bringing you into new territory.

Beloved, I do not forget you. O, no! I have a marvelous plan for you. I have great plans for all My people. But there is a timing that is necessary for the orchestrating of all things.

Child, I have set the time for you to do what I want you to do. That is why you will hear Me say: "Wait on the Lord" or "Be still and know that I am God." And you will hear Me say: "Speak to this one or pray with that one." This is why you will think at times that there is no movement of My Spirit at all. You may also think that your Lord has forgotten you or is not concerned about your situation.

But beloved, even in these times I am preparing you. Yes, you will find that the wilderness is the best training ground. So, trust Me. Enjoy My peace, and let Me do the directing. Let Me be the conductor, and you shall see a new day, a new beginning. You shall see the hand of your God at work both in your life and in your circumstances. You will see this, My loved one, in My timing.

So child, keep on trusting Me for in trusting Me there is great peace. Keep on in My Word for you shall be fed. Keep on in prayer for your prayers shall be answered. O loved one, My timing is perfect.

December 3

HE CHANGES NOT
Hebrews 13:8

Child, do not think that I forsake you, that I do not keep My Word, that My promises are empty and without substance. O dear one, just the opposite is true. I do not lie. My Word is forever fixed and true. My promises are real and genuine. I am the same yesterday, today and forever. I do not change.

So beloved, take heart in what I tell you. Have not I

285

said that I love you and because I love you I will rescue you, and that I would protect you? Have not I said that you are My dwelling place and that no harm shall touch you? Have not I said that I hear your call and that I answer and save you out of all your troubles? Have not I said that I will deliver you? Have not I said that the arrows shall not come near you?

My child, observe what I say. Believe My Word. Trust Me beyond a shadow of a doubt, so that when the pestilence comes you will not be devastated. When the arrows fly you will not be afraid for you will know that I am with you. You shall not be overtaken by the enemy. He shall not overwhelm you either mentally, materially, physically or spiritually. For you are Mine and I love, protect, deliver and comfort you.

Beloved, think on these things. Consider what I say. Know who I am. Yes, the pressures will come, but I will deliver you out of them all. So rejoice, dear one, deliverance comes with the dawning of hope. It daily comes to those who praise Me. And great peace comes to those who trust Me regardless the circumstance.

So child, believe Me. Believe that I am for you, not against you. Believe that I am greater than he that is in the world. Believe that what I say is true and that it is for you. Yes, it is for you today.

December 4
BELIEVE FOR THE IMPOSSIBLE
Matthew 19:26

Beloved, all things come from Me and through Me for all good and perfect gifts come from above. There is no variation. This is truth. For all things were made by Me, and by Me all things consist. There is nothing made that I did not create. There is nothing that exists that I have not put together.

So beloved, if I can form and shape the world and the entire universe, is there then anything too difficult

286

for Me? Am I not able to speak a Word and all heaven rush to My command? O loved one, look up and enjoy your Lord. I do not withhold from you. No, I care for you. You are precious in My sight and I jealously watch over you.

My child, see My majesty. See that I am able to produce what I say I can produce. See that I have all you need. See that it is yours. O, believe, what I say. Count on it, even when everything looks absolutely impossible and only a miracle could change the situation. Believe, that I am the God of the impossible. Believe, that I call forth things from that which does not exist.

So beloved, trust Me and lean not on your own understanding. Yes, in everything acknowledge Me, and I shall order your steps. Look up, there is no reason for your head to hang down, for your God is on the throne and He cares for His own.

O rejoice My child, for I am with you, and I uphold you, and I tell you to fear not for I am your God. There is nothing impossible for Me.

December 5

A KING AND A PRIEST
Isaiah 61:6; Revelation 5:10

Child, I have called you and all My children to be a king and a priest. I have called you and all My children to minister to each other. I have called you and all My children to minister unto Me. I have anointed each to bring good news, to bring hope, to bring joy and gladness, to proclaim liberty and freedom to My people.

Beloved, I have called you and anointed you to do what I have planned for you to do. You need not be concerned with the tests and trials, for I have ordered that you shall feast on the wealth of the nations. I have prescribed a double portion of your inheritance to you; a double portion of My blessings; a double portion of My Spirit; a double portion of the land to possess; and a double portion of Me to meet all your need.

Child, I do not hold back, as you think I do, but rather My timing is perfect. Know that I do what I do so that all may see and acknowledge that I am the one who blesses My people.

So, rejoice for I am at work and you shall see those around you grow in righteousness. You shall hear their praise spring up before you. It shall be on their lips, for they shall see the majestic hand of your God at work. They shall know that it is Me who blesses the people, the one who changes darkness into light.

My beloved, as I have anointed you to bring good news, so I bring you good news. Is not what I am telling you beautiful? Is not being a priest of the Lord good news? O child, I have made special provisions for My kings and priests, for they shall receive their portion from the wealth of the nations. Yes, My child, you are a priest and a king, and you are blessed.

December 6
GREAT AND PRECIOUS PROMISES
Psalm 145:13; 2 Peter 1:4

My child, I indeed share with you of My divine nature. It is yours through believing and claiming the promises that I have given you. I have made every provision to meet your physical, material, social, emotional and spiritual needs.

I have given you great and precious promises so you can know Me better, so you can know My will, so you can become an imitator of Me, and so you can participate in My divine nature.

O beloved, search out My Word. Seek and lay claim to what I offer you. Let My promises bring assurance, confidence and boldness to your life. Let My promises bring peace, joy and contentment. Let My promises bring health and healing to your body.

Dear one, let My promises bring you prosperity. Let My promises bring you favor, both with Me and with those around you. Let My promises bring peace from your enemies. Let My promises bring you comfort. Let My promises bring you through the wilderness into a great and spacious land.

Child, let My promises bring you into possession of all you need for life and godliness. Let My promises, My Word, which comes from My goodness and glory, bring you into the sharing of all that I have for you.

So rejoice beloved, for there is no need too small or too big that I am not willing and able to meet. Nothing is too insignificant or too immense for Me. Nothing is beyond My interest or capability.

Yes child, I have given you exceedingly great and precious promises. Go search and find them, and lay hold of them. Let them become your life. Believe them, and as you do, you become a participant in My divine nature. You become like Me.

December 7

THE LORD IS OUR HELPER
Psalm 118:6-7

My dear child, I am your helper, and with Me you need nothing more. Anything else will only bring disappointment. But confidence in Me never goes unrewarded, for there is nothing too difficult or impossible for Me.

Beloved, trust in Me, for who can help like I do? Who can rescue like I do? Who can bring into existence that which does not exist? O loved one, there is no other helper like Me. In Me you need never fear what man can do to you. For I will never leave or forsake you. In times of imprisonment both physically and mentally I come to your rescue.

Child, the only thing that really counts is faith and trust in Me no matter the situation or circumstance. And I honor that faith and trust. O dear one, I give songs in the night. I turn darkness into light. I make crooked places straight, and even in the midst of difficulty and pressure, I bring joy and peace. Have not I said that the joy of the Lord is your strength?

So rejoice beloved, I am your helper. Nothing escapes My attention. I rescue you in all your trouble and bring you out on the other side with gladness in your heart. I know the way through the wilderness, and I will lead you through. So, do not be afraid, I am with you, and I am for you both now and forevermore.

December 8
HE ALONE IS MY SOURCE
Isaiah 45:2-3

Child, do not I tell you that I am in control, that I turn sorrow into joy, and sighing into singing? Do not I tell you that I comfort and lift you up? Do not I tell you that I give strength to the weary and hope to the lost? Do not I tell you that I level the mountains and raise the valleys? Have not I said that I break asunder the gates of brass and the bars of iron, and that I go before you and make the crooked places straight?

Beloved, do not I tell you that I will prosper you and multiply that which you already have? Do not I tell you that I put My Word in your mouth, that you are to simply open it and I will fill it? Do not I tell you that you are My people, the sheep of My pasture? Do not I tell you that I am loving and caring, kind and compassionate, and that I am your Heavenly Father?

O child, do not I tell you that there is no other, that I alone am God, that I alone am in control? So, rejoice child, I alone am your source.

HE IS THE I AM
Exodus 3:14

Child, do you not see that I AM; that I AM all knowledge, all-powerful, and everywhere present? There is nothing that can hinder or change what I have planned? For I AM the Almighty one. Nothing is too difficult for me.

O My beloved, everything is under My feet. I AM the King of kings and the Lord of lords. I AM the Way, the Truth, and the Life. I AM everything you need, and you are precious to Me. I hide you in the shadow of My wings.

My child, I know you, and I love you, and I show you great and awesome things. I show you My majesty and splendor. I show you My power and My might. I show you My love and compassion. I show you My great plan and your part in it. O loved one, I AM.

FREE FROM THE CORDS OF THE WICKED
Psalm 129:4

Beloved, I make even your enemies to be at peace with you. They have no control of your spirit. They cannot destroy the real you, for if I be for you who can be against you. Have not I promised that no weapon formed against you shall prosper?

Yes child, you have My presence with you at all times, the very power and might of My Spirit. Nothing can touch you without My permission. So, rejoice beloved, I cut you free from the cords of the wicked, free from the wicked one.

HIS INEXHAUSTIBLE GIFT
2 Corinthians 9:15

Beloved, I pour out My love to you in ways you have never dreamed. It is My desire that you experience more and more, the rich, unlimited, and inexhaustible gift of My love.

Child, it is My desire to fill you with My presence, so that you will be full and running over; that My love will rise up within you and overflow to those around you. For, loved one, My love is endless and complete.

Beloved, My love is real, it does not vanish. It is genuine, it does not vacillate. My love comforts, it does not hurt. My love heals, it does not wound. My loves forgives, it does not hate. My love restores, it does not separate.

So child, let My love come through. Let it bathe you in My presence. Let it hold you close to Me. O child, let My love motivate you in everything you do, feel, hear, and say. For, loved one, I have so much love to give, and it pleases Me to pour it out on My people. All My people need do is to believe that I love them, and that I engulf them totally in that love.

O beloved, today, right now, receive and experience My love anew. Let it be fresh to your soul. Let it calm every storm, every care, and every problem in your life. For truly, I love and care for My own.

Dear one, you cannot escape or hide from My love, for I am with you always. Do not think that what you are experiencing is sent by Me to torment or plague you. But rather, know that in the circumstances, in the pressures of life, My love can flood your soul and carry you through. You will come out of the pressures and the tests rejoicing over the blessings you found in them.

HE HAS ORDAINED PEACE
FOR HIS CHILDREN
Isaiah 26:3-4, 12

Beloved, I have ordained peace for My children. This peace is for all times. Have not I said that I will keep him in perfect peace whose mind is fixed on Me, the one whose attitude and desire is for Me, the one who commits everything and all things unto Me?

Yes child, there is peace available, even in the midst of storm. There is peace available, even in the center of adversity, for trust in Me and commitment of all things to Me brings peace like a river.

Beloved, it is simple, just trust Me no matter the situation. Believe that I have everything under control. Know that I orchestrate all things together for good. And though the storm may rage and the waves roll, and though things appear to be disastrous and it looks like there is no hope, remember that trust in Me brings peace.

O child, I give you peace for I am the Prince of Peace. I am your peace. Nothing or no one can give you the peace that I give, for it passes all understanding. So, look at all things through My eyes. Trust Me. Fix your mind, your attitude, on My ways and let My peace settle you, calm you, and bring you hope.

O rejoice, dear one, for I give you peace. Let not your heart be troubled, neither let it be afraid.

ONLY TRUST AND BELIEVE
Mark 9:23

Child, nothing is impossible with Me. Nothing is impossible for Me. Nothing is impossible to Me for all things are possible when you believe, when faith is put into action. Have not I said to have faith in God? Have

293

not I said you could move mountains, if you believe? So, believe that you receive what you ask for, and it shall be yours. But ask wisely, not foolishly. Ask in My name. Yes, command in My name that the mountain be removed and that it must go. Simply believe it.

O child, let the faith in you become fully active, for there is no better way to live than by moment to moment faith. Live by trusting and believing that what I say, I will do.

Beloved, live by trusting and believing that you can do all things through Me. Live by trusting and believing for the impossible. Live by trusting and believing that I bring life where there is no life, and hope where there is no hope.

Yes, child, with Me all things are possible, only trust and believe.

December 14
THE ONE WHO DELIVERS
AND RESTORES HIS PEOPLE
Jeremiah 30:17-22

O child, does it not thrill you to know that I am the God of restoration, the God of deliverance, and the God that cares for His people? Indeed, dear one, I am such. And though you may fall, know that you will not be utterly cast down, for I am there to help. I am there to raise you up. I am there to set you upon a rock. Yes, I am there to deliver and restore.

Child, I take you into a beautiful place. I take you into the center of My blessing, and I restore your land. I make the desert bloom. I restore your fortunes, for you are Mine. You are My people. Beloved, I make you like a well-watered garden, a beautiful garden. I turn your darkness into light, your sorrow into joy, and your mourning into dancing.

O child, there is so much of Me that you have not yet experienced. So, simply let Me do My work in you.

For I am at work, and I have written on your mind and in your heart My Word and precepts. I have redeemed you from bondage. I have delivered you and set you free. And I set before you a banquet of good things. So, come and dine.

Beloved, I restore My own to places greater than ever before. So come, join Me in the heavenlies and enjoy the presence of your God, the one who delivers and restores His people.

December 15

WHATEVER HE SAYS WILL BE FULFILLED
Joshua 21:45

Beloved, whatever I say will be fulfilled. Nothing can hinder or stop it. My Word is true. You can count on it. And dear one, those things that I whisper in your ear, and those things I tell you in conversation with Me are true. They will be fulfilled. Have not you experienced this over and over again?

O rejoice, child, for I am for you to bless you, watch over you, and to care for you. So, consult Me always. Hear what I have to say on every matter, and then proclaim it. You will always see Me honor My Word.

December 16

HIS TIMING IS PERFECT
Ecclesiastes 8:5-6

My child, I indeed care for My own. I care for them even when it looks like I do not. Even when there is pressure that seems more than they can bear, I care. Even when they are in the wilderness, I care. Even when they are in great sickness, I care. Even when their emotions tear them apart, I care. Even when it appears that there is only great devastation, I care.

Beloved, even when there is no food on the table, or no bed to sleep in, I still care for My own. For I put all things together. I call for My blessing at My timing. I bring My people to holiness and to the end of themselves, so that I may lift them up.

Child, I do not leave My people grieving. I do not let the enemy sift them. No, for in sharing in My sufferings a little while they become strengthened, established, restored, and settled. They are My children, and I call them by name. I have redeemed them, and I have given them great and precious promises.

So beloved, lift up your head. Know that My timing is perfect, for I do not call My children to make them miserable, but I call them to be conformed to My image. I call them, not only to be My children and heirs, but also to serve Me with their whole heart, and to be an instrument of blessing and praise.

Yes child, I have made all the provisions. So, know that in due time, at the right time, all things will come together and will fit perfectly unto the praise, honor, and glory of My name.

O child, this is a Word of encouragement. This is a Word to rejoice in. I care for My children. I instruct them. I lead them and I correct them with love to bring them the best that I have in store for them. So, rejoice, for My timing is perfect.

December 17
THE WELL OF THE LIVING ONE WHO SEES ME
Genesis 25:11

My child, I am mindful of you at all times. I know you. I see you. I watch over you. I surround you with My presence. I am the living one who sees you, and I guide you with My eye.

O beloved, I have a vast supply. My well is full and overflowing. I have all that you need. So, ask that your joy may be full and that My joy may be fulfilled in you.

Child, know that it pleases Me to bless and care for My children. I watch over them always, to protect them, love them, gather them to Me, hold them, talk to them, anoint them, dry their tears, and kiss their hurts away.

O beloved, I am not some distant, and reluctant deity. I am not one that needs to be appeased by all kinds of fleshly mutilations. No, I am the kind and loving Heavenly Father, and I walk with you, and I instruct you. I tell you what to guard against, and I tell you what is good.

Child, I am always approachable. I do not hold you off at a distance. But rather, I welcome you into My presence, for I desire that My children come into My presence with singing and rejoicing.

Yes loved one, I am the living one that sees you, and I have a well full of living water, refreshing and cool. And that well springs up within you, into life eternal.

December 18
AT HOME IN MY HEART
Ephesians 3:17

My child, know that I love you beyond measure. My love is immense and marvelous. And out of this love I came to live within you, for you are My dwelling place, you are My home.

Beloved, have you not invited Me to be at home in your heart? Have you not asked that I be Lord of your life? Have you not offered your body as a living sacrifice to Me? So, loved one, you are My home, and it is good to be welcomed and at home with you. It is good for you to be welcomed and at home with Me. Child, My desire is that I am given the freedom to be completely at home in your heart, and that in everything it be My life living in and through you.

Beloved, think of the warmth and closeness of home. Think of the good things of home. Think not of a place or a shelter but rather think of security, love and togetherness. For it is not the structure that makes a home, but the life that is lived within it.

Child, the structure may be a tent or a mansion, but without My presence it is nothing. Yet, loved one, with My presence, even the tent becomes a palace. For I am there, and I bring all the best of home with Me. I share it with you.

So beloved, let us be at home together. Let Me be completely at home in your heart. You will never be alone. There will always be provision. There will always be fellowship. There will always be security. There will always be peace and harmony. There will always be love.

December 19
AN HONOR TO SUFFER
1 Peter 4:15-19

Beloved, think it not strange concerning the tests and trials for they are permitted so that you may grow in the nurture and admonition of your Lord. They come to bring you into holiness. They come so that you may always look to Me and not at the situation.

Child, tests and trials come so you may exercise the fruit of the Spirit. They come so that you may be able to help others. They come to prove to you and to those around you that your God is greater than any problem or difficulty. They come, beloved, to teach you patience. They come to instruct you in My principles. They come to train you in godliness.

O dear one, despise not the sufferings, the tests, and trials. But rather, rejoice for they lead to perfection. Yes, they lead to the fulfillment of My purpose in and through you. So rejoice, in that you are a partaker with Me in My sufferings.

Yes child, consider that the sufferings are not yours to bear, but Mine. For have not I said to cast all your care upon Me, because I care for you. So, count tests and trials as pure joy, for they are necessary in conforming you to My image, and they result unto My praise and honor.

O beloved, consider it an honor to suffer for Me and with Me. For the benefits, in so doing, bring great reward.

December 20

ALL THE POWER OF HIS PRESENCE
1 Corinthians 4:20

My child, nothing shall be impossible to you, for you have all the power of My presence living within you. I have fully equipped you, for your life is My life. I live in you with authority, strength and power.

O beloved, I assure you that by faith in Me you can move mountains. I assure you that I meet your every need. I assure you that I provide wisdom and understanding. I assure you that I make a way in the wilderness. I assure you that there is nothing too difficult for Me. I assure you that you have authority to speak in My name. You may take authority over every situation.

My child, know that I live in you through the power and presence of My Spirit. So dear one, settle the doubts. Think not that things are out of control, but rather, speak order to them. Command the chaos to flee, and in its place divine order to follow.

O, lay hold of this, dear one. You have authority. My authority has been given to you. And by that authority, you may speak, and it will be My voice that will be heard. You may speak, and the obstacles must flee. You may command, and the mountains shall be removed. But doubt not, regardless of how the situation looks, for I am the God of miracles. I am the God of resurrection.

O child, you have everything you need to change any circumstance, for you have My presence, My power, and My love. So, go and do as I lead for I will whisper: "This is the way, walk in it." And the mountains will flee, and the crooked places will become straight, and My name will be glorified.

December 21
JOY AND GLADNESS SHALL OVERTAKE ME
Isaiah 51:11-12

My child, I have declared that joy and gladness will overtake you, and that sorrow and weariness shall flee away. Loved one, this comes through praise; for praise makes all the sighings, all the frustrations, all the weariness melt before you, and in its place comes everlasting joy and gladness.

Yes, I have declared that joy and gladness is yours, and that it will overtake you. So, look not at the cares or at the mountain of things to do, or at what appears to be about to overwhelm you, but rather come to Me. Come to Zion with singing and rejoicing in your heart. Yes, come with singing and praise for Zion is a place of worship, a place of joy.

Beloved, Zion is the dwelling of the Lord, and you are that dwelling. So, be quiet and listen. Zion is a place of rejoicing and gladness. It is here, loved one. It is in your heart.

Yes, sorrow is for a season, but gladness and joy come in the morning. So rejoice, child of Zion, and go forth in song and praise, for joy and gladness will follow. And you will be exceedingly glad, for everything else must flee away.

December 22

HE HAS A PLAN
Psalm 138:8

My child, I have a plan, a divine plan, and that plan shall be fulfilled. It shall come to pass. And loved one, you are in My plan. You are a part of it. That divine plan, designed before the foundations of the world, includes you.

Yes beloved, I have a plan for you. And as I accomplish My plan and purpose, so shall you accomplish the plan and purpose that I have designed for you.

Child, what I say, I will do. What I speak I will accomplish. For I know the end from the beginning. I know what I am doing. I know the glory of what I do. O dear one, are you not thrilled that you are a part of My plan? Are you not thrilled that I have made you a part of what I do, and a part of My glory?

Beloved, remember that My ways are perfect. They are right. And the plan that I have for you is also perfect and right. Know that I am in control, and that as you desire and seek My direction, you shall never be put to confusion. For, loved one, I will make known to you what I have planned for you.

Child, you shall not miss it. You shall not make the wrong decision. You shall not fail, regardless the circumstance. For man looks at situations differently than I do. What seems as failure, poor timing, or disaster to man, is no more than My plan at work.

So relax, beloved, and let Me direct you. I will remove the stress and the strain, as you simply trust Me. O child, do not fret for I have a plan, a divine plan, and it is perfect. Come, let us walk in it together.

December 23
WILDERNESS BEAUTY
Isaiah 41:17-20

O child, am not I, indeed, a mighty God? Am not I a God of wisdom and knowledge? For I take the wilderness and turn it into a garden. I make it bloom like a rose. I turn the desert into a place of beauty, a place of growth, a place of strength, a place of

301

learning, a place of blessing, a place of refreshing, and a place of provision.

Beloved, though it may not seem a good place to you, and though it may seem harsh and barren, look around and you will see the springs bubbling up. You will see the trees beginning to rise from the barren waste. You will see the fruit of those trees, and you will see that fruit multiply.

Child, you will see the beauty of the wilderness, as I make it spring forth and bud, as I make it grow, as I make it beautiful, and as I change it to a place of beauty. For the changes I make are good, and they last.

So, look up, for the desert is beginning to grow. It is beginning to bud. O beloved, as you see what I am doing, you will say: "My Lord was here all the time." You shall say: "Thank you, Lord, for loving me and for blessing me." You shall also say: "It was good for me to have been in the desert."

Yes My child, without the desert, without the wilderness, there would be no opportunity for Me to bring forth beauty from barrenness, strength from weakness, and refreshing from weariness.

So loved one, despise not the wilderness, for I am there and I will meet you there. I plant your desert with trees of strength and character. I cultivate them, and I bring the wasteland into a place of beauty, a place of rest, and a place of sufficiency.

December 24
HIS WORD IS BEAUTIFUL
Psalm 119:72 & 165

Loved one, is not My Word beautiful? Does It not warm your heart? Does It not thrill you? O child, It should, for My Word tells you everything you need to know. My Word introduces you to Me. My Word is as alive today as It was when I first gave It. For My Word has the same power today as It did yesterday, and by My Word, you may come to know Me better and better.

Beloved, when I tell you that I am with you, does this not bring you joy? Is not there joy in this assurance? When My Word tells you that I love you, does this not also bring joy to your heart? When My Word tells you that I am your helper, does this not also bring joy? When My Word tells you that I alone am God, and that there is no other, does not this bring you joy? When My Word tells you that I care, does not this also bring you joy?

O child, there is great joy in My presence, and My presence is found in My Word, and in My precepts and principles. So, walk today in My Word, rejoicing that I am your God, that I am your Savior, that I am your sufficiency, and that I am your life. For My Word tells you that you are Mine, and that you need not fear, for I am with you always. Yes, rejoice in My Word, for I have made It My light to shine upon you.

December 25
THE GREATEST GIFT OF ALL
Isaiah 53:10-12

Child, see the totality of My love. See the unselfish and pure demonstration of the love of the Father. Did not I give mankind and you the ultimate sacrifice, so that, once and for all, your sin, past, present and future, could be removed and remembered no more.

Beloved, what I did for you was most difficult. Yet, for the sake of all My people and the sake of all mankind, I gave everything that I had. I did not hold back. Rather, I willingly went to that cross, and there I gave My life. I did it for you. I took your place. I paid your penalty.

O My child, this alone should cause you to greatly rejoice, both now and forever, for I have purchased your redemption. I have given eternal life, which is life in abundance. There is no longer eternal damnation, but life everlasting in the presence of your Heavenly Father. Beloved, what I have done for you is as fresh and new as the day it first took place. The effect of My work has changed the world. Yet, dear one, it is so simple, for all one need do is to believe and receive it.

Child, what I have done, is the greatest gift in the entire universe. It is the gift of the Father for all men to have right standing with him, through the forgiveness of sin. Yes, I am the Father's gift to man. And there is so much to that gift, for it includes love, peace, comfort, healing, hope, joy, prosperity, My Spirit, a new nature, life eternal, and all that goes with it. O beloved, rejoice and be glad, for I am your gift, I am your Christmas.

December 26
LAY UP TREASURE IN HEAVEN
Luke 12:21-31

My child, set your affection on things above, not on things of the earth. For I have said to seek Me first, and all these things would be added unto you. Yes, loved one, do not seek after material things or earthly praise and glory, but rather seek to please Me, and these will follow.

Beloved, know that the things of earth are only temporal. They do not last. Know that there is no value in fame and fortune, if I am not in it. It has no meaning in eternity. So child, lay up treasure in heaven. Lay up things that last. Let your life count in matters of the Spirit, and be not overwhelmed by the hardships, the pressures, and the sufferings. They, too, lead to great spiritual benefit.

Beloved, do not be anxious over anything, for there is nothing to be worried about. Simply, trust Me and turn everything over to Me, and I will take care of the rest. So, seek Me first. Seek to do My will. Place Me first in your life, and as you do, know that I pay great dividends. Know that your labor is not in vain. Know that My compensation is beyond earthly compensation, and it is something you take with you wherever you go. It lasts.

Yes, I reward you My child, and you shall share in the riches of My kingdom, the power of My Spirit, the wealth of My presence, the splendor of My holiness, and in the magnitude of My glory.

December 27
TO OBEY IS BETTER THAN SACRIFICE
1 Samuel 15:22-23

My child, to obey is better than sacrifice, for faithfulness is grounds for great reward. Loved one, no matter what I ask you to do, there is no need ever to be put to shame. For I give purpose to life. When I tell you to go this way, or when I lead you in that way, it is because there is a reason and a purpose.

Beloved, what I ask of you is obedience. So, hear My voice, heed My Word, and follow Me. Let Me lead you in the paths of righteousness that I have marked out for you.

Child, I am your refuge. I am your rock of salvation. Those who put their trust in Me, their blind trust, need never fear. They will never be put to shame. And, in spite of what is visible to those who stand and watch, trust in Me brings peace and confidence. Those who put their trust in Me will never be ashamed of what I ask them to do.

O beloved, trust Me. Obey Me, and you will see miraculous things take place, even more than ever before. For I respond to trust and obedience. And you shall sing My praises to the heavens, and those who stand and watch shall be amazed, while you do what I tell you to do.

December 28
THE RIVER OF HIS SPIRIT
Psalm 46:4-7

Beloved, from the river of My Spirit come streams of blessings, streams of My presence. And that river flows freely and makes glad the dwelling of the Lord. Yes loved one, that river rises within you, and out of your innermost being flows rivers of living water.

O beloved, let My Spirit rise within you. Let My living waters flow over and out from your soul. For there is a river whose streams make glad the city of God.

December 29
THE GOOD SHEPHERD
John 10:11

Child, I am the Good Shepherd, and you are sheep of My pasture. I know My sheep, and I call them by name. Yes, I call you, and I lead you forth. I lead you where it is safe to go. I lead you into shady green pastures, where there is all the provision you need.

Beloved, I do not lead you where I have not been before. Rather, I lead you carefully through all the crooks and turns. And though it may seem dangerous, and though it may seem barren and dry on the way to the pasture, know that I have marked out the path in advance. I have gone before you and have made all the crooked places straight and the narrow places safe. The path is clearly marked, and I lead you along that path.

O My child, look not to the right or to the left. Look not at the heights, or the depths. Let them not cause you to fear, but rather, keep your eye on Me, as I lead you. I will not let you fall. For I lead you to pleasant pastures, waving green in the breeze, and to refreshing streams and waters flowing beautiful and peaceful.

Beloved, because I am the Good Shepherd, I came to give you life in abundance. I did not come to destroy you, but to rescue you and to bring you into My presence. And, loved one, wherever I am, there is blessing. Wherever I lead, there is sufficiency.

O indeed, My child, I lead you and I shepherd you. I watch over you, and I bring you to the place I have prepared for you. And, you shall rejoice and be glad, for My leading is done with tenderness and with great care.

Beloved, listen for My voice, and you will hear it. You will not be led astray. Yes, I am the Good Shepherd, and I know My sheep, and I care for My own. No one can ever take them from Me.

December 30
YOUR INHERITANCE IS SURE
Psalm 37:18

Child, your inheritance is sure. The land is before you. Go in and possess it. There is nothing that can stand in your way, for I go before you, and I fight your battles for you.

Though the odds may look astronomically against you, remember that you are favored by your Heavenly Father. Am not I the author of grace? So, let nothing hinder. Go in and possess the land. Everywhere you place your feet, claim it, for it is yours. Child, have not I said to be strong and of good courage? Have not I said that I will be with you, and that I will never leave or forsake you? Have not I said that you share in the power of My resurrection?

O yes beloved, there is nothing that can hinder, and nothing that can stop Me from completing what I set out to do. And you are a part of this plan. So, look up. Take authority over the situation. Take command, for the enemy must flee. You will see, in the middle of the battle, the goodness and glory of your Lord.

O child, let nothing, no word, no action, no deed, no disaster, sway you from pressing on, from taking possession of your inheritance. And though there may be giants in the land, I am greater than any giant. Yes, the enemy is there, but I am greater than he that is in the world.

But you say that you are weak, that you know nothing. O beloved, remember, that when you are weak, then I am strong. Remember, that I have said that if you lack wisdom, just simply ask for it. Remember, that I bring things into being, when there is no possible way for them to be so.

So rejoice child, the best is yet to come. Go in and possess the land. The enemy cannot have it. It is yours. It is part of your inheritance. Believe it. Claim it and walk in it, for through your God you can do anything, of this you may be sure.

Beloved, I give you the land. Your inheritance is sure, and I strengthen you to the task at hand.

December 31
HE LEADS ME
Genesis 12:1-9; Exodus 33:13-14

My child, as I led Abraham, and as I led Moses and the children of Israel, so I lead you. For I go before you in My name, and I conquer all your foes. I go before you by My Spirit, and I turn difficulty into blessing. Beloved, My name is the Word of God. I am the King of kings and the Lord of lords. Everything is subject to Me.

So, do not lose heart. Do not be discouraged, for I go before you, and I fight for you. You are not alone. I bring you to a land, to an inheritance promised long ago. It is the inheritance of My blessing, a land flowing with milk and honey.

So, press on beloved, and fear not. Can you not see My hand in your life? Can you not see that I have brought you this far? Yes, the door is open before you. The land is waiting for you to possess. And, dear one, I am there with you, and I will go before you. I will lead and guide you, and show you where to go. I tell you what to do. So, listen for Me. Hear My voice, and you will not be distracted to the left or to the right, but will go into the land following Me.

Beloved, there is so much ahead for you, so much that I desire to share with you. So, move out. Take no thought of the obstacles, but move at My instruction, and stand still at My command, and you will see Me do great and marvelous things before your very own eyes.